# Cherry Blossom Children

One Foster Parent's Story

## DANI VALDIS

**Grosvenor House Publishing Limited**

This book is published by
Grosvenor House Publishing Ltd
28-30 High Street, Guildford, Surrey, GU1 3EL.
www.grosvenorhousepublishing.co.uk
Registered in England No. 5184603

ISBN: 978-1-78148-754-9

*This book is non-fiction and is based on the author's experience. The events recounted are true. The names of all individuals have been changed to protect the identities and privacy of all characters.*

# Life's Gift

*Many years ago as a student nurse I had the privilege of caring for a young boy, Gary, who unfortunately had a terminal condition. I became quite close to Gary and his family and though his death left me with a devastating emptiness, his journey towards that day was filled with a great deal of happiness and joy as his zest for living and ability to make others smile was wholly uplifting. In 2011 I found myself needing to search for the only photograph I had of him, this search became a week long drive of determination to find that photograph. During my search I discovered all the memorabilia and information that I had saved over the years about the children we had fostered. None should be forgotten. I hope this book encourages others to help and support other children. All children are inspirational so I hope that readers of this book will be inspired by and give inspiration to the children in their lives. Thank you Gary for my journey, you and many other children gave me the inspiration I needed.*

# Dedication

I wish to dedicate this book to two very influential people in my life, who, for very different reasons and through completely differing channels, have brought life and meaning, as well as understanding to the purpose of sharing our family experiences with others.

'Jake'- a special young man, who could be described as being 'small but power packed.' His influence on our family had a huge impact, as I am sure it did to the lives of many others he met throughout his short life.

My thanks also go to Janet Simpson who provided me with the channel of insight, the encouragement to continue writing, and the patience of a saint, as I relived our family experience as each chapter emerged in print. I am forever indebted to you both.

# Acknowledgements

I would like to offer my sincere thanks to all those wonderful people who gave me the confidence to complete this book. My very patient family, who gave me the time to write and faced their experiences of our life together. My husband, who painstakingly vetted this book as well as tolerating my determination to write it! I would also like to thank all of those who offered to read the manuscript to give me their true opinions with direct honesty and criticism. Finally, I would like to thank every child that joined our family throughout our fostering years for the life and laughter they gave to us.

# Foreword

*"How many children do you have?"*

*A straightforward question that is usually responded to in a straightforward way. I for example would answer "Two, a girl and a boy."*

*The author however looks at you, smiles and then explains.*

*This is her story, the struggles, the highs, the lows, the tears, the laughs, the parties, Christmases and the achievement of her dream.*

*Believe me when I say that this could only have been achieved by a very special person and her remarkable family, so if you are considering fostering or adopting this is a MUST read for you. It will prepare you in a way no other book can.*

*Janet Simpson*

# CHAPTER 1

# *Decisions In Life*

Very early in life I made two very clear decisions that were to affect my future. My mother would say that I made three! Perhaps she was right given the unfurling of my future. However I might suggest that the third decision was a necessity rather than a planned event based purely on the second major decision! I recall being a rather miserable child, one of six, and if it is possible to be the middle one of six, then I held that position. Never considered to be grown up enough to join my older siblings but considered to be too old to be a part of my younger siblings' games and activities. But as with all youngsters there were some very simple almost unavoidable events that were to influence the direction my life would take.

I was five years old when I had to go into hospital to have my tonsils and adenoids removed. This was back in 1957 when the norm was for the mother to take the child to the children's ward at the local hospital and leave them there for the duration, usually a week. During this time the children received no direct contact with their family at all. They were to go through this traumatic experience very much alone, along with their fellow sufferers who were total strangers and the seemingly unsympathetic ward staff. The theory was that the children would be least affected emotionally. How little they knew. I can only recall that experience as a week of unpleasant memories that frightened me, left me fearful of being alone, and never feeling I could trust what adults said. On arrival I was given a bed and a bedside locker, told to say goodbye to my mother with a faint promise by the very strict nurse, who snapped at me, that my mother would collect me in a weeks time only if I was good, did as I was told and stopped crying. This message was given to each child as they watched their mothers leaving and as their tears began to fall. We were all admitted on the same day, operated on the day after and allowed home six days later assuming there were no complications. Shortly after my arrival I needed the toilet, was desperately in need but there was no one to ask. I recall going in search of it, wandered into a room, which must have been the ward sister's office. I heard the distant sound of voices but they were coming in my direction, so I hid behind the door, barely breathing in case they heard me. But my need for the toilet was imperative; my whimpering behind the door could not be held back a moment longer and my hideout was discovered. I was hauled out of my safe haven and told to go back to my bed. I was petrified of the nurse and I am sure she considered me to be the most exasperating and difficult child she had cared for.

Playtime on the ward I cannot recall, however I do remember the nurse (perhaps it was the same one?) trying to teach us to gargle some brightly coloured, awful tasting antiseptic liquid, over the bath. I could not do it to save my life, either before my operation or even worse afterwards. I was told that I would have to stay there forever if I could not do it, as my throat would remain sore forever and my voice would never return to normal! I tried so hard between the tears, but the exceptional sore throat accompanied by the fear of the nurse's threats during that time never allowed me to acquire the skill to gargle.

Eventually the day arrived when we could go home, but we had to wait patiently for our mothers to arrive. One by one each child was carried off the ward to be returned to the care of their Mum, to be taken home to their family once again. But I was left behind, I strongly believed now that the nurse had meant what she said after all my voice was still strange sounding and the art of gargling a complete mystery to me. My mother had not arrived and my usual chest heaving wailing began. This caused my nose and throat to bleed, bringing ward sister and doctor to attend to me. They reassured me, held me close, stopped the bleeding and made me feel better; they explained that I could go home when my mother arrived providing I could be happy and the bleeding ceased. I smiled probably for the first time that week. I had discovered that one could feel good when comforted by a stranger, as easily as one could have their feelings and emotions destroyed by the harsh words of a stranger. New children were being admitted for their operations, which began to fill me with doubt about my own position, but eventually towards the evening my mother arrived to take me home. The relief was enormous, but from this point onwards I knew I wanted to be a nurse when I grew up!

I was desperate to own a nurse's outfit. I was eventually to be given one, a much-prized Christmas gift that, as a five year old, meant the world to me. It served as a reminder of my recent experience, but more than that, a symbol of my future intentions. In my five-year-old understanding, I was going to be a nice nurse, one who understood how children felt, someone who could make them happy and not be worried or frightened. My promise to myself was made; I just had to wait the passage of time to fulfil my intentions. I was so sad when eventually I grew out of my nurses' outfit. The next one I wore was for real, many years later.

About the time that I grew out of my first nurses' uniform, age seven, I experienced another life changing event. Playing with our neighbourhood friends was an everyday occurrence as it is in everyone's life. We met on the 'green' at the top of our hill, where we played endless games using our imagination and limited experiences to while away the hours. We were overseen by our older siblings who played their games separately but within calling distance so they could yell out their instructions, which kept us clearly in line. The green was the place for all seasons, playing among the spring and summer wild flowers, where we made daisy chains, checked out each other's love of butter using buttercups and singing rhymes as we picked the bluebells, my favourite flower. We were that gaggle of girls giggling as they changed the words of the traditional version of 'In and out the dusty bluebells' dancing aimlessly together. We played there too in the autumn and winter kicking the leaves about or building the communal snowman. Our numbers were variable from day to day according to who was available to play, as minor illnesses and bad behaviour affected us all from time to time. But on one particular day our numbers were markedly depleted. The children from the family who lived across the road didn't join us. Neither did they the following day, nor the next, in fact they were not to be seen in school or ever again.

The parents were still living at the house but their children had disappeared, seemingly into thin air. What

4

made it worse was that if any of us asked about their whereabouts we were instantly hushed and shushed. Adults talked in whispers about it among themselves but never to us as children. I constantly asked if I could go and ask the missing children's parents when they would be back but was scolded and threatened against going near their house. Only after the parents moved away too, did I learn that the children had been taken away from their parents by the then social care department. Yet again I found myself having sleepless nights, living in fear that this could happen to us, to me.

I had no image of how they could have been taken, or where they had gone, if they would ever return and if they did would they find their parents? Where were they being kept? Were they in a sort of jail? My mother reinforced all of these thoughts and ideas, as she and our older sister would throw out the threat that if we were not good the same would happen to us. In view of the endless scoldings we received, I was convinced that we too would disappear in the middle of the night. My seven-year-old brain could not accept this idea and yet I was fruitlessly searching for clues that this was inevitable and I needed to be prepared.

Strangely, I am unsure what this preparation involved or what it was all about, I only remember praying to God at night to leave me in my own bed until morning, and clutching my doll, Julie, tightly so that I was not alone, knowing that if I was taken she would surely come with me.

Whilst going through this uncertainty, being unable to accept that the missing children were safe or indeed that my siblings and I were, I found myself thinking about other children that this must have happened to. I questioned how they would have felt, their fears, their safety and their futures. It seemed to fill my waking hours and kept me awake during the night, I spoke to my teacher at school as to why such things happened, she was always sympathetic but suggested I should not worry over such things and to stop frowning!

Then, in the spring whilst playing at the local recreation ground known as the 'rec' to all of us, I had a revelation. Skipping through the park I saw pink trees, yes, pink trees! In my limited life's experience trees were green, but I had found pink trees. They were beautiful. As a matter of fact they were the most beautiful things I had ever seen. An avenue of perhaps twelve or more pink trees, I had of course seen these same trees many times before but they were always green or leafless. Pink trees were magical trees, and as I skipped towards them I planned what I would do when I grew up to help children taken from their parents, they would be safe, they would not be frightened, above all else they would be happy.

I spent that afternoon under the cherry blossom planning my house, the children's rooms, how I would care for them, the toys they would enjoy, the lessons they would learn, the life style we would have! Such plans, such expectations. I visualised a boy's room and a girl's room, shoes beneath the bed, each child had their own space, a place to put their own belongings. They played together, looked after each other, in my mind's eye they were always happy, bad things never happened, they never needed telling off or reminded of what not to do! My ideal world of childhood was based on the ultimate adult expectation, total perfection. That afternoon was a wonderful world on my own whiling away the hours planning my future and that of the children I would care for, until one of my siblings would remind me of when we were to go home for tea.

My fantastic idea, why had I not thought it all out before? To me it was the perfect solution, I could not change the lives of my friends but I could make it better for other children. Of course I could, well at least I could when I grew up! But at seven years old I had a lot of growing up to do, I had a great deal of experience to gain, as a matter of fact I had a life to live first! In the meantime I had plenty of time to formulate my master plan in my mind's eye so when that time came I would be ready. So my second promise to myself was made, and as the years rolled by I never deviated from either of my promises, though my imagined plans, ideas and intentions evolved towards their moment of fruition. My idealistic views on childcare became more realistic and sensible. I was to discover that children who had negative experiences in life needed and deserved their own space far more than those who enjoyed a positive life experience.

So several rooms to my imagined house rapidly replaced the impractical illusion of a girl's room and a boy's room. Unconsciously I had made my third decision as predicted by my mother! Consequently I found myself regularly searching the local paper for a large house suitable for my family home, this search started soon after my resolution, and my mother frequently accused me of 'getting above my station'. She would say "big houses, big bills!" We lived in a three bed-roomed terraced house, with six children, as well as my mother's younger brother living with us after both their parents died. My mother found life very hard being the wife of a trawler cook, my father, whom she saw for three days in every three weeks. I believe she also found it hard to listen to this irritating child who talked of having a nursing career and a houseful of other peoples children. She felt it was her duty to bring me back to earth on a regular basis and would remind me that "Girls like you don't do nursing it means doing exams", always adding that "You'll have enough with your own kids without having other people's", then came the inevitable "anyway you will be too busy working to do either because you need to pay your way". Of course she was right I would have to pay my way! I would need to learn to do that if I was to have a career and an extended family. I am not too sure how my mother envisioned my future but I was frequently accused of having ideas of grandeur, exaggerated notions or 'our Dani's big ideas'.

Big ideas for a youngster they may well have been, but telling me they were unachievable for the likes of me was a waste of breath as it only served to make me even more determined to fulfil my intentions, my promises and my premonitions, which is how it felt.

So throughout my childhood I dreamed, planned, prepared, worked out and on the pros and cons of such a venture. Each step taking me closer to having the extended family we have today. Every year to this day during springtime I am reminded of the reason for my existence. Pink trees appear in full bloom in gardens including my own, in parks, on roundabouts, at road junctions, in fields, they are everywhere. They are truly magical, they bring out the child in me, no longer just a reminder of ideals of long ago but also proof that I was right to do what I did. Spring is my favourite time of year, as it marks the end of winter, one can look forward to the long days of summer and the freedom each day brings.

Looking back on the stepping-stones of life, I can truly believe that our pathway is drawn ahead of us. The distance between the beginning and the end is too great for us to handle, so we are given small manageable steps that guide us to our ultimate goal. On reflection we can see how each event in life changed us in some small way throughout our development, to offer us the ability to cope, survive, move on, share our experiences, so teach and guide others as they undertake their own life's journey. There are times we do not offer ourselves with enough credibility to achieve our aim or we diminish our efforts when we feel we did not put in the determination and time that perhaps we could have or should have! Sometimes we feel we are standing at a crossroads uncertain of which route to take, though I feel all routes need to be explored to make that informed decision, only one route can be taken. Perhaps this is when having made our choice we have to accept it may have been a wrong choice, do we then backtrack to that same crossroads or do we move forward to the options given to us at the next one?

For a child to survive as a freethinking individual, he/she needs to learn to be discernable with his/her thought processes. Learn to make and take decisions to their ultimate conclusion. Above all, to have confidence in his/her decision-making, whilst at the same time, hold the confidence to recognise when a decision was not one of the best, therefore making a u-turn to make an alternative decision would prove to be the sensible course of action.

Making and taking decisions was never going to be easy in our large family of six children especially when you are stuck in the middle. The dynamics of family relationships seem to allow for mockery and jeering of anyone who stepped out of line. Judging by the amount

9

of sibling jousting that I endured I obviously stepped out of line far too frequently! But that knocking of confidence, witnessing their mistakes, at the same time as coping with my own trials of growing up, gave me invaluable experience that I doubt I could have gained so close to home had I been part of a smaller family unit. There was strength in a family group, though any weaknesses that we dared to show would be seen by the others as trophies to be gained and waved to all. Such embarrassment quickly taught us to either cut and run at the earliest possibility or stand up and be counted for what we believed in.

Looking back I had an interesting childhood, or so it seems. Perhaps it was no different from the average youngster growing up in the 1950's and 60's. But one thing I have learnt is to reflect on my own life, my own positive and negative experiences, and to analyse the reasons for the decisions that lead to the behaviour exhibited. Do I really have the answer? No of course I don't! Most of us would be unable to explain why we did most things, especially as children, and I am certainly no different. In the words of the average child (or adult!), "Just 'cos" is good enough as an answer, it's all we know, that is until either someone explains this to us or we are encouraged to understand ourselves better, the only reason we do anything is because we can, the consequences of our actions are not anticipated or understood initially.

However we all learn through different methods, the fact that a class of children can all be taught by the same teacher, yet all absorb that teaching to interpret it differently is so dependent on our individuality, as well as our experiences. Though surely this is exactly why the world has such an abundance of fascinating and interesting people. I for one feel very privileged that I have been fortunate enough to meet so many. A child is moulded and shaped by those around him, but more amazingly also by those we have a brief encounter with, as these experiences, whether negative or positive, can provide the spark for each of us to create a memory locked within us, that widens our experience and serves to surge us forward in our development. Take a long look back to your foundation, think of your own brief encounters that shaped and moulded you, are these not the stepping stones you chose to take when standing at the crossroads that determined your direction in life?

*"Before I got married I had six theories of how to bring up children, now I have six children and no theories".*

*John Wilmot (2nd Earl of Rochester)*

*English Libertine Poet (1647 - 1680)*

# CHAPTER 2

## Childhood Experiences

I believe that we spend a lifetime making memories, so not only do we gain valuable experience and rise up the ladder of life's lessons, but we can also enjoy and reflect on these memories when we reach the stage in life of being unable to make many more. Of course not all of our memories are positive or even beneficial but we do have ownership of them, they are unique to us. Another part of life's rich tapestry!

Shortly after my tonsillectomy times my older brother decided he wanted to go to the park to play, but when he asked our mother her answer was "Only if you take Dani." He was not impressed, after all how could he enjoy himself with his miserable little sister hanging around. He had wanted to go to Sidney Park a far more exciting park to play in than the local 'rec', it even had a boating lake for model boats, but he had been specifically told that he was only allowed to go to the 'rec'. Somewhat aggrieved he reluctantly accepted the terms for his freedom. Holding my hand as we left the house, he quickly let go as we descended our hill heading towards the 'rec', my little footsteps would never allow me to keep up with him so all to soon I found myself having to run to try to keep up with him but was constantly lagging behind which disgruntled him all the more.

We were in sight of the recreation playground that Mum had agreed to when my brother formulated his master plan to get his own way, embroiling me into his devious plot of misdemeanour. Turning towards me to offer the biggest smile only a big brother up to no good can, he offered me sweets from his pocket. He told me that if I walked faster he could show me another park, which was much nicer to play in, and had so much more to offer, and he would give me extra sweets if I promised not to say anything to Mum when we returned home. He filled my head with images of a fairyland to play in. I believed him, he was my big brother after all, so why shouldn't I? Sibling secrets hidden from Mum, Dad or in fact any adult is the stuff of childhood and I felt very special to be taken into his confidence. I agreed with the whole of my being feeling ten feet tall alongside him. My brother must think such a lot about me, he was taking me to see a new and special park, and this was to be our secret and extra sweets into the bargain! Could life get better than this? My brother took me by the hand as we laughed and giggled all the way to the park.

He was right, the new park was so much more attractive, so much brighter with hidden gardens laid out with colourful flowerbeds that weaved in and out to lead to hidden sanctuaries with park benches. He showed me the wonderful arch that formed a gateway into one of the flower gardens, made from the jawbone of a whale that had found itself stranded on the local beach. I stood in awe of the size of a whale's mouth eternally grateful that I hadn't met the whale when it was alive! The playground had not one but two slides and two roundabouts, two sets of swings to accommodate all age groups. It was wonderful! There was an enormous playing area with a line of bushes ideal for endless games of hide and seek. There were several tennis courts, though I had no idea what the game these people were playing was called at the time, it still fascinated me. But the most irresistible feature of all had to be the boating lake, which is where my brother wanted to be.

The lake had groups of young boys dotted around the edge admiring each other's wooden boats that were attached to string to prevent them from sailing into the centre of the lake out of reach of their owners. Engrossed in his passion my brother quickly forgot about me, his kid sister who was now clearly no more than a nuisance. I was tired, fed up, lonely and after what felt like a lifetime began to wish I had never agreed to this stupid idea. I felt let down by my brother who had now ignored me for what seemed like endless hours. But then suddenly I saw someone waving at me from the other side of the boating lake; well at least I thought they were waving at me trying to get my attention. I waved back as I stood up from the grassy banking I had squatted on and started to walk towards them. In my five-year-old head I knew I just had to walk in a straight line, keep my gaze fixed on where the young person waving was standing. This was exactly what I did! Foolishly, naively I headed in a forward direction, a straight line, eyes fixed on the waving youngster ahead of me, until I stepped into that sinkable pond and began to flounder in the depths below. All I remember is the intense coldness of the water numbing any other feelings I could have had, apart from the sharp searing pain that entered my head as it filled with ice cold water that rushed into my eyes, my mouth, my nose and even my ears. I had never been swimming, I had no idea what to do, the cold prevented me from responding in any way at all, then suddenly in one swift action I was snatched from the water by someone, but I never knew who my rescuer was. I was taken back to the grassy bank where my brother had been forced to join me. Adults around were telling him off for leaving me on my own insisting he was to take me home immediately. He was not impressed after all he would have some explaining to do when we returned home.

Heavily drenched and dripping from head to foot, I followed my brother who was now furious with this drowned rat of a sister. Once again I was struggling to keep up with him as he strode ahead of me. I was cold, frightened, miserable and dejected. A sorry pathetic sight, my feet squelching in my wet shoes, I pleaded with my brother to wait for me, he was so cross and no doubt equally frightened of the inevitable telling off that he would receive from our mother. Nothing he could say to her would hide what we had done or help him to salve his conscience. I cried, I wailed. My dithering, cold, tired, wet bedraggled body blundered on behind him exerting every last possible effort under the weight of the wet clothes. We had about two miles to walk home, with both my appearance and the snivelling racket drawing attention to ourselves from the neighbouring households. Two older women stopped my brother to demand an explanation for my sorry plight; he told them that I had fallen into a puddle. Some puddle! Then one of them approached me as I drew alongside them, I reached out to my brother but he was being told to run on home to fetch our mother. Reluctantly he sped off shouting a promise to me that he would soon be back, no doubt relieved to relinquish responsibility of his embarrassment, me! Although I was with the two women

I felt so alone, they were strangers who were ushering me inside the house. My only thought was would my brother remember where he had left me?

The inside of the house was dark with dingy décor and the brown painted surfaces increased the darkened smoky atmosphere but the room we entered was lit up with a blazing fire. Sitting in a chair at the fireside, was a man I presume to have been the husband of the lady that had taken over my situation, he was smoking a pipe. He said nothing. The lady's insistence that I was to take all my clothes off by the fire so she could dry them broke the silence. I said nothing, not a sound came out of me, but my tears burned my cheeks. Wet clothes were heavy and uncomfortable but they were better than no clothes. The man continued to watch us and I stared back frozen and fearful still wondering if my mother and brother would know how to find me. She took off my hand knitted cardigan, my socks and my dress. I was down to my vest and pants and not prepared to part with them. In it's wet state my underwear clung to me as much as I clung to it! However the lady of the house had a different idea, she brought in a big blanket wrapped it around me and rapidly peeled the remaining clothing from my cold little body. She then picked me up and put me on the fireside chair opposite the silent man who was still staring, making me feel really uncomfortable. The lady disappeared into the kitchen then returned bringing a clothes horse with her to set around the fire to dry my clothes on. She promptly started to hang up my clothes to dry by the heat of the fire. The soporific atmosphere created by the blazing fire in the hearth, increased by my blanket cocoon of warmth coupled with the unlit smoke filled room caused my eyes to wearily droop. I had to stay awake I just had to. The man opposite stared as he continued to smoke his pipe, so I stared back watching his every move. Occasionally he would wink at me, or give me a half smile, to which I refused to react. I continued to try to fight against sleep but the steamy smoky surroundings enveloped me, encouraging me to drift into a dreamy slumber. I was exhausted. The long walk from our home to the park, our afternoon of play, the frightening experience of launching myself into the water, the responses of those around at the time, finding myself with strangers, the effects of shock, all of these had all taken their toll on me and though I could hear voices I was no longer aware of what was going on around me, nor did I care.

I awoke some time later to the sound of familiar voices, the lady who owned the house, was talking to someone; the other voice was my mother's! I had longed for her to come for me but now I was afraid of what she would say. She actually said little to me, but an awful lot to my brother who was getting the roasting of his life. I was hauled to my feet, dressed very quickly in warm clean clothes, throughout all this my mother was thankfully apologising to the woman for all she had done alternating with angry remarks thrown towards my brother who appeared very sorry for himself. Then came the ultimate embarrassment the very worse thing to happen to a grown up five and a half year old, the most extreme indignity that I was ever to be afforded. My mother put me in my youngest sister's pram! How could she? How dare she? I was mortified, I knew this would lead to payback time, my brother will have to share this with all the neighbourhood children and I will be the laughing stock. I recall trying to bury myself in the pram blanket, lying as low down as

I could so no one would see me. I dreaded the thought of anyone peering into the pram, as people are prone to do. The only consolation I could gain was that I was not being blamed for the escapade I had shared with my brother. On this occasion he had to shoulder all the blame.

The resilience of children is often spoken about in terms of how easily they appear to others to be unaffected by their experiences in life. Is it less about resilience and more about survival? Life's challenges do affect all of us and the manner in which we cope is dependent on so many factors. These include the attitudes and behaviours of role models around us, our ability to keep a perspective on given situations, our previous experiences and their outcomes too. We all prefer the positives in any circumstance we meet, and most of us can find at least one even in the depths of our despair, but nevertheless the occasion will leave it's mark on us in some way. Even as that almost six-year-old youngster I was able to pick up on my own deviousness, I knew at the time I was in the wrong in allegiance with my brother! However I have no idea what possessed me to think I should be able to walk on water! Even when I reached the water's edge I continued to step out even though I knew where I was but my concentration was on something or rather someone else. This focal point caused my mind to side step understanding, resulting in my demise. This whole experience put me through a huge range of emotions from both ends of the scale.

There is no doubt in my mind that in childhood our coping mechanisms and our emotions may be immature but they have a true grasp on the reality around us, the inherent dangers that lurk, and the effects these have on those involved, in line with the level of maturity we have reached. Children are able to pick up on the cues that adults give out, whether they are cues of reassurance, fear, uncertainty, pleasure or despair. How they react to them is dependent on what they witness in others. This of course starts in babyhood watching and learning from the world around them. They will only interpret the information as positively as it is presented. Sadly for far too many children their best positive could be very negative. Therefore the trigger to their response on a negative event in life can result in an exaggeration in behaviour. To others this behavioural response appears even more unacceptably infantile. Until such time that the emotional development has a chance to catch up with the physical development the child will be disadvantaged. This creates so many problems for them that frequently lead to failing or struggling to form good relationships not only with their peers but also with adult figures, especially those in a position of authority as they are viewed through contradictory eyes. Lessons I had yet to learn, but would quickly gain from the children who were to join my future family.

We all too often subconsciously reflect on our lives during conversation with friends, colleagues, and relatives or even with strangers. Their story related to us triggers our minds to reminisce and impart similar experiences of our own which we may choose to share. Each time we air any such occasion I suspect that we examine aspects of it, making it more acceptable to us and gain a perspective and understanding which provides emotional growth thereby improving our maturity levels. Events of long ago are frequently recalled years later. These are the very stories that affected our thinking, our view on the world, were the touchstones of our lives and are related in a humorous manner.

Sweets were very much a treat in our house, and, more often than not were restricted to Saturday evenings, bath night. So for us to find a chocolate bar on the mantelpiece midweek was indeed rare. But on one particular day there was a small bar, still wrapped in its red paper. Only one square had been eaten. My younger brother and I asked if we could have some, Mum said no. Then our older brother and sister came in asking the same question. Again Mum said no. But later that day someone did help himself or herself!

She asked who had eaten it; this was her chocolate, her special chocolate, more than half the bar had been consumed. No child would admit to stealing or eating the chocolate. To reiterate her message mum lined all six of us up in age order, youngest to oldest. She held the remaining chocolate in front of us all. In a very stern voice my mother insisted on knowing which one of us would dare do something so awful. She paraded up and down the line wagging her finger at us filling us all with such fear and guilt as she demanded to know which one of us had committed the crime. "I will find out, even if you don't tell me, I will find out. When I do I will tan your backside so you can't sit down for a week"! This phrase, still echoes in our ears. Our silence was our strength, not one of us dared admit to such a heinous act nor were we prepared to point the finger of blame at each other. Oh boy was she angry, she meant every word thrown at us. I am certain that we all shared the opinion that this punishment could never happen; whoever committed the crime had eaten the evidence! This was never going to be solved. Wrong again! Any child that believes he or she has fooled Mum is only fooling itself! Mum had to go to work, so we were left with our older sister to look after us and in order to keep us in line she could be tougher than Mum! I strongly suspect my sister felt she was being supportive in her attempts to persuade one of us to admit to taking the chocolate but none of us would.

During that evening I developed really painful tummy pains and felt very ill, I constantly had to run up and down the stairs to the toilet. An early bedtime was on the cards for me and I suspect having one in bed was one less to look after for my sister. Even so I wore the carpet down several more times trailing back and forth to the toilet with diarrhoea and awful cramping pains leaving me feeling exhausted and tired. Eventually I fell asleep. Much later I was abruptly awoken, jerked out of bed; my eyes could see nothing in the pitch black of the night, though my backside felt every slap I was given as my mother fulfilled her promise to tan the hide of the one who stole the chocolate. Words were not spoken they were not needed. I was hurled back into bed confused and bewildered as to what had happened and why. I returned to the depths of my dreamland but when I awoke the reality of my stinging backside was proof enough that I had not imagined or dreamed my punishment. My mother had indeed caught the culprit; her evidence was my 'illness'. The chocolate laxative bar had found me out!

Lessons in childhood are constant and necessary. Everything is so new to each of us. Some we embrace and accept so readily, some we dispute, rebuke or dismiss. They are the building stones to our character. A child's limited speech can reduce his ability to express his understanding but we have all heard children succinctly offer a one-word summary that says and conveys everything. Children absorb so much from around themselves, our language, our behaviour, they reflect our personalities and our understanding. One short but hefty slapping in the middle of the night spoke volumes to me! I eventually learnt why I had been slapped but at the time the punishment was totally disconnected from the crime committed and I was left confused and befuddled, and oddly enough in the pitch-black night, more asleep than awake, I really had no idea who was slapping me but the episode left an indelible mark on my life. The lessons learned were simple, i) don't steal; ii) always give a child a full explanation he can understand and relate to; iii) never eat laxative chocolate!

Before we can begin to understand the life of a traumatised child it can be helpful to understand one's own traumas. No matter how big or small the experience the resulting effect on one's life will offer a significant impression and affect one's thinking as well as one's behaviour, I had been taught not to steal, that had had a profound effect on me that was reinforced by another incident when someone stole from me. The injustice of the incident was enormously humiliating.

My mother made me a dress, a simple cotton print frock with a semi-flared skirt, which buttoned down the back to the waist; it had a fixed belt that tied at the back. The background colour was in my favourite shade of blue, a royal blue with beautiful multicoloured cakes depicted all over it. I loved it. This was mine and no one else had ever worn it, only me. No one else had one like it. Having two sisters older than me meant that hand-me-downs were my usual clothes. Wearing this pretty dress made me feel so good and always happy, as my siblings or my friends would pretend to eat their favourite cake off it or count how many they could see. Youth provides such simple pleasures. I just adored wearing it at every given opportunity.

My older sister planned to take four of us to the local beach for a few hours. So armed with sandwiches and a drink packed in a bag with one towel between us we set off. Of course I was wearing my favourite blue dress. The sun was shining as we played on the beach. We had taken off our shoes and socks. My brothers were busy making a sand boat whilst the girls were making a sandcastle and collecting shells to place around it. Then one of my brothers suggested we ought to make the seawater run towards the castle to fill the moat. This would mean digging a trench from the waters edge all the way to the castle, there were five of us and with teamwork we should be able to achieve it easily. My dress got very splashed which upset me as the sand was sticking to the wet patch, so my sister suggested I took it off to dry out leaving it by the towel. We then spent what seemed like a long time trying to persuade the water to reach the castle.

Eventually came the time for us to go home. We all ran back to the bag and towel to argue who would be the first to dry their feet. First one had a clean dry towel to use; last one would have a wet, well-used sandy towel! In turn we dried and de-sanded our feet as best we could, put on our shoes and socks, then I went to put my dress on which I assumed was in the bag. I couldn't find it, the remains of our lunch was in the bag but nothing else, I looked around in case it had blown away, but my beautiful dress was nowhere to be seen. Panic rose inside of me, but maybe it was possible that my brother had hidden it, but out on the open beach where could he hide it?

He was furious about my accusation, and used a few choice words to me, which only added to my distress. Sitting close by was a woman watching over her two children, she had seen and heard us arguing among ourselves, occasionally glancing over. My sister remarked that it was possible that the woman may have noticed whether anyone else, other than us, had been near our belongings. We approached her but she denied knowing anything. What else could we do? We were in a dilemma, if we spent any more time searching we would be late home and risk the wrath of Mum, to go home without the dress would definitely be meeting that wrath! I was feeling sick at the thought, not only would I have to face Mum, but in order to get home we had to walk quite a long way and cross a busy road, all this in my underwear! Feeling very vulnerable, being teased by my siblings I turned away to do that which I was inclined to do at times like this. I cried. There was no comfort, not only had I lost my dress I had also lost all credibility with my siblings. Yet again I was a total embarrassment to them, relegated to either walk several yards behind them or in front of them but certainly not with them. To further my punishment for putting them in this position I was expected to carry the bag. Through my tears I asked if I could wrap myself in the towel but was vehemently told 'no', as I would look stupid. How could I look any more stupid than I did already? I cried all the louder, increasing the risk of abandonment by my siblings altogether. Reminded of this by my sister and brother, I could see the sense and calmed the howling to a constant sobbing which I kept up until we reached home, then fear hit me again as I faced my mother's exasperation.

Frightened, cold, feeling foolish wearing only my underwear and footwear, I had dragged myself behind the family group all the way from the beach, along the sea front, out onto the streets to wend our way home. It was a long haul, not helped by the jeers and taunts of my siblings. My attempt to retaliate with words and threats of my own was tempered by my need to be with them, that group strength was essential; I would need their support when I got home, so tolerating the taunts and teasing was necessary, though did not prevent me from snivelling behind them!

So my best blue dress had gone, disappeared into thin air, never to be seen again, but my mother's warnings and threats remain with me to this day. How could I have been so stupid to lose my new unique dress? What did I think I was doing? How dare I walk home undressed showing everyone up? I was bombarded with all the words that reiterated my incompetence. I would never be allowed out again or have any new clothes ever! My mother never knew when to stop when she was in full flow, and as a child there was no option but to shake in your shoes, listen and take it. Cry if you dare, because that would only add fuel to the fire, as she demanded you stop making that racket thereby prolonging the reprimand.

Sometimes children find it hard to recognise the correlation between events when they find themselves on the one hand aggrieved by what they have done to others, but on the other hand equally aggrieved by what others have done to them. They can feel the strength of their own strong feelings regarding an incident that leaves them totally dejected or rejected, as they are the victims of the circumstances. However when they are responsible for committing the crime, feelings of remorse can be overridden by self-pity, totally untouched by the intensity of feeling in their prey. Empathy is beyond them as they are nursing their own wounds at being found out, unable to reach out to offer consolation to those they hurt. Without an explanation of the effects on others how can a child gain insight or appreciation but how many actually get one? Far too often parents or those in authority are quick to chide and reprimand, which dents a child's self esteem, but slow to show them the balance between good and not so good. Reprimands can put boundaries around behaviour, but discovering the root cause and effect to gain clarification of an incident offers an awareness of alternative methods of coping in life, allowing self made boundaries to be made, not imposed ones. Growing up is not easy for any one of us. Different stages of our development provide us with a different perspective on the events of our life. A parent's responsibility is to keep pace with their child's changeable emotional swings, this of course must be in tune with their own emotional swings, which can lead to a whole lot of fun and frustration when they are out of tune! The more of you there are in a household the greater the likelihood of emotional swings becoming entangled, in which case the adults spend more time freeing these sensitive, friable emotions or in our case searching for an elusive magic wand to wave.

> "Each day in our lives we make deposits
> in the memory banks of our children."
>
> Charles Rozell Swindoll
>
> Evangelical Christian Preacher and Author

# CHAPTER 3

# Growing Up

Eventually of course I emerged from childhood to enter the turbulent teens! The least said about this era of my life the better. If I was to share such times how would I be able to hold my head high in front of my children? They believe there are times in their lives, especially their teens, of which we as parents know nothing about. I would doubt the truth of that, as I am sure we got to know the majority of their misdemeanours and antics from a variety of sources, but that does not entitle them to get to know mine!

Leaving school was not going to be easy for me, I had loved my time there and had wanted to stay on an extra year to take my exams, and this was optional in the late 1960's. My parents were not keen; the need for a contribution to the household was essential. However I was determined, as I so wanted to do the nursing course much against my mother's wishes. (Though secretly I think she was rather pleased but was unsure about how important this was to me). Maybe she thought it was no more than a childhood whim that I had carried with me but would not succeed in. In time my parents agreed to let me stay at school to achieve my first real set of qualifications, on condition that I did not do homework at home, as our home would not allow me my own personal space to work, and I was expected to offer a small contribution to the household as well as earn my own spending money. The former was easy to do, there was always the local library and as school librarian I had access to the library and spare time in school to work. That would then leave me time to work to earn. I had a newspaper round both morning and evening that rewarded me with five shillings a week. If I delivered the bills to the customers for the papers and collected the monies I could earn an extra two shillings. Sometimes at weekends and school holidays I had the opportunity to work in a bed and breakfast establishment, covering for a friend whilst she was on holiday. Then I was introduced to the local confectioner who had several sea front shops as well as a couple of shops in town. This was brilliant, between all of these I had earning power to fulfil my obligation to the family, have my own financial independence, and gain the qualifications I would need to go into nursing. At our school we only did the CSE's (Certificate of Secondary Education) of which I gained eight. I had mainly grade A's and B's, but when I looked into qualifications required for nursing they quoted GCE's (General Certificate of Education). To gain these I would need another year at school, this time at the local Grammar School, if I could get a place!

By the end of 1969 I had the necessary qualifications, but I was still too young to enter the profession unless I started as a pre-nursing student which only added an extra two years on to my learning curve. Not what I needed. With little support and a huge lack of confidence I was uncertain which direction in life to take. I continued to work at the confectioners, a brilliant family firm that let me work the sea front shops in summer and the town shops in winter. I learnt so much there, organisation and money skills, the retail aspect, people skills, health and safety of the business (our ice cream machine was the cleanest in town and always passed it's inspections). I could pull a Whippy ice cream and create a '99' with the best of them, candy floss on a stick or in a bag was a doddle! Beef burgers, hot dogs (with or without onions) as well as fresh made doughnuts (I loved that machine), seaside rock of all flavours, I knew them all and was taught how to display the various types to their best advantage. The seaside working experience was a wonderful time, my employers gave me trust and I gave them loyalty, truly the best time of my life.

I began to have doubts in my ability to complete the nursing course. Yes me! I had made that decision at five, stayed with it all these years. I had become a member of the British Red Cross Society at seven years old and stayed with them until I was almost eighteen. I had represented the Division and County at the Red Cross Centenary celebration at Buckingham Palace. I had been buying the Nursing Times since I was fifteen years old, even though I didn't understand half of what I read. But careers advice was in its infancy and those who advised were too! If they had given me an application form and an addressed envelope I would have easily applied, but I really did not know how to go about becoming a student nurse. So I stayed in my comfortable rut. However my main employer, the brother in law to the family firm, took me under his wing, a wonderfully dedicated man who encouraged me to learn more about the business but also took time to learn about my aspirations. On one of our delivery runs between shops he gave me a good talking to, he told me he valued me and the work I put into the company, but the world was bigger than the rock shops and I had to stop being a coward and raise my expectations and go for it. Good advice, such easy words to say, but not so easy to act upon. Doubt rose again.

Maybe my mother was right all along. Perhaps I didn't have the brain to study, to learn all those difficult medical terms, to achieve my dream. If I didn't embark on the training, then I wouldn't prove that I was the failure others believed I might be. This logical conclusion went against the beliefs of my employer. Was there a truth or a reality in what he said? I had reached a crossroads in my life. Unsure of the direction I should take. Who should I be listening to, which one of them knew me better than I knew myself?

About the time of this confused period in my life I found myself in hospital for a spell, which gave me time out to think, and also reinforced my original convictions. I really did want to be a nurse. A staff nurse who was married to a GP befriended me. After I left hospital I was invited to visit them. They were to become a very important part of my life. In time I was to live with the family helping to look after their three children. They persuaded me to take a nursing auxiliary post at the local cottage hospital. They also actively encouraged me to apply to three nursing schools, the local one in Grimsby, the county hospital in Lincoln, and a city hospital in Sheffield. My application to Sheffield was responded to first, they offered me a place to start training in February 1972 to undertake the three years State Registered Nurse Qualification. All I had to do was find my way to Sheffield and I was on the starting block, ready and raring to go. I wore my new nurse's uniform with pride, but those darn caps were a work of art to make and to keep on your head.

Three years later I had accomplished my childhood dream. I had become a nurse. My tutor's tolerance had paid off. I was a fully-fledged State Registered Nurse and I even had the certificate and a badge to prove it. Amazing!

Towards the end of my training, through the nurse's family, I met my future husband. Though ten years my senior his experience of life made up for my inexperience. I still worked in Sheffield whilst he lived in the Outer Hebrides. Such an incongruous contrast but it worked for us. The geographical difficulties meant that we met up infrequently, usually every six to twelve weeks or so, occasional letters and weekly telephone calls helped to cement our relationship and led him to ask me to marry him, in fact he asked several times, but my mapped out career was calling and I was reluctant to give in. Eventually at the end of 1975 I accepted. We married in the heat wave of June 1976, had our honeymoon in Tenerife, where it was cooler than Britain, and then headed for the Outer Hebrides, which the heat wave had not found! Life took a new turn altogether. Island life was certainly different and took some adapting to, Lawrence had lived there for about ten years having gone there in his RAF days so in some ways was very established. He was manager of the local agricultural supplies depot. I worked in the local fifteen-bedded hospital. For the next two and a half years we were to discover each other's strengths and weaknesses, with few distractions and excellent friends, both from the local community and the Army, we were to enjoy a good life. December 1977, our second Christmas in the Hebrides gave us our first son. He too benefited from island life.

The fresh air, mild weather, freedom, tranquillity and the pace of life suited us all. However during the following months we had reason to rethink our lives. Together we agreed to return to the mainland.

This led us to starting a new life in Yorkshire. Finding a home was the first hurdle. One we could afford and one that would in time allow for our joint commitment to foster children. We looked at new and older properties but could not find anything to compare to the house we were living in which offered us what we needed. In it's prime it had been the original farmhouse for the area. When we moved in it had been up for sale for several months and was in a very poor condition. Owned by Lawrence's new employers, they allowed us to live in it whilst we searched the area for a new home, however, we made them an offer to buy, which they accepted. With only two bedrooms it lacked the inside space we would eventually need, but with approximately two thirds of an acre of rough pasture surrounding the house it had potential for extending. There was to be a lifetime of work ahead of us but we were young enough to tackle it and make it home for all who came to stay. What we lacked in cash we made up for in hopes and dreams and to top it all at the head of the drive was a cherry blossom tree just waiting to show it's full glory! This was to be home for more than thirty years and for every child that came to share our lives.

In 1980 our second son was born. Our two boys were to give us the parenting foundation and insight required to feel we were ready to contemplate fostering. Aaron our older son would always be 'big brother' to the children and our younger son Gareth, would always be their 'friend or partner in crime'! They were raised knowing that eventually other children would be living with us. The house would need to grow to provide us with the accommodation we really needed and the field outside was to become our garden, a therapeutic de-stressing area for everyone! So the house grew, we doubled the size of it providing ourselves with a spacious four bed-roomed property and the garden was gradually taking shape. Our boys spent much of their lives outside learning the art of gardening. Together we cleared the debris, dug it over and planted many trees over the coming years. The first trees were planted alongside the drive, one for each of us, leylandii, which the boys took a great deal of interest in as they grew to represent each one of us, bemusing all as they were in height proportion to us. Over the next few years we were to plant many trees, one for every child that joined us. A symbolic way of putting down roots which for some was very important. Anniversaries, birthdays and other celebrations involved planting of some new treasured shrub; the garden was big enough for all of them. I would like to think that our children at some stage of their lives saw this planting as accepting and celebrating new life.

We approached our local Fostering and Adoption Unit during 1983 to explore the possibilities. Though our interest had been registered, the department was short of staff so were unable to pick up our application until 1984. Early that year we were invited to attend an introductory meeting. Young Aaron was very disappointed when we returned from the first meeting without any children. These sessions were an opportunity for us to join with other prospective foster parents, gain insight into what may lay ahead of us and for each of us to explore our own roots, our own expectations, also to review our own understanding and misinterpretations of life events. I think it was also a filtering of the determined from the uncertain prospective guardians of little souls. Several meetings later all of which took place in our own home with Emily, a very experienced and dedicated support social worker, we emerged with an assessment that would be presented to the panel of experts who would decide our suitability to foster. This form was designed to collect and present information about prospective substitute parents to include a profile on each of us, our relationships, parenting capacity, limitation of family size, family lifestyle, motivation and preparation, and our expectations of any future placement. No stone left unturned. The assessment concluded: -

*"A very close and happy family consisting of mum, dad, and two sons. A little geographically isolated but not isolated socially having several good family friends. Very child orientated."*

Our friends were an enormous support, at times our rock. We had no relatives who lived close by and if our children, or we, ever exasperated them they hid it well. That is apart from one who always kept my feet on the ground by telling me it straight, which I have always valued! The isolation came to be a godsend as our children were protected, when they were displaying their worst, from judgemental critical eyes. This also gave them freedom to be themselves without causing problems or distress to others, at least whilst they were on home ground.

*" Lawrence is very much a family man, intent on giving his children as best a start in life as possible. He is ambitious and hardworking, having built up a business from near scratch in five years, yet continues to remain calm and patient…"*

Indeed he was and remained so even though that patience was tried and tested to its very limits. Not always by the children I hasten to add! But also by my demands on him to be a strong presence within the family, he rarely had time to sit quietly to unwind after a day at work, as one youngster or another would need taking to or collecting from an event, or a model needed making, homework to be helped with, or a story to be read. I would remind him endlessly that a change was as good as a rest! He had a head for facts, and an excellent command of the English language, so useful for project homework, and his head for maths concepts was second to none, so he frequently engaged the youngsters in quizzes and maths games, which kept them on the ball.

*" Dani presents as a determined person, prepared to take on challenges, and very much the one to lend a helping hand to others in need. She has proved very supportive of Lawrence during his first few years in business, showing her strengths and dependability."*

We were a team; we worked together whether it was work or family, we each had our limitations and we had a pact that we were not allowed to be downhearted at the same time! It was the responsibility of the other to support and uplift whichever one of us was low! This became a necessity in the years to come. Any child's behaviour can try the patience of a saint; some of the extreme behaviours we were to deal with were to take us to the very edge of sanity!

*"The Valdis' see themselves as an open door type family, making everyone feel comfortable in their home. They are definitely cuddlers and are very supportive of each other both in everyday living through*

*to making major decisions. The household rules are quite flexible, the main consideration being respect for each other and each other's property, attempting to teach children to primarily respect themselves. The roles of the family are very much shared, with everyone expected to muck in regardless. Their degree of flexibility is such that they would not envisage a great deal of difficulty in helping a child to fit in with their lifestyle. They are very child orientated and treat each one as an individual, responding to their individual needs, whenever possible, although academically the house is quite busy and so time is set aside at bedtimes to accommodate this."*

Our doors were always open to the world and its wife! Sleepovers were a regular occurrence for our sons' friends. The lack of close relatives in the area brought us closer to our friends. Being involved in the community brought us closer to so many other people. Life was full and our boys were a big part of this. Though I think our 'respect for others' rule was lost on Aaron when as a young boy of three he overheard the road planner explaining to us that there were plans to build a by-pass that would involve taking part of our drive and garden, the main area that we had worked on, planting trees and daffodils. He had been playing quietly oblivious to the conversation, or so I thought! When he suddenly unleashed his feelings on the poor man kicking with his slippered feet wailing at him that we had just planted trees and flowers and "No, he could not have our garden to make his road!" Our own children had their own extremes for us to deal with and this was only one example! Recognising individuality was vital, we were all different, held differing views, had our own strengths, weaknesses and emotional responses. But we were there for each other, regardless of the situation we faced.

*"Dani and Lawrence have had varied experiences of other people's children from baby-sitting and caring for sick children to caring for Dani's brother's three children, permanently for a considerable length of time following a house fire. A very sensitive time for these children as it was to be their second traumatic experience in a short space of time. Dani and Lawrence recognised that children cannot always articulate problems and that parents need to be alert to signs of unhappiness and stress and to give them opportunity to talk. Dani has been involved with running a playschool and has completed the Pre-School Playgroup Association course. This has involved her with children from a variety of backgrounds, given her insight into many of the problems faced. Lawrence has a relaxed and straightforward attitude, which should help him to achieve a good understanding of a child's difficulties, which has recently been demonstrated whilst looking after a friend's child with learning problems.*

Our lives had always been intertwined with children around us from before we married. I don't think either of us had ever given it any serious thought. Children were a strong part of our lives both individually and together. We had met through a mutual friend, well my friend and Lawrence's cousin, I helped look after their three children one of which was Lawrence's Godson whom he had come to visit. Other children included my two nephews and the young brother of my friend from my student nurse days; I took all three (at the same time) to visit Lawrence in the Hebrides. I wonder if subconsciously I was putting him through an endurance test? If I was then he passed with flying colours to the next stage of life. Some of my nieces and nephews were frequent visitors to our home. Every child is loved and cherished for its unique qualities; each one has something special to offer. I am a great believer in look for the good and you will find it, look at the not so good and that is all you will see. A child needs more loving when he least deserves it, keep this in mind and you will only move forward.

So as the cherry blossom bloomed in May 1984 we were 'presented' on paper to the panel and accepted as foster parents. At last we were ready and raring to go! Room ready, boys as prepared as we could have them be until the reality of sharing parents, home and life were to hit them between the eyes.

Excitement and anticipation filled our home. Constantly awaiting a telephone call to take a child or two into our home and offer the support we longed to give. How many years had gone by since this idea first came to me? That child had grown up and was now in the position of fulfilling the promise made. My second childhood decision was also to come to fruition! Over the following months we waited and waited but no telephone call came. We were offering a home for children in care, we had been prepared, accepted, celebrated our achievement, but still no children were brought to us. Christmas came and went as did the New Year and winter with it. We were almost of the belief that we had been forgotten or our file had been filed away. Then Spring arrived along with the cherry blossom in full bloom and with it the long awaited telephone call: -

*"Mrs Valdis would you be prepared to look after two children, a brother and a sister? Dad is out of the country and Mum is unable to care for them effectively. There is a history of neglect. Family do not live in the area, the length of their placement is uncertain."*

I had been preparing tea for our family at the time; this was a bolt out of the blue. I confidently said yes of course we could, but deep down I was in a state of panic!

Overnight we would be doubling the size of our family, I was to care for a little girl, boys were easy, but would this little girl fit in to our boy-orientated world? Would they like us? Would we get on with them? How would the boys cope with strangers taking our time? Were we really ready for this? The next few months would answer all these questions and more.

Our real test in life was about to begin. The Social Worker and her two charges arrived, out of the black car stepped Carrie aged six years and her brother Carl aged two. Life was about to take us to a whole new dimension.

*"Don't worry that children never listen to you; worry that they are always watching you".*

*Robert Fulghum*

*U.S. Author*

# CHAPTER 4

## Our First Arrivals

Two small pale fearful youngsters stared at me as we were introduced to each other. Their wide-eyed expressions were unemotional but striking. They said nothing. What were they expecting from us? What was going on in their minds? How must they feel about being plucked from their own environment and suddenly finding themselves in ours. We could only try to imagine, as we did not have their inner turmoil of emotions, we could only anticipate their feelings and thoughts but to empathise with them was the closest we could get. Aaron, with his natural desire to make others feel at home, took a grasp on the situation. He suggested they went on a tour of the house to find their bedroom; Carrie went with Aaron and Gareth whilst Carl sat in Lawrence's arms giving me an opportunity to do the necessary paperwork with the children's social worker, gain contact numbers for support and to be given a potted history of their circumstances, it felt like signing for a delivery, which I suppose it was. She assured me that she would call us the next day to see how the children were settling. She offered encouraging words of reassurance to the children reminding them she would be back to see them soon, after all she was the bridge between all they knew, home, and us, the unknown. With a quick wave and a smile to all of us she climbed into her car and left. We were now on our own.

Carl was a dear little soul, not your normal active almost three-year-old full of vitality and wanting to discover the world around him. He lacked animation, carried a vacant expression and constantly dribbled out of the corner of his mouth. His skin was very dry, he always seemed constantly tired, and he was also extremely bowlegged with scrawny limbs, only walking when he really had to, as it seemed to take such a lot out of him. His tummy was quite distended and I began to question if he should be having medical attention. For one so young he was too quiet for long periods, rarely cried or reached out for affection. The natural inquisitiveness that one would expect did not exist in Carl, exploring or playing was unknown to him. But he watched our boys, if they moved he would follow them around the home which increased his level of activity, though there were still times when he would just give in, usually if they went upstairs he would sit at the bottom to wait for them to come down again. This was not because he was unable to climb stairs, nor through idleness or laziness, Carl lacked the physical energy to do anything, for much of the time he was extremely tired and just could not make any effort. Everyone who was to have reason to pick Carl up commented on his thin limbs and the feeling of holding a rag doll, he just lolled in your arms and I just wanted to hold him and love him to give him strength, physically, psychologically, and emotionally, to discover the true character of this little soul.

Carl's remarkably blonde hair framed his equally exceptionally pale face; his tiny head emphasized his thin features. He had the most gorgeous long eyelashes and big blue sad vacant eyes. His bland expression of sadness spoke volumes of the neglect he had experienced. His speech was virtually non-existent; Carl made very little effort to try to make sounds, not even to gain attention or to have toys, food, or treats. Playtime had little if no meaning to him. He lacked 'oomph' as Gareth so aptly said; he was right. Carl's get up and go had got up and gone, if indeed it had ever been there at all.

Carrie was a few month's younger than Aaron but much smaller and thinner for her age. She had long fair hair swept back in a ponytail; this style accentuated her small eyes and pointed features. She had very thin lips that rarely smiled but an inquisitive expression that asked so much without the use of words. Her inability to speak clearly stemmed from her dental problems that we were to find out about fairly quickly! She appeared very sullen, almost morose, but yet there was a keenness of spirit itching to be released. She loved having Aaron and Gareth's company but gave little attention to her own brother but I suspect she was relieved to hand over the reins of responsibility for him to someone else. She dreaded being left alone and frequently asked if we were leaving her by herself, seeking reassurance regularly that this would not happen. Carrie's memory was very poor indeed, her powers of concentration were very limited but she was able to mimic the behaviour examples of those around, which is why I suspect she enjoyed our boys' company so much, they gave her the lead to follow. A sensitive little girl, Carrie craved for love and acceptance, but did not demand it, however when given these qualities she would respond with caution. We would have to work hard to gain her trust.

Family history was limited. Dad had been working abroad leaving Mum to manage alone, which she struggled to do. Mum had some support from the extended family but her mental health difficulties and drinking had pushed their support to the limits. She frequently left the children alone in the house, which explained why Carrie desperately needed to be reassured that she would not be left alone. It seems Mum had given the children Mogadon tablets periodically; these were sleeping tablets prescribed for Mum's needs but instead were used to subdue the children. When the children were collected by the social worker to be brought to us, she could find no real evidence of food in their house apart from an almost empty box of cereal. Carrie's attendance in school was not good. The lack of stimulation in the family home, along with her poor school history and general neglect, explained her lack of progress and limited appreciation of the world around her.

They were to stay with us for almost five months, during this time we would have less sleep, spend a great deal of our time at the Dental Hospital, the weekly wash of course took longer, and the food bills and petrol usage were to double. Homework time would increase, with additional teaching time and valuable playing time to be given to Carrie to spur her along to catch up with her peers. We played endless children's songs in the car wherever we went, partly to help relax the children but also to increase their vocabulary, pronunciation and intonation. This worked beautifully especially for Carl who wriggled and jiggled to the music trying desperately hard to sing the words and join in with Aaron and Gareth. Carrie struggled initially with our endless 'in car' singing, perhaps through embarrassment or because she was not familiar with the songs, or maybe the noise was far too much for her, however she was eventually to be the initiator of this activity, demanding certain cassettes to be played, then she would shout out the words with gusto, several decibels louder than everyone else. The other children would continue to sing along but covering their ears, I suspect to prevent them from becoming damaged from Carrie's bawling!

This relatively quiet duo fitted into our family ways fairly quickly, almost straight away. But their needs were great and we knew that the plan was for them to hopefully return to their own family as soon as the home situation had been resolved. We needed to pack in as much living for them as possible in the short time we may have, yet also give them time to recover from the physical neglect they had experienced and come to terms with the temporary loss of their family and cope with the suddenness of finding themselves in ours.

The few clothes they had brought with them were not clean and had been stuffed into plastic bags in a bundle. We could cater for Carl easily with out grown clothes of Gareth but what about Carrie? A quick call to my friend Cath resolved that difficulty as she had a little girl slightly older than Carrie with an abundance of redundant clothes. Over night I managed to wash, dry and iron their own clothes just so they could wear something of their own when they awoke, something recognisable from their own life.

Our first evening together was more about getting to know each other, letting them find their way around the house. I was concerned about the level of freedom they had previously, in case they tried to get out of the house, perhaps even try to go home. However I needn't have worried at all, going outside was to prove to be an ordeal for all of us. Carl was afraid to go out, and Carrie always thought she was being taken home whenever we went in the car. We all had tea together that evening during which both of them appeared to struggle to chew food. Carl needed help to finish his meal as he was overcome by tiredness. Bath time was over very quickly as this was an anxious time for them both. We were to discover that this was actually an infrequent event at home so they had never learnt to relax and enjoy playing in the bath as most children do. A few bedtime stories later and they were both fast asleep. Exhaustion had taken over, and they slept all night. Time was given to our boys to allow for us to answer their endless questions.

*"How long are they here for? Does this mean we now have a brother and a sister? Where have their Mummy and Daddy gone? Why do they look so sad? Why can't Carl move properly? Why does he dribble like that?"*

On and on went the interrogation, better that we had it rather than the children. We pointed out how little they had brought of their own so it was very important that they (the boys) shared toys, games and time with them. They were intrigued, but showed compassion and concern for our newcomer's plight.

Our first morning started early, as every morning was going to do for a long time to come. Carrie would wake about five-thirty most mornings, awaken Carl, and then be hell bent on waking everyone else in the household. She was cheerful enough with it, but her anxiety and need for others to be around was enormous as she was so afraid of being left alone. First of all she would shout at Carl or sing in the loudest voice possible with decibel levels that would pierce your ears. Who needed a cockerel to herald the dawn when Carrie could do a better job? Thank goodness we did not have neighbours.

A whirlwind of a week lay ahead of us, new family dynamics, trying to accommodate everyone's needs, treating all of the children as individuals was a challenge. I had to learn to awaken before Carrie or at the first sound of her calling out to Carl, at least then the others had a chance of a longer sleep. We had to consider which school Carrie would attend, should Carl go to nursery or would it be wiser to keep him at home with us, arrange dental and doctors appointments for both children. Make their bedroom feel more homely and personal. Squeeze in shopping time and do the general household chores. This all gave new meaning to the old saying of "a woman's work is never done." But I doubt that Lawrence had much time to himself either. Playtime was essential for everyone, children learn by example, so that is what we had to give, and lots of it! Among all the work we had to find time to enjoy having the children, this meant silly times together, something that was alien to Carrie and Carl. Perhaps they thought we were all crazy but they needed to learn free expression but within the boundaries we created for their security.

Our family GP was of the "old school" type, a typical grandfather figure, though once described by Aaron as being "like Father Christmas or maybe his brother as he hasn't got a beard!" We all knew what he meant. The doctor was friendly, rather rotund with a shock of white hair. He wore glasses and laughed a lot. But he didn't suffer fools gladly, he gave a great deal of time to his patients, but with the old system of turn up and wait to be seen, his patients gave a great deal of time in his packed waiting room too. Having taken Aaron and

Gareth to school I then joined the long wait to see the GP with the two youngsters in tow wondering how they would cope with this ordeal. They were too good; they just clung to me the whole time we were there, so I read stories to them whilst they glared around the room at the other patients. Eventually our names were called, the children were examined, and I was told that Carl was on the verge of rickets and scurvy, was teething, and had a chest infection and a skin infection. Carrie was diagnosed as needing dental treatment; was short of vitamins and she had an ear infection. Both had severe dietary deficiencies. He finished by saying that it was nothing that couldn't be fixed by a dose of antibiotics, vitamins, good food, exercise and fresh air, and a good dose of Valdis' living! However he did choose to set the wheels in motion for Carl to see an orthopaedic consultant about his legs. "Bring them back in a month, if you still have them, and let me see the difference you've made" he added.

To make it easier on the children to visit the dentist I arranged a 'family appointment', this simply meant that all six of us would go so that the children were not singled out and had the opportunity to watch how Aaron and Gareth coped with this. Our boys were old hands at going to see the dentist, who was called Mr Wolf. The imagination of a child who had not met him or was unaccustomed to visiting a dentist could have been enough to give them nightmares before their first appointment. This is where we discovered the real damage to Carrie's teeth. Apart from the moderate odour of bad breath and the plaque on her teeth through lack of care and regular brushing, an unhealthy diet, and having had too many sweet drinks, we established that she would need several teeth removed as the decay was so bad the gum appeared to be protruding through the teeth and some teeth would need fillings. We were aware that she had toothache but the extent of the treatment needed in one so young surprised us. Specialist help had to be sought from the dental hospital and we were to spend one day a week there for a few weeks to come to resolve the problem and give her a chance of healthy teeth and gums. Carrie loved to get the stickers that dentists willingly gave out, so accepted all the treatment very well as long as she was supported with lengthy explanations of what was to be done and given a sticker that she so proudly wore on her jumper. We were to become very familiar with the waiting area in the children's department, the cartoon murals on the walls, the story books on their shelves, the best toys to play with, we knew them so well.

Our doctor was right, the children changed so much within the first three to four weeks, they gained weight, found new energy, slowly learnt to play, accepted going outside, not only in the garden, but also gained confidence in outings. With Aaron and Gareth as role models they started to use their imaginations, to play and learn. Carl began to show signs of straightening and therefore standing taller. They had got over their infections, ate well and willingly tried new foods. They even smiled and laughed, such a wonderful sound to hear for the first time from children whom, only weeks earlier seemed to have nothing to laugh about. But the early morning warning call from Carrie was still in force and had to be reckoned with!

Lawrence and I may have been the organisers of their daily routines and various appointment times, we may have been the guardians of their hurt feelings, we may even have been their protectors, but their real teachers were Aaron and Gareth. Our boys were loving and tolerant with them, they played so well and without realising it taught them so much. On one particular day they were all drawing and crayoning around the table before going to bed, they chattered away together talking about what they were drawing when I noticed that Carrie had only used black, browns and purples, the dark colours of life, which I suspect said more about her inner feelings than I appreciated at the time. I could oversee this activity whilst I was ironing and casually suggested that she used some of the brighter colours to liven her picture. Carrie stopped what she was doing, looked down at her own picture, then at Gareth's and then Aaron's, with a deep frown she nudged Gareth and said, "Which ones are the bright colours?" He looked at her, smiled, and said, "they are all bright colours, just that some are brighter than others, but girls usually like red, pink, yellow and orange, I think that's what Mum means." Thereafter flame coloured pictures from Carrie were bestowed upon us all as she experimented with these new colours in her life.

Aaron took on the role of helping her to learn the alphabet mainly through a Mr Men jigsaw that we had as well as teaching her how to read using the 'Dick and Dora' system from school. We had decided that it would be far better for Carrie to attend the small private school that our boys enjoyed, as she would get the one to one attention she needed in the short time that she would be with us which had been intimated at being only a few weeks. School was school to Carrie, the type didn't matter but the regular attendance did, she made a huge effort to keep up with the boys and loved the homework time with us, a way of gaining individual time and show off her new skills. This was also a time when she would share her feelings about her Mum and although she wanted to go home she was frightened to go in case Mum forgot to look after them properly and left them alone in the house again. Both boys just adored Carl, and whilst Carrie and I had our own time together they would be down on the floor crawling about mimicking animals or playing with the toy garage and cars, teaching Carl all about different colours. They would read him stories or chase him around the house, which always gave rise to raucous laughter and high excitement and gave him plenty of exercise too. Playing outdoor games was essential, endless 'hide and seek', racing games and ball games, anything to keep them on the move to get lots of exercise and happily tire them out? This would ensure a quiet evening once they were in bed but did nothing to prevent that early morning reveille.

One morning about four weeks after their arrival, I was in my bedroom combing my hair, dressed and ready for the day. The door was open and in came Carrie, she stopped in the doorway and with a big "Oh" emanating from her, and she just stood and stared. I asked her what was wrong as I rechecked myself in the mirror and couldn't see what the problem was. Eventually she managed to put words to her feelings. "That's the dress you wore when I first came here." I asked her if she didn't want me to wear it as it so obviously brought up memories and feelings that I wasn't sure she was comfortable with, she then ran towards me, threw her arms around me and shrieked "Yes keep it on it makes me feel nice." She also made me 'feel nice' as it was her way of letting me know how happy she was about being with us. Here was a little girl who was described as having a poor memory and yet on that first day with us she had taken in more than we realised. First impressions last, so they say! Thereafter I found it very difficult to wear that dress again without feeling self-conscious and recalling their first day, the arrival of our first foster children.

During the review that took place six weeks after their arrival, it was stated by the social worker that 'Carrie settled very well into the foster home, almost too well.' I began to question if we had got it all wrong. Were we doing too much, I only knew one way to look after children and as far as both Lawrence and I were concerned we did not differentiate between our natural born sons and our foster children. We knew that eventually they would be going home and this fact was never hidden, but trying to find the balance of giving them the best experience that we could, without taking over their lives or lead them to disappointment, was difficult and something I agonised with often late into the night. We did not go to the vast expense of bestowing gifts on them; treats were small and had to be earned. But time was the greatest gift of all, was in short supply for us to give to these children so every waking moment would be filled in some way. Carrie and Carl had an access visit organised at their home. They were to spend a few hours with Mum, which would hopefully encourage a connection or at least remind them that she was still there at home and all that they knew still existed. The experience was not a good one, Mum did not cope with the children, and especially now they were more lively and playful. This set the children back considerably,

Carl was quieter and less lively for several days and Carrie became more frightened about returning home, she also developed a psychological cough, needing endless reassurance and love. The emphasis was on waiting for Dad to return from abroad before making any long-term decisions for their future.

Birthday excitement filled the air for the boys, as Carrie was to celebrate her birthday a week after mine, and Carl had his two weeks later. This was almost a month after their arrival. But two birthdays in a week and another to quickly follow within the family was 'feel good factor' time. They talked incessantly about birthday cakes speculating on the type or design we would give Carrie or Carl, ideas for birthday presents, having friends for tea etc. All this seemed to confuse and bemuse Carrie and was way over Carl's understanding. Gareth and Carrie were playing outside whilst I was gardening, and I overheard yet another conversation between them about her birthday. She sounded even more confused than ever. Eventually young Carrie strode towards me; with a quizzical expression she questioned why Gareth thought she needed a birthday present and a birthday cake. I explained to her that that is what you get on your birthday to make it special. I went on to explain she would have seven candles on the cake and she could blow them out whilst we sang to her. The lack of comprehension was fixed in the expressionless face, then I realised that birthday celebrations were probably an unknown experience for her. Before Carrie was in a position to make the most of any celebration for her birthday we were going to have to work on her lack of experience and increase her understanding to have any chance of enjoying her own special day.

We searched for storybooks about birthdays or parties, our family favourites for the youngsters had always been the Topsy and Tim series as they are well illustrated, easy to read and relate to real life scenarios that children meet. We had dolly and teddy tea parties in the garden to re-enact the events. We made birthday decorations to hang up for these parties and used balloons to make signs. We practised party games, which were played with great enthusiasm once the rules were understood. All this new excitement would have Carrie awake even earlier just so she could play 'party time' with her dolls at dawn!

Carrie loved every minute of my birthday celebrations especially the birthday cake, blowing out of the candles and all the family joining in! So a week later, when her day came, I was surprised at her level of apprehension, however this quickly evaporated at breakfast time when she was inundated with presents and cards, which were opened with renewed enthusiasm. She loved it all. Joining in with the preparations for her birthday tea party she could not wait to see her birthday cake. She had chattered on about it all day, "what would it look like? How many candles would it have? What colour would it be?" She questioned constantly all day to anybody who might listen. The excitement of having her own personal cake was far more meaningful than any friends that might be joining her for the party tea. During the interim between my birthday and hers I had let her peruse the book of celebration cakes for children in the hope of establishing what kind of cake she would really like to have. She had intimated a castle shaped one at first, but having heard the story of Hansel and Gretel she finally chose a house shape with the roof made of chocolate finger biscuits. This had proved to be quite a challenge to my cake making skills but the final result held some resemblance to the picture in the book. I had even created a garden around it made of sweets. There were only a few family friends that joined us in the celebrations, all of whom Carrie had spent time with. The anticipation of this new experience had been quite daunting for Carrie, being the centre of attention was also an embarrassment to her, so to relieve the pressure we chose to play outdoor games which gave everyone natural freedom, with fewer constraints, so was far more relaxing. Having exhausted all the children outside they then raced inside for tea. Aaron pointed out to her that as the birthday girl she would have to be at the head of the table so everyone could see her. Although a little shy she soon revelled in her newly acquired role, loving every moment of her special day. Then the moment came for the birthday cake to be brought in ceremoniously, her face was a picture, her jaw dropped when she saw the 'house' cake as everyone sang 'Happy Birthday'. The moment was filled with emotion for all of us, when she shouted out "I love it, it's the bestest ever!" These were such simple words and yet so meaningful.

If Carrie had ever celebrated her birthday before she had no memory of it. However after her seventh birthday she started planning her eighth! Again I hoped we had not set her up to be disappointed in the future. Unfortunately most of her planning took place very early in the morning before the rest of us wanted to be awake! For the sake of our sanity this early waking had to be stopped and soon.

We had talked to Carrie about waking early, making several suggestions to her as to what she could do whilst waiting for others to wake up. We placed a great deal of importance on her new age status! Now at seven years old she was a third of the way to being grown up, so this was the time to try to show some grown up ways, of which one was to show respect for others, especially if they needed more sleep than she did. To encourage this we extended her bedtime by half an hour as proof of her growing up needs. We gave her several books at the side of the bed to occupy herself quietly, which seemed to work initially but after the first week she announced that reading a book with someone else was better than reading alone. New tactics would be required. Although Carrie was unable to tell the time we decided to give her a clock and set the alarm to seven o'clock. To reinforce this time we helped her to make a cardboard cut out of a clock with the hands coloured in bright red to indicate seven o'clock also. This was stuck to the wall just above her bed to remind her what waking time was acceptable to the rest of us! This really did help, she quickly realised that she needed to wait until the hands on the real clock matched up to the picture of a clock, though some mornings we had our sleep punctuated by her talking to herself quite loudly, saying, "Nearly there, just got to get to the top, yes it's nearly there" then there would be a call to all "It's at the top you can all wake up now." On days that she actually managed at the very least to stay in her room until the appointed time, we would offer endless praise which she loved.

Our friend's daughter and Aaron used to go horse riding each week; Carrie had asked if she could go too. We felt that this would improve her self-confidence and we could use the sessions as a treat for her staying in her room and not disturbing others in the early morning.

It worked! Once she was over her initial fear of climbing on the horse she must have felt twice her size as she really enjoyed the lessons, which she looked forward to so much. She knew that the horse riding lessons were considered to be a reward for Aaron based on certain achievements gained each week, so she happily accepted the price she would have to pay to enjoy the same experience. She took great pleasure in getting the allotted points each day on the chart for remaining in her room and not disturbing others. This fast became her routine. The early waking still continued, but she came to respect the needs of others to not be disturbed, and was able to use that waiting time more constructively to occupy herself. At about this time she was also gaining confidence in us to not leave her on her own at any time.

Little man Carl was also making strides. Looking more robust and having more energy, he enjoyed playing games of all kinds. We referred to him as being Gareth's shadow. Carl was never far from Gareth's side. Gareth's never ending patience with him was wonderful; they played endless games of road building using wooden blocks, the remains of laying the hall floor! The blocks would be strewn all over the floor to form roads branching off in all directions, with small cars, and play people interspersed. They loved these games together making endless car noises, counting cars, discussing the colours of the cars and talking out the game. Carl's parallel play, his ability to follow Gareth's games, noises, and his own input and interaction led us to believe he was ready to cope with play school. His speech was slowly developing, as was his own personality. We chose to arrange for him to attend three sessions a week in a local playschool that I had been involved in running when our own two boys were younger. I felt confident that he would settle well in that small caring environment and I knew the staff well enough to be assured that if he met any difficulties they would be recognised and he would have the relevant support to cope. Once he managed to overcome his initial reluctance to leave my side at the playschool he would head for the water trough to play and pour water to his hearts content. This usually meant he was drenched through before the middle of the morning even though he wore protective waterproofs, but the experience gained and the rise in his confidence was worth sending those extra clothes for him to change into.

Slowly Carl's vocabulary began to increase, he could sum up a whole sentence in a single word to get his message or needs across. This was a wonderful achievement coming from the doleful soul that he was on arrival. His expressionless face was replaced by total animation that lit up his now bright eyes and turned up the corners of his mouth into a beaming smile taking away that endless drooling. He loved mealtimes and ate anything that was put in front of him consequently the thin listless body gained weight, sturdiness and had newfound energy. He loved to sit up on Lawrence's knee or mine and used this position as a vantage point to talk to us of his day's events or to have a book read to him or just to watch the others play. Carl still showed a slow reaction when asked to do something, but as realisation of what was expected dawned upon him his face slowly changed. The intense concentration that registered on his face was replaced firstly by one, then two, raised eyebrows, then his eyes would look up and make contact with whoever was speaking to him, then very slowly, like raising the brightness with a dimmer switch, the biggest smile would spread across his face quickly, followed by the biggest chuckle that rocked his body, only then would he spring into action and respond to whatever was said. He loved to be hugged always putting his arms around you, holding on so tightly, making you feel that he didn't want you to let go. His legs were straighter but still had a slight bow causing him to walk with an exaggerated side to side waddle. Carl's shoe size shot up considerably very quickly, he barely had time to scratch one pair when the next size was needed. No longer afraid to play outside, at least as long as the others were, Carl would happily play on a scooter or a tricycle chasing after the boys and his sister on their bicycles.

The transformation of the two children was remarkable in such a short space of time. But eventually we knew we would have to prepare them to go home. I just hoped they were ready as a family, that the children now stronger, could retain that strength and with revived lives could continue to move forward.

One particular outing, Carrie's loudness and incessant chatter had dominated the whole of the car journey; everyone's nerves had jangled with exasperation, as nothing encouraged her to calm down. Especially as many of the questions she asked were repeated or our answers were interjected with 'why' or 'when' responses. Consequently on our return home I decided to take her to her bedroom to talk out the event with her hoping she could gain some insight into her actions and the effects these had on others. She listened intently to every word I said, with complete eye contact throughout. She gave not one verbal response. Eventually, somewhat surprised by her lack of response I asked if she had anything to say or maybe to ask. She raised her head and looking straight at me asked, "Auntie Dani, will you teach me how to cook one day?" I sat back, now it was my turn to say nothing, I simply answered "Yes, of course", gave her a hug and she went downstairs. Who taught whom what during this session! She must have switched off from listening to me, giving me time to air my feelings. Perhaps this was how she coped at home with Mum. I have to say though that the car journeys were never again as traumatic as that one had been.

Swimming was a shared family activity, especially on rainy days when the children were fractious and irritable. This simple activity was a great confidence booster and a marvellous way of using up surplus energy. It also gave the children attainable goals to strive for. From learning to accept going into the water and staying in, to floating with swimming aids, then moving on to using momentum, to move independently, to actual swimming without aids was quite a feat. After this the children were encouraged to gain distance badges, which I painstakingly sewed onto their tracksuit jackets to show off their achievements, their certificates were equally displayed for all to see. The first time I took Carrie and Carl to the swimming pool I left Carrie in an adjacent cubicle to change into her swimsuit. It never crossed my mind that she may never have been swimming before, until that is, she called out she was ready, appearing at my cubicle wearing her swimsuit over her underwear and still wearing her socks. Lesson one, how to wear a swimsuit! I never took this for granted with future children! The less a child showed us what they knew, the more we worked at it. To her credit Carrie loved the water, and with our boys' influence to spur her on she rapidly learned to swim. Before leaving us she had achieved three distance badges, ten, twenty-five and a hundred metres. She loved to show these off to everyone and we were so proud of her too.

We frequently visited the Yorkshire Dales, taking our caravan to spend some of the school holiday time. This gave the children a sense of responsibility, a sense of freedom and a sense of adventure. On one of our trips we drove to Kilnsey to visit the fish farm where the children would enjoy feeding the fish. Aaron and Gareth loved this venue and loved showing it off to our dynamic duo that were initially taken aback at seeing so many fish coming to the surface at once in a lake. They stood on the decking both of them hanging over the fence throwing in the food pellets, fascinated by the fish competing for the food. We could hardly persuade them to leave when it was time to go. I had taken a simple photograph of the children with Lawrence but this captured the moment and was a favourite photograph for Carrie. I decide to have it enlarged and turned into a jigsaw which they all enjoyed doing. Through this photograph Carrie relived that experience. But I think she also took great delight in 'making the family' piece by piece.

The time came to put away the jigsaw to replace it with the play people game to play out the events of returning home. Mum had been in hospital for help, but had returned home stating she was ready to take back the children. Dad had returned from abroad and the couple needed support to reunite their family to try again. So much rested on Mum's ability to cope. Carrie and Carl were reluctant to allow their play people figures to go to 'Mum and Dad's' figures initially, insisting they stayed with the figures that represented our family, but eventually both accepted that this is what would be happening. They helped to choose some of their favourite photographs that I compiled in an album illustrating their time with us. I hoped this would give them a point of reference for the future, also help to revive memories that they could share with Mum and Dad to fill the gap that would exist for them as a family. The date was set for their return and a calendar chart showing how many 'sleeps' were left was hung in the kitchen to help them understand some time concept to this. Carrie diligently crossed off each day before going to bed. I wanted their departure to be a positive experience both for them and our boys so we marked a leaving party on the calendar too which gave Carrie and the boys something to concentrate on as they planned what they would do, who would come, and what party food to have. Carrie insisted we have a special cake with their names on, so a leaving cake had to be designed too. The party was planned for the day before they were to leave to give a sense of feeling of being together yet also recognising the need to be apart. This was as important for Aaron and Gareth as it was for Carrie and Carl. The parting was to initiate emotions and feelings in all of us, but whilst Lawrence and I had made choices, the children were having this foisted upon them. Being positive in our attitude and our approach was important and including the children in making decisions and plans was vital as it would help them to cope better and feel they could share their feelings and be supported.

Party day came, the weather was grey and threatening rain all morning, but half an hour before friends would be arriving the sun peered through the clouds and it just got warmer. We had a lovely afternoon playing outdoor games. Cards and gifts wishing the children well were given, but hidden to be opened in the evening when we could offer the children personal one to one time, reflecting on their day and the friends they had made with us. They loved the party atmosphere, the 'leaving' tea, and talked to friends openly about going back to Mum and Dad. We felt privileged at being able to have the opportunity to give such a positive experience as all too often children were returned home with far less planning involved. All too soon the party was over. Friends had departed.

We sat with all the children sharing time as they opened their gifts and cards reflecting on how each person had fitted into their life with us, as we helped Carrie and Carl try to understand how much they had meant to us in the short time they had lived with our family. The underlying sadness of our parting was over ridden by the positive feelings that were shared between us. The children went to bed that night and for the last time were tucked up to the action rhyme that we did every night.

*Here's a body,*
*There's a bed.*
*Here's a pillow,*
*There's a head.*
*Here's the curtain,*
*There's the light.*
*Here's a kiss,*
*And so goodnight.*

*Thomas Hood*

*British Humorist and Poet (1799 - 1845)*

Leaving them in bed, lights out with the door slightly ajar I came downstairs saying as always, "see you in the morning dawning" which the children also repeated. I wondered how they would be at bedtime the following night when they would be at home. How much of the life we offered would carry with them, be remembered?

The following morning was just the same as any other; Carrie awoke early but read her books quietly waiting for others to awake. But today she didn't even come out of the room at seven o'clock. I called them all down for breakfast. After this Aaron and Gareth played with Carl to keep him occupied whilst I took Carrie to help with the final packing up of clothes, books and toys. We talked together, reflecting on memories attached to the items we packed, she shared her feelings of being scared, we laughed about the events of the party the day before. With the case packed and toys, games and books all in bags ready to go we joined the others downstairs. We left their belongings by the door to wait for the social worker to call. Carrie had refused to pack the photograph album opting to hold it in the car, so we put this on top of the bags until it was time to go.

We then sat around the kitchen table as we had often done to do jigsaws. Watching Carl trying to find where pieces would go, often getting the wrong place, listening to Aaron and Gareth encouraging him with suggestions of where to put his chosen piece. Watching Carrie concentrating hard on the shape of her jigsaw piece and possible places for it, always with her tongue sticking out between her teeth. They reached across the table to help each other. I realised then that we had done the right thing, this had worked for us and for all the children. Sad though it was that Carrie and Carl had

had the need to join us, we had done our best to give them a positive experience to fall back on. I hoped they would remember the good times regardless of what lay ahead of them.

Eventually the social worker arrived, everything was packed into the boot of her car, final hugs and kisses given. Any apprehension carefully hidden behind smiles and laughter, each child carried their own farewell gifts and cards, Carrie held tightly on to the photograph album as they were fastened into the safety straps in the back of the car. We stood at the top of our drive and waved them off as their arms waved furiously back at us.

Then we were a family of four again, with a huge cavernous gap in our lives. But these were only two children, a small representation of the real problem out there. We were only one family, an equally small representation of foster parents. Our lives would never be the same again and we knew it.

We owed our boys time to come to terms with how they were feeling, to cope with their loss and the change in family dynamics. Fortunately it was the school holidays and we had plans to take the caravan to Kent to see Grannie, this would be a good focus for the boys to look forward to at the same time give them quality time to understand the reasons for the children's need to stay with us. Aaron, being the older one had more insight accepting the situation, but Gareth was left feeling very uncomfortable about the whole thing, blaming us for letting them go home. He also voiced his own fears about what would happen to him if anything happened to Lawrence and me. His thinking cut deeply, but he was still determined to have other children to come to stay. Gareth really missed having a younger one around, and during the holiday we witnessed him watching other peoples' toddlers and he would refer to some of their behaviours being like Carl. Lawrence and I agonised whether we were being fair to either of the boys if we continued to foster, but it was also made clear by the boys when they were ready for the next children that needed us.

> *"Children begin by loving their parents;*
> *as they grow older they judge them;*
> *sometimes they forgive them".*

*Oscar Wilde*

*Irish Writer and Poet (1854 - 1900)*

# CHAPTER 5

## My Family

Gareth, our younger son, was a very sensitive young fellow with an air of permanent mischievousness about him. Blonde haired with a round face out of which constantly beamed the biggest smile. Totally different to his brother yet he had to follow in big brother's footsteps throughout his school days, which he was not at all pleased about. But this young lad, our son, would give anything to anyone if he felt they needed it more than he did. His generosity knew no bounds and his friendship was valued by many. He had the ability to reach out to others with an understanding that was beyond his years, and I believe it was this that helped him to unconditionally accept anyone who came to stay at our home, whether friends, family or foster children.

Gareth enjoyed playing, formal learning was a nuisance factor in his life that he had to accept, but not willingly I hasten to add. Looking back in his 'Baby Development' book I had written a comment that read "Gareth needs a hard line taking with him", strong words considering he was little more than a year old. Strange to relate that through the years to follow my view has never changed! He had a wonderful imagination that he could use to his best advantage and to ours. He was not a child that fell back on the words "I'm bored" because he was always able to find something to do. In his imaginary world of make believe anything could happen and frequently did! He has always loved to tease and trick others, but would also be there to defend and support especially his brother and their friends, and in time our foster children too.

From an early age Gareth ailed endless ear and chest infections and seemed to be taking antibiotics permanently. When he was about sixteen months old he had to be admitted to hospital with a high temperature and horrendous earache and leaky ears, which gave us all quite a scare. When he recovered from this his demeanour was to change from being a happy cheerful baby to a miserable toddler who struggled to connect to those around. He hated going out in his pushchair and would cry incessantly, if visitors came to our home he would hide under the lounge chair sucking his thumb and feeling the underside of the chair until he eventually wore it away. I concluded that 'God had given Gareth to us as no one else would cope with him!' During the next two years he was to struggle with life, as we were to struggle with his behaviours. However at about the time he started going to playschool we realised that he was not always responding when called. This was more noticeable as he was spending more time playing in the dining room whilst I was in the kitchen. Then I heard an almighty argument between him and his brother over the volume of the television, as Aaron turned it down, Gareth would turn it up. This triggered warning bells and we had his ears tested, his hearing was very poor indeed, caused by the condition known as 'glue ear' the result of the endless infections and need for antibiotics. A quick referral to the ENT specialist arranged for him to have his adenoids removed and grommets put in his ears. Learning from my own childhood experience I had no intention of leaving him on his own. However surgery techniques and recuperation periods had changed over the years since my time and Gareth was only in hospital overnight. But the transformation was incredible. It seems he had been living with an ever increasing hearing loss and a low-grade earache, no wonder he had been so miserable and was cutting himself off from those around. Perhaps it was this experience that had given Gareth the ability to occupy himself so easily.

His sense of fun and humour grew and no one was safe from it. He could turn any serious situation into a moment of laughter for all. As a small boy he loved theatre and magic. Determined to be a magician he would pester Dad to teach him new tricks and make props, which frequently challenged Lawrence's abilities. I had to make him his magicians' outfit, black with gold and silver sprayed on stars and moons, complete with a large pointed hat decorated to match. We once took him to the Theatre to see 'Paddington Bear's Magical Musical', he was three years old, mesmerised from the beginning to the end, he then demanded to see it all again and could not accept that it would not be on anymore. We had to carry him out of the theatre kicking and screaming. He loved to take on and act out roles of his heroes 'He-Man' and 'Super Ted.' These were his favourite characters of the time. They were much loved by him, and gradually taking over our world around us. On one particular Sunday in church the vicar of the time was explaining the importance of raising funds for the church and the repair or replacement of the organ, he referred to the cost of running the church and the running costs of the endless repairs. The emphasis was on the word running. During this part of the service we had been struggling to keep Gareth quiet and from irritating his brother endlessly. Then he suddenly became quite controlled, concentrated on the vicar's words before standing on the pew sporting his best Super Ted and He Man stance. Picking up on the word running, and in his loudest voice Gareth gave his greatest performance... "Run, run as fast as you can, YOU can't catch me, I'M the Gingerbread man". Nothing was going to stop him; nothing could make him sit down until the performance was over. The vicar lost the concentration of his entire congregation and as all heads turned to stare in our direction Gareth felt the strong power of an audience and judging by his enormous smile loved it, whilst we were searching for the proverbial hole to crawl in to! This was to be the first of many performances he would give both on and off the stage.

Gareth's daredevil behaviours and risk-taking demeanours were to keep us on our toes to maintain his safety, but were to prove to encourage our additional children to take chances, to try something new, to achieve and attain skills they may have never thought to try. If Gareth ever thought of doing something new and at first it wouldn't work out for him, he rarely gave up, but would study the issue, discuss what to do, then set his mind to do it. He could ride a bicycle at three years old without stabilisers because they broke and he still wanted to use his bike. Though he fell a few times he eventually mastered it. Swimming was a great family pastime; Gareth loved the freedom of the water but detested the drains. He developed an irrational fear that he would go down the drain hole if he stood on it, consequently he would swim faster over that area. He had learned to swim by the time he was four years old but whenever he visited a new pool always checked out where the drain holes were so that he could avoid them whilst in the water. By the time he was five he had gained several distance-swimming badges but his ultimate goal was to achieve the mile badge. In typical Gareth style he worked out how many lengths this was. Recognising that by telling him it was 64 lengths, the number would not have a great deal of meaning, and I then told him it was twice the 32 lengths he had achieved. In his mind Gareth saw the number 2, which was only one more lot of 32, which he knew he could do. So he set his mind to do it during his next swimming session, nothing was going to talk him out of it or tell him he may not be physically ready to achieve this. So we organised him to do it as a sponsored swim for the Candlelighters, a children's charity. Needless to say Gareth, aged five achieved his mile badge and raised the total of £70 for the charity. His determination was something we were going to have to live with, would at times lead us to total exasperation but would also give him the strength of character he would need to cope with, to guide and to teach our future children. He would always be their playmate, their friend and their mentor.

One of life's deep thinkers he looked for philosophical answers from a very early age! Whilst waiting for his brother to come out of school I looked down at Gareth to see him with his right forefinger stuck up his nose, when I suggested that picking his nose was not the thing to do, he replied, "Why do they give you a finger that is the same size as the hole in your nose then?" I have often wondered why he did not offer his schoolwork the same level of scrutiny; just think what he could have achieved.

The overall comment on his school report aged four years and ten months was: -

*'Gareth is a polite and reliable pupil. He shows enthusiasm for all aspects of his school life. He has maintained his satisfactory progress. His powers of concentration and application have continued to improve.'*

I should have found a magic spray to keep him that way. There came a time in his schooling when I questioned why we were paying out such large sums of money for his education, as he seemed to have little interest but to test the patience of his teachers and entertain his peers with his antics. Lawrence's response was "well if he wants to be a clown, so be it, at least he will be an educated clown!"

However I know he thought very deeply about the children that joined us, and their circumstances that brought them to us. He had a level of compassion and understanding that taught Lawrence and I how to move forward with some of the difficulties we were to face in the future. Never underestimate what a child can offer, never dismiss his views as lacking in understanding, they may lack maturity but sometimes their level of reasoning is what may be needed for a situation, whereas our own level is actually beyond the requirement. Certainly parenting Gareth gave us a foundation for dealing with the unexpected, the unexplained, and a touch of humour to survive all that lay before us.

In complete contrast, Aaron, his older brother by two years and nine months was slim, very dark haired with a swarthy appearance and red rosy cheeks. There were the usual brotherly similarities yet their personalities were totally different. Aaron had a confidence of one much older, had a determination to achieve and was incredibly competitive. He had a 'love to have a go attitude', and though his younger brother was a force to be reckoned with and a permanent thorn in his side, Aaron was fiercely protective of him not only at home and in school but also wherever they went. This was born out on so many occasions and commented on by others who had responsibility for them in our absence, such as play schemes and holiday camps. This protective approach was exceptionally beneficial to our foster children and he comfortably accepted the role of being protective big brother to all. His position in the family was very important to him and we realised that this had to be kept in mind when accepting new children.

Aaron enjoyed school, taking it all in his stride, he got on well with his teachers and his peers and was never short of friends. Learning was a challenge to him and he did not give up on anything. He had a spirit of adventure, the word 'no' was rarely used by him if he could say 'yes.' An avid reader, some of his favourite stories were by Roald Dahl, 'BFG,' 'Charlie and the Chocolate Factory' and the 'Great Glass Elevator.' He loved to be outdoors and took great pride in working in the garden alongside me, often trying to do more than his young years should expect. Aaron would set himself little projects to achieve, clearing an area of garden ready to be dug over by Dad, then he would enjoy planting his vegetables, a pastime he has carried into adulthood. Whenever we went camping he would be first to organise his brother, and later any other children that were with us, to fill the water bottles and help set up the caravan. He could be trusted implicitly but as one school report said:

*'Excellent achievements, Aaron works with an eager approach and enjoys the challenge of new topics. The only faults in Aaron's behaviour come from his not having patience with lesser intellects.'*

He was seven years and seven months. What the school did not see was his endless patience teaching and supporting our youngsters at home when they struggled to grasp certain concepts. His patience with their slow phonetic reading was endless and a credit to him. Especially when he had to start all over again the very next day as the child involved had 'forgotten' and the learning experience needed reinforcing?

A very sociable child who was never short of friends, though preferred to have stable long term type friendships rather than the whim of the day type. He loved to have 'sleepovers' so it was not unusual for us to have extra children around especially at weekends or for him to stay over with friends at their homes, which gave him the status of one who was growing up. Aaron, who responded beautifully, and rapidly became my second in command in Lawrence's absence, took our habit of stressing the importance of being seven years old to heart. If Mum had asked the children to do something, Aaron would do his level best to make sure that they all reacted appropriately. He tried to be a good role model, offering a good behavioural example, and his patience was limitless with his brother's antics, and culminated in his tolerance of some of the negative behaviours we would endure in the future.

Aaron's main hobbies included playing board games especially Monopoly, Scrabble and Coppit, which would involve the whole family or anyone who was around.

These were the days before computer games when family time was quality time, in theory, in between family 'arguments' and sibling rivalry when a parent's role was that of a professional referee! He also had a love of horse riding, which was his weekly treat. For two consecutive years he spent a week at a riding school in Lincolnshire on a children's holiday camp for extra tuition, mucking out stables and learning to take responsibility for a horse on a daily basis, which also included a Gymkhana on the last day. He revelled in his achievements, knowledge gained, and the inevitable rosettes he would bring home. The interesting thing was that although he was Mr Ultra Clean at home, his suitcase of clothes was barely disturbed, with the excuse that "I thought I would save you from doing all the washing." Such a thoughtful boy! But nor did he find that extra £2 hidden in a pocket of a clean pair of trousers for a surprise, or my endless 'hello' notes that were hiding in various pockets, between layers of clothing or in his wash bag! These were fun notes to stave off homesickness.

Swimming was as much enjoyed by Aaron, as by Gareth. He was busy keeping ahead of his kid brother with the distance badges and the Personal survival badges too. He had achieved the Bronze, Silver and Gold (Swimming Teachers' Awards) by the time he was seven. His best stroke was the backstroke, which could be a nuisance to others in the water during a general public swim. He worked hard to perfect a good diving technique and took pride in being able to swim under water for one length even at this young age.

Aaron rarely ailed anything but if he got a childhood cough, cold or virus he usually managed a heavy dosing that would knock him flat for a day or two before he bounced back to full health again. Though my mother's attitude of 'if you can put two feet to the floor and stand then there's not much wrong with you' had been implanted in me and I suspect I had done the same to Aaron.

Musicals were firm favourites of Aaron, 'Joseph and His Amazing Technicolor Dream Coat' had hooked him very early on. So this music was played endlessly. He had a love for singing and desperately wanted to be in the Cathedral Choir at his new school, unfortunately did not pass the audition but was happy enough to accept this and joined the school choir instead.

Aaron was a great note taker; this was a skill he would use many times when he felt the need to report to us any seemingly strange behaviour given by children, in our absence, when left in the care of our child-sitter. She was in fact a family friend who had been Aaron and Gareth's first infant teacher. A lovely, lively lady who could cope with any child's behaviour, interesting or otherwise, and knew how to use Aaron's leadership qualities to his and her best advantage. When Aaron became a young teenager he was to work with her again in running youth groups and courses.

Aaron was a strong character, who worked hard, played hard and reaped the rewards for his efforts. I cannot recall a time when he objected to having his life shared by so many others. He challenged the thinking of others if he felt they were not heading in the right direction, especially his brother! Unfortunately, this attribute was once challenged by a teacher, who felt that Aaron's ability to recognise right from wrong, lost him credibility with his peers. I felt if this was the very worse that could be said about him both of us would cope!

Aaron had known from a very early stage in his life that he and his brother would never be the only children in our lives. I believe he accepted this as he did most things in life, as just another challenge or another difference in his parents, that he did not find in the parents of his friends. He defended our cause to the hilt and we have been eternally grateful to him for that.

So over the next few years, indeed for the rest of their lives, both boys were to be a part of 'our team' in helping every child that walked through our doors, whether the children who joined our family liked it or not! But one thing I do know is there were times for all of them when they depended on Aaron or Gareth for some aspect of their life. For the boys' part they were endlessly tolerant of some terribly antisocial behaviours, they were sometimes ridiculed or witnessed children treating us with far less respect than they would ever be allowed to get away with, but not once can I recall either of them suggesting we stop fostering or wish a child away from us. On the contrary if we felt we were not making progress with a child they would defend them wholeheartedly and give us countless reasons for continuing. I have seen them have their belongings deliberately taken and broken; their peaceful evenings or night times disturbed by rampaging behaviours of disturbed frightened youngsters, and still they have not asked us to stop supporting foster children. The boys have been thrilled by the arrival of new children, challenged by children's natural parents' behaviours, struggled with slow progress of some of the youngsters, and been devastated and emotionally drained by the departure of every child that has left us, regardless of how much preparation we offered to help them to cope with the event.

I recall one such time when Gareth was going through a difficult patch coping with the departure of children which he found too painful to put into words, I always felt that this stemmed from his need to blame someone, and that someone was usually me! This would then make him feel guilty so withdrawing was the easiest route. I could not allow him to do that. It wasn't fair on him. We had talked at length about the present children of the time, and I gradually helped him to recall any other child that he missed and needed to talk about. I wrote the names Mum and Dad on the top of a piece of paper and suggested we then wrote the names of the rest of our family. Consequently I then wrote Aaron and Gareth, and the names of our present children, he then recalled by name all the rest of our children, each and everyone. In his young mind there were sixteen children to our family! He knew that they were not his real brothers and sisters but for each one he still held a special place within himself. They had touched his life as strongly as he had touched theirs. Years later I was to witness both our boys greet children of years gone by as though they had only seen them the day before. This had a profound effect on the returning teenagers as it also did on Lawrence and me. We had anguished over the consequences of some of the negative behaviours and situations that they endured but to give up was never an option and this decision came very clearly from the boys. Perhaps there was always hope that the next child or children would be easier but that was never to be the case. The challenging behaviour would simply prove to be different.

Born to a middle class family in February 1942 in Herne Bay, Kent, my husband, Lawrence was the older child of two. Three years older than his sister, and a much-wanted son. So many females, mother, sister, grandmas, great grandmas and aunts surrounded him. The husbands of all these family women (apart from Mum's) had died as young men either as a result of illness or because of the two wars. His father was still around in Lawrence's younger days, though being an officer in the RAF he had been posted to Canada, and did not return until Lawrence was in his third year. Sadly, almost three years after he returned he was taken very ill with 'flu like symptoms, was diagnosed with poliomyelitis and died leaving his wife, Mary to cope with two small children. Mary was a very capable person and as a single mother of these two youngsters took the practical step of taking up a half share in Lawrence's paternal grandmother's home, where Lawrence would openly admit to 'being spoilt' as he was now the only surviving male within the family. When he was ten years of age his mother took a live-in post at a boarding preparatory school where Lawrence stayed until he went to Grammar School as a boarder aged eleven years six months up to the age of seventeen years old. He then left school to enter the Royal Air Force as an officer, aircrew, eventually to be trained as a navigator where he stayed for twelve years travelling to many places and gaining experience of life.

By the time I knew him he had left the RAF to settle in the Uists, Outer Hebrides, Scotland. Being a loner he loved the lifestyle the islands offered and he was quite at home in the wilds of nowhere, fishing and shooting according to the season, enjoying the peace and serenity, the wildlife of the area, and a few well chosen close friends. Some were from the resident Army base, others like the vet and his wife were incomers, some were the softly spoken island folk that accepted him into their midst. Content with his life and his beloved St Bruno and pipe, which epitomises him so well! So how did he meet me? After all I was based in Sheffield, but I came from the east coast of Lincolnshire, he was based in the Scottish Islands but came from Kent. Our backgrounds, our experiences in life and our aspirations were completely different. He was ten years my senior. At twenty years old I was just finding my feet, at thirty years old he had found his! He was worldly-wise and I had a great deal to learn, though so different we complemented each other, oh so well. We were to meet through his cousin who lived on the east coast. Lawrence was Godfather to her youngest son and I had lived with the family helping with the children, frequently staying there on my days off from nurse training. Our acquaintance turned into friendship as his visits to his Godson suddenly increased from an annual call-in visit en route to Kent to visit Mum, to three or four a year that seemed to coincide when I was there too!

Our relationship changed from friendship under the influence of a New Year's Party when he asked if I would like to visit him in the Outer Hebrides where I could stay with friends of his, he was still billeted within the Army Officers Quarters. He sent me a single orchid for Valentine's Day with a message that read 'Happy New Year.' This confused his Godson who thought that if this flower was really from his Uncle Lawrence, he had made a mistake and had forgotten why he had sent it!

For my twenty-first birthday he bought me two cassettes, the one I loved the most was Andy Williams - Home Loving Man, was there a hidden message? We were to meet up so infrequently but this gave me the opportunity to concentrate on my studies and gave

Lawrence time to sort out his new job and a new home. To describe Lawrence was easy, he was tall, slim, dark and handsome, well in the eyes of this beholder he was! His attention was always taken by his first love, the bane of my life, his St Bruno and the smoking pipe that was closer to him than I could ever be!

I do remember a time when I was so looking forward to seeing him; we were to meet at his cousin's home. I was to drive there after finishing my shift, as I entered the house he came down the stairs sporting a full-grown beard. I couldn't believe it, this was not my Lawrence. He registered my distaste before I had time to say anything, returning back upstairs. Moments later he came downstairs minus the beard, never to be seen like that ever again.

We were married in June 1976 on one the hottest days of the year, enjoyed two weeks in Tenerife, which was cooler than Britain at that time. Then returned to Britain to live in the Outer Hebrides. Our bungalow was on the edge of Locheport, a beautiful spot, though at times the weather could be wild and wilful, the landscape was amazing, at least it was when you could see through the haziness of a traditional Scotch mist, on those occasional clear days. Whilst we lived there we had a succession of friends and family to stay with us. But after two and a half years, and with one son at a year old, we knew it was time to return to the mainland.

Just as Andy Williams's song had predicted, Lawrence was a home loving man, and though family life was not what he was used to, he adapted very well! He had always known how I felt about fostering, and was prepared to do his best too. His background did not lend itself too well to cope with some of the attributes of 'our' children but he deserves full marks for all the effort he put in. He has had a gentle strength that I know has been pushed to its very limits. Lawrence has a quick fire mind and a dry humour that can leave a few standing, questioning what he really means, this has certainly allowed the children to stand back and think before they make their next move especially those that turned into teenagers! He is a man of few words, and is willing to ignore an awful lot. But when he does speak out it has more impact, as those around will certainly know about it. He is a lover of crosswords and quizzes, and also a gatherer of useless information that he holds in his head until he really needs it. This latter skill came in very useful at homework time, along with his amazing ability with numbers and maths. Lawrence's command of the English language was second to none, and his use of it confused the children at times. On several occasions they would come to me asking for a translation of what Dad just said! There was a wonderful moment when we were on a short break holiday in a cottage near Whitby. We had six children with us and they were having a 'debating session' it was lively, argumentative, fun and very, very loud. I had been listening to it all from another room and had no concerns about the liveliness of the one-upmanship that was going on. However the more excitable each youngster became the louder they got until Lawrence could cope no more, he stormed into the room and demanded them to "Stop this cacophony of noise!" in a voice that boomed so loudly they almost fell off their chairs. The instant silence was broken by Gareth who burst into fits of laughter, which the rest followed suit, none of them knew what he meant, Gareth had called out "Mum, what does Dad mean by cacophony?"

then realised that Lawrence had actually made more noise than they all had. That day they all learned a new word, and this has been used frequently ever since, when the noise levels raise and is always said with the same volume and intonation as used by Lawrence.

Sadly after leaving the Hebrides, Lawrence had little time or opportunity to fish or shoot, but the kit is still there, just in case! But his work took up most of his time and he developed new interests in the up and coming computers. He has always held on to his love of sport, especially cricket and motor racing that he has shared with all our sons. Through the years he has tolerated taking boys to Leeds United football ground, he never found it a pleasure but endured it for their sake. He became a Cub Scout leader for a few years in an effort to keep the local group open for the duration of our younger son's time. This also involved organising and attending camps, which his ageing bones struggled to cope with. To encourage the children to overcome some of their own fears he has had to face one or two of his own including his fear of heights. Several events have led him to have to scale our rooftop when children have hurled things up there, causing blocked gutters or disturbing roof tiles. Lawrence has abseiled with them; climbed rocks to retrieve children that have managed to get up but can't work out how to get back down again. He has tackled aerial obstacle courses to prove to children that if he can so can they! The most challenging one for him was the Leap of Faith in Cornwall on a 'Family Bonding Holiday' when he found himself about 30ft in the air on top of a narrow telegraph pole wavering in the breeze. Fear ran through him as never before but his 'What the hell' approach paid off when he finally found the gall to go for it and not only achieved it but much to his amazement survived too! This combined with endless 'support runs' for the children gave very little time for hobbies. Life became our combined hobby. Extending the house, taming the wild field that was to become the garden. Lawrence became an expert in court affairs when supporting errant youngsters who found themselves with one foot on the wrong side of the law. He held the position of head of projects in the household, irrespective of what the project was. Taxiing youngsters here, there and everywhere was almost a full time job in itself especially when we reached the stage of having seven children between six schools spread over a fifteen-mile radius. He learned the art of being able to sleep on a 'washing line' at a moment's notice if that was the only way to get rest! Believe me sometimes sleep did elude us. He did all this and so much more as well as earning a living to keep us all going. On one occasion after watching Cliff Richard perform on the TV, I asked him why it was that Cliff, who was a similar age to Lawrence, looked so young in comparison. He remarked with such a stunned expression, "Well for starters he is not married to you, nor does he have all these children!" Point taken and accepted!

Lawrence was a man of principals that would not be demeaned by anyone, sometimes those principals got in our way, but usually for the right reason. At trying times and moments of pure stress he would seek the solitude of his study, switch off from the world by switching on his computer where he could be found playing solitaire, that is if you caught him quickly enough before he clicked to minimise the screen to show a spread sheet. The uninitiated believed he was working, those of us who knew him so well knew otherwise!

DANI VALDIS

*"Family life is full of major and minor crises — the ups and downs of health, success and failure in career, marriage, and divorce — and all kinds of characters. It is tied to places and events and histories. With all of these felt details, life etches itself into memory and personality. It's difficult to imagine anything more nourishing to the soul."*

*Thomas Moore*

*Irish Poet and Singer (1779 - 1852)*

# Chapter 6

## A Little Visitor

I was in the middle of baking cakes and biscuits, clock watching to make sure I was not late in leaving to collect the boys from school. The telephone rang as I was taking hot trays out of the oven. Our support worker was on the other end of the line, "How do you feel about looking after a toddler for a few days, we're not really sure of all the facts as yet, he is two years old, an only child of a teenage Mum who is unable to cope at present" How could I say no. We had all missed Carrie and Carl so much since they returned home. Life had seemed mundane, too easy and too straightforward for all of us. We missed the children terribly and that cavernous hole in our lives still existed waiting for someone else to arrive. One small two year old would fit perfectly into our family.

It had been a long three months since Carrie and Carl left us. Never a day went by when one or other of us would mention their names, or recall things they had said or done. Carrie's colourful pictures still adorned the kitchen walls. Any toys played with or books read would remind us of games played with Carrie or Carl. Getting two boys organised for school in a morning suddenly seemed so easy with time to spare to play before leaving the house. Whilst we had anticipated having children in rapid succession this did not seem to be happening.

We were ready to start again, face another challenge, and if this little chap needed somewhere to stay then we were ready, willing and able!

We were not to expect him too soon as he was currently being checked out at the hospital. This gave me time to collect the boys from school, prepare them for the evening's events and prepare a room for our new guest. On hearing the news the boys whooped with delight, though sorry to hear that something may have happened to the little boy they were thrilled at the thought of starting again. They gabbled on and on all through tea wondering if he would be like Carl. "What would he look like? Could he talk? What kind of things could he do? Could he walk?" The relentless questioning continued until eventually at about seven o'clock we heard a car coming up the drive. The child's social worker got out and immediately went to the back of the car to retrieve a serious little boy from the escort who then gathered up the belongings of young Robert. It was a cold dark evening, the day after bonfire night, I ushered them inside to the warmth of the kitchen where the boys were finishing their homework for school. Robert was beautiful, gorgeous dark brown hair, clean and shiny and smartly cut. He appeared well developed, wearing clean clothes appropriate for the time of year. He had a warm jacket on and very smart leather boots. He was pale and tired looking and unsmiling. But considering the time of day and the ordeal he had gone through, which had culminated in him not having his Mum with him, but instead finding himself surrounded by strangers in an unknown environment, his level of confusion must have had his tiny head in a whirl. Though his eyes were tired, he was alert and watchful especially in Aaron and

Gareth's direction. I suggested they should take him to find the toy box to look for something to play with. His little face broke into a slow beaming smile, though coy, he willingly left the knee of the social worker to hold the boys' hands to go in search of toys. His tired but expressive brown eyes had the longest eyelashes I'd ever seen and would be the envy of many!

The usual paperwork was completed and I signed for our 'delivery'. I was then given more details about events leading to Robert's admission into care. The length of time he would be with us had not been determined as yet. The social worker handed me a note from Mum that she had hastily written so she could send it with him. It read: -

*'Robert wets the bed so I've sent some nappies for night use. This bag of clothes has been washed but need drying please. Please look after Robert well for me until I get myself right, he needs a lot of attention at the moment.'*

My reaction was to feel desperately sorry for this young Mum who was obviously trying hard to do the best she could for this little chap. She had reached out to a stranger on behalf of her son, she had made an effort to provide for his needs at short notice. Robert's Mum had put her trust in us to do the best we could, to do for him that at the time she was unable to do or not being allowed to do. The full reasons he had been brought into care we had yet to establish. I looked at Robert being gently pushed around on Gareth's old ride around 'Billy Bumper'. He had kept his smile as they talked to him encouraging him to steer as needed. If having a child of your own is a gift then looking after someone else's gift was indeed a privilege, I felt exceptionally honoured to look after this little fellow.

We were to discover that Mum was going through a stressful time and had hit Robert in the mouth causing a cut that bled. I had to look very carefully at Robert in order to find the cut, as it was so small. Mum's immediate reaction to her own behaviour was to contact social services for help. Robert's Mum had had a troubled upbringing, which frequently led her to being brought into care. She had asked for help and support from the very same people that had supported her but instead had her child taken away. It felt to me as though Robert was the one being punished, being separated from his Mum. She had gone to the shops whilst Robert was left in the care of a close relative, it was during this time that he had been removed to care. How must she have felt returning from the shop to find Robert missing? I might add that around that time there had been reports of bogus social workers taking children from their parents. I dread to think what must have gone through her mind. For now our concentration had to be on Robert, caring for him, and keeping him as happy and content as his Mum had obviously tried to do in spite of her recent setback.

Once the documentation was completed and our farewells had been said to the social worker our attention turned to young Robert. Lawrence and I watched him play with the boys; he enjoyed the attention given to him, though he said little he clearly understood everything that was said to him. When he became bored with the toy of the moment he would aim for the toy box to discover another toy to play with. Whatever he pulled from the box made him smile that expressive beautiful infectious smile that spread across his face resulting in the rest of us smiling too. His responses were those of any other two year old. He really was a delightful little boy and I found myself questioning why he was in care based on the information we had received.

After playing for almost an hour we needed to bring the excitement levels down and persuade these boys to get ready for bed, hopefully without upsetting Robert. Aaron and Gareth took control of this whilst I went to run the bath. They helped him up our steep stairway, and set the example that he was only too willing to follow. They undressed and jumped into the bath water, with little help so did Robert. They played pouring games and blowing bubbles, so did Robert. They washed and then washed Robert too as he giggled with them. The boys got out of the water, dried and dressed quickly, as they did so Robert stood up and reached out to me for help. I dried him, put on his nappy and played peep-bo as we put on his pyjamas. We all sat on Gareth's bed to read a story before settling them all down. Robert happily accepted our routine, but then he must have been one very tired little tyke only too glad of the opportunity to sleep.

Robert slept all night. I had been on alert duty in case he woke up and wondered where he was. We had a safety gate at the top of the stairs but I always worried that if an agile child tried to climb over the top they would fall headlong down the stairs. Our stairway was much steeper than the average and I was very aware of the dangers it could hold to those not used to it. Our boys woke first and their chatter woke young Robert. He showed his delight in seeing the boys again and playtime began for all three once again, even though school was on the agenda for the older two!

Whilst the boys were in school and Lawrence was at work, I settled down to get to know young Robert a little better and also to establish a few more facts surrounding his admission to care. He had been brought in to care under a Place of Safety Order section 28 of the Children and Young Persons Act, 1969. The reason given, 'His proper development is being avoidably impaired or neglected or he is being ill-treated'. We were also to receive a form that gave further details of Robert, under the heading of 'Child's temperament and interests' it stated the following: -

*'Normal lively child could possibly be undisciplined.'*

Our little friend was two years old responding in quite a mature manner for his young years. Looking back I am unable to recall any negative behaviour or tantrum aimed in our direction. On the contrary he was a very positive responsive happy little boy. There was no defiance, he had a placid nature and warmed to any suggestion on offer without even a mere hint or sign of the terrible two's syndrome.

Under the heading of 'Details of any difficulties experienced by the child' it simply stated: -

*'Bed wets.'*

There are few children that would get through that second year of life without an occasional enuresis episode. I was beginning to despair!

Yes I understood and accepted that Mum in the heat of the moment had hit out towards Robert and caught his mouth. But realising her mistake she had turned to the services for help, these were the same people that had helped her when she had a need as a child. Perhaps she viewed the services as a 'parental substitute.' She had admitted her mistake but was this helping the situation? Separating Mum and toddler did not shout out support to me, and though I recognised that Robert had the right to protection, I knew I could easily witness far, far worse in the average supermarket, where a frustrated angry mum would verbally lash out and at times physically lash out at their annoying tiresome offspring screaming the place down like a wailing banshee. The events of the day before were clarified. It seems that after Mum had telephoned social services, Robert had indeed been taken from his uncle in Mum's absence, transferred to the local hospital to be checked out. It was here that Mum caught up with him and the social worker trying to explain the reasons for her actions. However social services' actions had been to protect Robert first then establish the situation, this was based on information they held from Robert's early baby days.

When Mum had Robert she was living in a children's home, and had displayed signs of short temper and some aggression aimed towards Robert, as she had difficulty coping with his demands. She was just seventeen years old. Consequently Robert was placed on the NAI Register better known as the Register for children at risk of abuse or injury. He had also been made a Ward of Court with a Supervision Order. Steps in place to protect him had to be responded to. However over the two years since his birth, Mum's care of Robert had stabilised and the Supervision Order had lapsed three months before to his arrival with us. His name had also been removed from the 'At Risk Register'. Mum's boyfriend had been held in custody recently, since then Mum had found it difficult to cope resulting in her taking her temper out on young Robert.

The social worker had responded to Mum's plea for help, but needed to give her the opportunity to settle down, accept what she did by taking the responsibility and the consequences of her actions, as well as protecting Robert. She had been given time to prepare a few things for him to take to prospective carers as well as a chance to write the note we received. I felt more relieved when I knew these facts. I did not want to think of her not having support, she was little more than a child herself and Robert was a credit to her care. I hoped my words of reassurance sent via the social worker would reach her.

In the meantime we really loved having little Robert around. He was pure innocence and a pleasure to look after. He played beautifully, had powers of concentration in play, keen and eager to listen to stories being read, and enjoyed picture books. He loved doing jigsaws with anyone prepared to give him time or to draw and colour. Robert would copy the actions of the boys when playing with cars or when running around. There were four playmates for him to choose from depending on the time of day and he lapped up the time given to him and the attention bestowed upon him. Being such an easy child to care for made it so very easy on us too. But this was to be short lived, common sense was to reign and Robert was to be returned to his Mum and rightly so.

Five days after his arrival arrangements were made for him to go home. Just as he entered our lives so suddenly, he was equally to exit our lives, though never to be forgotten, but then who could forget that beguiling expression, those gorgeous long eyelashes surrounding those big brown bright eyes, and his love of play. The innocence of childhood, if only it could be bottled!

Whilst Aaron and Gareth were at school, their little playmate Robert was collected by his social worker and taken back to Mum along with all of his belongings. He had gone happily into the car, unaware of what was happening though we had told him. We sent a couple of photographs back with him to share with Mum. I waved him off as he smiled back giving a gentle slow side-to-side wave back to me. What a little treasure he had been.

Our boys returned home after school quite crestfallen. They were in no mood to play at all, choosing to sit and mope, feeling very sad for themselves and missing the companionship of their newfound playmate. Instead of a story at bedtime, we decided to sit together and talk about Robert. This gave me a chance to help both boys understand how wonderful they had been to accept him, play with him and give him so much attention, but yet also for them to recognise how important it was for Robert to be back with his own Mum who did really love him and need him.

The following day the social worker returned unexpectedly with a bunch of beautiful flowers from Robert and his Mum with a little card attached saying-

*"Thank you for looking after Robert*
*With love*
*Robert and his Mum"*

The social worker reiterated the thanks stating that Mum had welcomed the support given to Robert but had also felt supported by the positive report I had submitted regarding Robert's presentation and achieving all expected milestones. I was very moved by their responses but also by knowing that common sense had prevailed and she had been given another chance.

Robert's stay with us only lasted five days. But they were five precious days of his life and also of ours. They could be viewed as five precious days missing out of his Mum's life too. She loved him and it showed, she wanted the best for him, but in a moment of stress and difficulty took her feelings out on her son, Robert. I believe she was shocked by her own actions which is why she reacted the way she did. Mum was only nineteen years old locked in life with the demanding needs of a two year old, and anyone involved with children will know what I mean. All the love in the world does not make it any less exhausting from morning till night, and if you are on your own with virtually no support, no one to turn to and no one to hand over to at the end of the day, added to that the financial constraints of a very restricted income, it is not surprising that the frustration and anger rose to the surface. The sad part is whom it was taken out on. The application for a Place of Safety Order meant that social services had the authority to detain Robert for up to twenty-eight days. This allows for the issues involved to be explored, a way forward to be sought and will involve a multi-disciplinary approach so those involved can have some input in providing the relevant support required. If this period of time out for Mum was needed, then so be it. Perhaps she gained more insight into her actions and the outcome for both of them. Perhaps she received a greater level of help and support as a result of it. I hoped there would be a positive outcome for her as this would eventually affect her future, and for Robert's sake I would like to believe that the aftermath was beneficial. Time by social services was not wasted in this case; they turned the situation around very quickly in comparison to some situations we were to meet.

The time we had with Robert was wonderful. It was like having the pleasure of the company of a relative or friend's child to stay for a few days. His arrival had been wrapped in excitement for us, his departure with feelings that were steeped in recognition that the right move was taking place, though touched with a selfish hint of sadness because his charm had us wrapped around his little finger.

The gift of time is never wasted and I don't necessarily refer to endless hours of play devoted to a youngster. Moreover, those singular seconds it takes to acknowledge the child's presence. All it takes is a quick reassuring word, a nod, a wink or a smile given. Perhaps as the child attempts to interrupt your conversation with another person, you reach out to hold his hand to ensure his silence until the conversation ceases, all of these moments are so important. All of these little interactions with a child remind him that you are there, that you care and that he is not being ignored. They offer the child boundaries, making them feel important, that they are safe as well as being recognised for the individual they are and teach them how to treat others. Surely it is only natural to gain attention through any channel that provides it, even if the channel is a negative display of tears and tantrums. You may find that you are the first person to offer the child in your care any real worthwhile time. I often used to say to my children "If you ask me a question at least give me time to answer!" On one such occasion my son answered, "But you don't need to say anything, your face says everything!" I can only surmise that he must have had my time in order to read me so well!

We had five days to offer him fun and games. Five days to give him a taste of family life. The chance to teach him how to do jigsaws, to construct things from Lego bricks, and of course to knock them down! Time to play in the garden or the local park where he could run, climb and slide, play ball and enjoy the company of other children. We had the opportunity to read our favourite family stories to him such as 'Mr Bingle's Apple Pie', 'The Topsy and Tim' series, and 'Bendomelena' that he enjoyed so much. We were certainly highly privileged to be trusted with his care and as a family we enjoyed a really positive experience. The boys have good memories of Robert's short stay with us and whenever they spoke of him thereafter it was always with a smile.

Robert was to come back to us the following February for three days as Mum was not well and needed a short stay in hospital. Then eleven months later, we had our little friend to stay again, this time for five days, again whilst Mum went into hospital, but this was a planned event, he was booked in with us in advance giving us plenty of time to be prepared, though we had a family of three children staying with us at the time. He was still a credit to his Mum, by then he was three and a half years old.

On each subsequent visit there was an air of 'déjà vu' as Robert seemed to recognise his surroundings, joining our family as an 'old hand', greeted by the boys on the same level as they would a cousin. On both of those occasions we had other children staying with us and he made our numbers up to six, still an only child, but he revelled in the company of all our children. It was about this time that we took on the identity of being a clan, three families combined by circumstances to function as one family. Somehow this helped all our children gain greater confidence in us as a family as we accepted that they had their own personal family, which deserved recognition and preserved their identity, yet gave them a sense of belonging which is so important to everyone.

Following the second visit I received another letter from Robert's Mum, it read: -

*Dear Dani,*

*I'm just writing to thank you very much indeed for looking after Robert for me.*

*Since he came home he keeps asking me if he can go and see the 'Lady' again. It sounds to me he thought a lot of you & misses you very much!*

*I hope he behaved himself at your house; it was nice of you to have him again while I was going through a bad patch at least I knew he was staying with you my mind was at rest.*

*I would also like to thank you for doing his washing & buying him the jigsaw, he gets the jigsaw out every morning without fail & has me fixing it up for him.*

*Thank the boys too for me because they've been really good with Robert.*

*I'm hoping to get pregnant again so Robert will have a brother or a sister to play with, an only child is a lonely child & I don't want that for Robert. It'll be nice for him to have a little playmate.*

*Anyway once again thanks. I must go now.*

*With Love*
*Robert's Mum.*

We were never to meet, and yet through the three occasions we had Robert, along with her kind notes, I felt we had. We were certainly building a foundation of trust between us, and if it helped her to know that there would always be a place for Robert in our lives and within our family should the need arise, then that was ok by us.

Young Robert aged three and half years old was a strong sturdy little boy and still had those beautiful eyelashes and that beguiling smile. His determination to enjoy life was very evident and he slipped into our family in his usual easy manner as though it was only yesterday that he had been here. He put a balance to life when we were going through some difficult times with other children and reminded the boys that fostering was fun too! The reason for this visit was because Mum had to go back to hospital for planned surgery and needed time to recuperate. Although this was to be another short visit nevertheless it was wonderful to be a part of his life once again, and hopefully help to stabilise his situation in Mum's absence. He had been fortunate enough to have the same social worker for the duration of all these visits, so the care system had provided him with continuity of care, which was always beneficial.

After Robert's third visit to us we received a letter from his social worker written the very day Robert left: -

*Dear Mr & Mrs Valdis,*

*I would like to take the opportunity to say thank you to yourselves and family. This being for the loving care you gave to Robert over his brief period in care.*

*It is hoped that we will not require any further placements, but if we do, then I shall give yourselves first consideration if you are available at these times.*

*Looking forward to working with you again in the future.*

*Yours Sincerely*

We did have the opportunity to work together in time but not for the benefit of Robert. We were never to be asked to care for him again, and I want to believe that this is because he never needed us. In my mind Mum gained strength and confidence to care for him herself, so no longer had a need for our services. I hope she had a good partner and that Robert had a sibling. Though I doubt we'll ever know.

> *"Call it a clan, call it a network,*
> *call it a tribe, call it a family:*
> *Whatever you call it, whoever*
> *you are, you need one".*

*Jane Howard*

*U.S. Writer (1935 - 1996)*

# CHAPTER 7

## Then There Were Three

After Robert returned home we were on countdown to Christmas, a wonderful and exciting time for all of us, but hectic. The usual gift buying and wrapping, card writing, baking to freeze, activities were well and truly underway. We had our church and school Christmas fairs to support. The excitement among the boys about what they hoped to be given. The hiding of presents out of sight of prying eyes and itchy fingers! Putting up the Christmas decorations overnight to surprise the boys in the morning. Learning of lines for Christmas Nativity Plays, Aaron's Choir practices to squeeze in, as well as the ordinary everyday events of living, washing, cooking, cleaning, shopping and ferrying children to school. Life as every mum knows it. But of course we also had to fit in Aaron's birthday on the 21st December with all the usual small boy celebrations, a party with friends, and try to separate this event from all the Christmas hype around, and preparations were underway for this too. So double the average excitement levels was the order of the day at this time of year.

Mid December the inevitable happened, just as I was managing countdown to Christmas quite nicely! We received a telephone call from our illustrious support worker. "Hello Dani. I thought I'd just run it by you to see how you felt about a placement this side of Christmas; you see we have a family of three, two girls and a boy. Their ages are two, three and five years. I realise it is very close to Christmas, but we are trying to place them without having to separate them, especially at this time of the year and we have very few possible placements at the moment." Those last words grabbed me. No way could I ever feel responsible for having this sibling group separated days before Christmas.

I felt sure we could manage; after all I was pretty well ahead of schedule with our festivity plans. I didn't have to think about this for long. "Of course we can, when can I expect them to arrive, do we have any background on their situation?" Foolish words! Social work terminology of 'can you' usually means ASAP and they rarely have too much information at the outset. "They will be with you mid-afternoon some time, their support worker will give you all the details. Thank you so much; we really have had a struggle to place them." Their struggle had come to an end but ours was just about to begin.

The batch of baking destined for the freezer that day never made it any further than the table, as it would be needed to fill the extra mouths that were on their way. Not knowing quite when to expect them, but realising that it might be around school pick up time I decided to arrange for Lawrence to come out of work to collect our boys, so that I would be at home in readiness for the children's arrival. I hastily made a vat of beef stew, mashed potatoes, with peas and carrots. I thought this could stew away slowly but be ready in time for our new arrivals without me having to give the meal much attention when the moment of truth came. I laid out the cakes and biscuits that I had baked earlier in the centre of the table along with a jug of juice and children's glasses. I had made a banner to go on the back of the kitchen door to welcome the children, wishing them a Merry Christmas, and also asked Lawrence to bring in three appropriate Advent Calendars for the children.

Eventually at about three o'clock they arrived. I cannot recall seeing such anxiety in three small children. The younger ones clung to their older sister, Jenna. She had dark brown hair, a rich chestnut colour, and straight with a fringe that parted in the middle, almost a pageboy style. She was petite and very pale and stared at me with questioning eyes but remained quiet. The smaller two were virtually a year apart in age; they had three weeks between their birthdays. Both were similarly dressed and had a mass of blonde shoulder length curls. One had a hand stuffed inside of its mouth, the other shook with apprehensive fear, but which was which? One was a girl, the other a boy but it was extremely difficult to tell the difference, they were so alike. I suggested they might like a drink and something to eat so I pulled out the chairs from around the kitchen table to encourage them to sit down. This they did, not taking their eyes off the plate in the middle of the table. I poured the children a drink having asked them if they would like juice or milk. As they drank, their eyes were still fixed on the plate, so as I walked across the kitchen to make a drink for the social worker, I simply said, "Help yourselves", nodding in the direction of the plate. I was mesmerised by the swiftness of three arms flying into the centre of the table to grab a cake or a biscuit. In the time it took to boil a kettle and make an instant coffee they had cleared the plate of every last crumb of more than a dozen buns and a dozen biscuits. The speed was unbelievable, neither a crumb nor a scrap lingered around any mouth or on the table for long, as their tongues would be licking and catching every last morsel. It was then I realised that it was hunger that was staring my way, as well as anxiety and fear of the unknown. This was to become quite a characteristic of this family, which we would have to learn to live with, to manage and control to make sure everyone had their fair share!

The social worker explained they had been monitoring the family for quite a while but their situation was getting worse. Mum had separated from the younger children's Dad but had had a rift with the new boyfriend. She found it difficult to concentrate on the children's needs, as it seemed her own were unmet. There was no food in the house, Grandma had periodically looked after the children but was unable to do this as frequently as was expected. They had all recently lost weight and concern was expressed about the little boy both physically and emotionally. I could not have agreed more as I shared their concerns about him too.

The social worker, Roger, was a pleasant, friendly man with a beard. Together we sat at the table with the children whilst he reminded the youngsters what would be happening. He would go to see Mum the following day to see how they could work together for her to have the children home again. But she might have to go into hospital for help. In the meantime they were to stay with us but he would telephone regularly to see how they were getting on, and would visit them in a few days time. Roger also explained that he hoped it would not be too long before they could return home for good, because he knew how much they were already missing Mum. I was impressed by his efforts to reassure the children, to offer them the explanations they needed to hear and include them in his plans as much as possible. He had been involved in the family for quite a while and was aware of the dynamics that had broken them. He gave them that all important element, time. This would build up their trust in him no matter how many times they were to be let down in the future. He was a very sincere man, although we were to eventually learn that he did not always agree with the system he had to work with, he would work along with it as well as he was able, but be prepared to challenge events where necessary and always for the benefit of the children. During our time around the table I discovered all their names as well as whether they were a girl or a boy! The older child Jenna, aged five years, asked a few questions, which Roger answered patiently and as fully as he was able, whilst the younger two sat and stared. The youngest one, Andrea, was the child with her hand in her mouth, this was her stance which developed into her having just two of her fingers frequently implanted on her tongue usually with an inane grin peering from behind the fingers and a girly giggle that in the future indicated to mean 'I'm up to no good'. Darren, was the middle child, he had an angelic, cherubic appearance, very quiet with wide eyes and an expression that emanated anxiety.

I enjoyed working with Roger as I held a great deal of respect for him. Sometimes children can be 'stuck' in the system, and at times it felt like they were used as pawns in a game for social services to achieve their own aim, under the guise of 'in the best interests of the children or family'. There was many a time I was to leave some of their meetings in a fury or be very upset because I did not agree with the actions they planned to take. But those 'essential actions required' came under the heading of 'professional decisions', by those who knew best! It was amazing just how many times they would be proven otherwise. But I did learn to control my feelings after such meetings, as I learned 'time' would indeed show us the truth, sadly often at the expense of many a child or their family.

Lawrence came back with our boys just as Roger was leaving. He had left their few belongings in the utility room for me to sort out. Clothes were few and the size of the clothes did not match the children. Mental note made to sort out clothes that would fit to get us through until I could go and purchase new clothes for them. They were all introduced to Lawrence and the boys. Aaron was a little disappointed that there was not a child nearer to his age, but Gareth and Jenna hit it off immediately, they were similar ages, both quite talkative and both loved to play similar games, so were content with each others company, they made good play mates. The younger two had a tendency to stick together, but Aaron was to have a soft spot for Darren as the only boy in the trio so took him under his wing to guide and mentor. Darren was quite a studious little chap and was evidently happy to follow Aaron's lead and teachings! Being in an all female environment had had quite a confusing effect on this little boy, without the male influences and being dressed similarly to his sisters as well as sharing the same hairstyle as his younger sister, his male identity was lost. This he was to discover and regain through the influence of our boys. On occasions this pairing off would leave one of them on their own. More often than not it was to be the oldest child, Aaron, or the youngest child, Andrea. I learned to use this to my advantage in a constructive manner to emphasise Aaron's growing up needs, giving him his own special time to play one to one games with him, when the others were well occupied and engrossed in play. Equally I was able to spend time with Andrea to engage her in some activity to encourage her speech and learning needs, as well as preventing her from irritating the others when they were playing so well.

I was glad I made that huge vat of stew. I expected to have plenty left, perhaps enough to freeze some for another time. But our new trio had other ideas. I gave them all average portions for children of their age and size. Aaron and Gareth had excellent appetites so I always leaned on the generous side when serving out. But these three could outstrip any of us! No sooner had I put the meal in front of them and they had devoured it staring hopefully at the casserole dish for the offer of more. Obviously they were very hungry, so I offered more, each child dived in to a healthy second helping that disappeared as quickly as the first, and their third helping was to go the same way. I scraped that casserole dish clean to satisfy their hunger. Their recent ordeal had not affected their ravenous appetites; they craved food in an exaggerated way that shouted survival. For many, many weeks those hungry eyes were to follow me around, as soon as they realised I was preparing a meal, they were there by my side. I would always lay the table well in advance, but when these children realised the cutlery was on the table they sat in their places waiting to eat. This escalated to them appearing in the kitchen the moment they heard the cutlery rattling as I took it from the drawer. I would explain that it was not dinnertime just yet and suggest they went back to play but as soon as I turned my back, they would have returned to sit at the table in readiness for the meal. I found this limping from meal to meal very disconcerting and very, very sad to witness but also extremely frustrating. I decided to involve the children in laying the table but only to do this at the last minute before we sat down to eat. The exception of course would be breakfast time, I was able to lay the table the night before which made it so much easier when the five trooped downstairs, because at least three would immediately shoot straight to the table creating order to my day with ease.

Breakfast time at this time of year was always enhanced by the excitement of opening the window in your Advent Calendar, discovering a small piece of shaped chocolate, and being allowed to eat it. Though not until they had eaten breakfast. This usually encouraged breakfast to be over rather quickly. Aaron and Gareth gave our trio their calendars on their first morning and identified the seventeenth window to be opened on each one. They all eagerly found their trophy and compared it with each other's before eating it. I then hung the calendars around the kitchen in easy reach so they could be seen and admired by their owners. I planned to let the trio eat the chocolates from window one to sixteen on Christmas Eve as a treat rather than spoil the opening of one window a day, which they seemed to enjoy doing. On about the third morning with us, I was ushering Aaron and Gareth to go upstairs to clean their teeth, as they still had to get to school and we were racing against the clock. One of them called for my attention so I left the three youngsters to find out why I was needed, I was only out of the kitchen for a few seconds but when I returned Gareth had joined them, demanding to know who had eaten all the chocolates from his Advent calendar. Jenna was clearly verbalising her innocence, whilst Darren stared, moving his head from side to side, shaking in his shoes, white faced and frightened. Little Andrea was sitting at the table, fist in mouth, smiling or was she smirking? I checked all five calendars, every chocolate had been removed and was nowhere to be seen or found. There was no evidence of excess chocolate on anyone's face. My immediate thought was perhaps Gareth had eaten his own after seeing the others had eaten theirs, but he was far too upset. No one gave anything away, but either on their own or in partnership, one or more of these children had committed the crime! But how had they had the deft skill to strip the calendars so quickly without taking them off the wall? That actually was quite an amazing dextrous feat. I expressed my disapproval in no uncertain terms to all the children, making it clear that eating your own was one thing, but to eat someone else's was totally unacceptable and disrespectful too. However this learning curve needed an upward turn, and I did not want to ruin the Christmas expectations and anticipations for any of them, so I did replace the calendars with new ones, but this time hung them well out of reach. But I removed all the chocolates from one to nineteen from each calendar for them to eat at a later date. I was very aware that the likelihood of the two younger ones with their insatiable appetites were likely to have been the culprits as partners in crime and were not at the stage of fully understanding the consequences of it. Survival was still their main theme in life and this had been a part of it.

Fortunately that year, Aaron's birthday was a simple arrangement, we had planned a party at home for him and a few choice friends, this meant in the December cold we would not have to venture far as the guests were coming to us. The day passed well, and Aaron showed off his new extended family to his friends with pride. The trio equally joined in the celebrations in a very positive manner. Bonus! They understood the meaning and importance of a birthday. Considering this event was only five days after their arrival, they coped exceptionally well. The party had also given them something to look forward to and focus on, which helped to ease some of the discomfort in their personal circumstances, and offered a stepping-stone to the kind of Christmas they would celebrate with us. In fact, prior to the children coming, we had booked to have our Christmas dinner and spend the afternoon at a hotel, a short drive away. The reason for this was because we had no immediate family in the area, geographically we were a little isolated and the day would pass without us meeting anyone else. We also felt that by doing this we would be able to give the boys more quality time but also allow us to enjoy some adult company. There was to be a children's entertainer for part of the afternoon, which would enhance the day and keep the boys away from television. But now we had three extras! I rang the hotel; they agreed to accommodate our trio, though I was the apprehensive one now. Taking two young boys could be a challenge, how much more so would taking five children! My mother had also agreed to spend Christmas with us and I wasn't certain about her reaction to the enhancements in the family.

Last minute preparations for Christmas were now in force, the children were young enough to fall into any of our plans and accept them with open arms. Their preconceived notions were not so indifferent, though I was acutely aware that Jenna had strong views on most things happening around us and would relate these to her own limited experience of life. Within a week of being with us she had informed us of her 'Cafflick' status, a fact we were aware of, as it was part of the information we had been given. Her announcement of this fact amused many of our friends, as she would inform them as soon as she met them. One friend who was also Catholic commented that Jenna made it sound like a disease. Realising we needed to maintain their links with the Catholic church we arranged for another friend of ours to take the older two to the Catholic church in the village along with her own two youngsters. They passed our house each Sunday and were only too willing to take them. This involved having the couple vetted by social services to be satisfied of their suitability. This arrangement worked well until Jenna decided she was fed up of being a 'Cafflick' a few weeks down the line! This arrangement also meant we could maintain our links with our own church. Lawrence had to work every Sunday so was unable to be a part of this; so I was greatly relieved to have our friends help. My main concern for Christmas was making it as special for our trio as we planned for Aaron and Gareth. I needed the time to establish their likes and dislikes, the type of presents they hoped to receive, the time to buy, wrap, and involve all the children in making the 'magic' of Christmas. I was running out of time, as Christmas day seemed to race towards us. This was before regular twenty-four hour shop opening occurred, so free to shop time was limited. Thursday evening was late night opening but that was also Lawrence's late night opening too. Fortunately the Saturday before Christmas gave me an opportunity to go shopping whilst Lawrence occupied the children. But I wanted the children to choose a small gift to give to each other, which meant taking each one out to buy four gifts. Lawrence took Aaron and Gareth, then I went out with the others so they could feel involved on that level too, and they chose Mum a gift as well. This was followed by a very exciting secretive session with each one helping to wrap and label their gift to give, and hiding them until it was time to place them under the Christmas tree. Fortunately Mum and members of their own family sent gifts for them to open on the day. This was so important as they would need those presents to connect with their own family, irrespective of the sadness that might arise from their appearance.

Usually before Christmas the boys would help me to make Christmas biscuits and home made sweets. The biscuits would be wrapped in cling film and hung on the Christmas tree, which could be enjoyed later. The sweets would be packed into little transparent boxes, the type that Christmas cards came in. These would have a ribbon tied around them to be given to anyone who called during Christmas week. This year all of the children contributed to these creations, and Jenna put aside boxes for her Mum and Roger their social worker.

Christmas Day 1985 was on a Wednesday. My mother had arrived a couple of days before and loved having the children around; recently widowed she was still finding it hard to cope with family celebrations without my father being around. She was looking forward to spending the day at the hotel, but also expressed her concern about whether the children would cope with the environment without spoiling it for us or for other diners. Being the mother of six she was only being realistic and I shared those same concerns. We had known the children for a mere week, better known as the 'honeymoon period' after which their settling in could well turn into the most unexpected behaviours being exhibited. The hotel might be just the right place to trigger such behaviour!

We could not have been more wrong. All the children were complimented on their behaviour by the hotel staff and some of the other guests, and for making their Christmas all the more enjoyable. We arrived in time to be seated almost immediately having enjoyed an aperitif first, this gave the children an opportunity to adjust to the atmosphere and orientate themselves. The festive laid table was a great incentive to sit down and anticipate what might happen next. There were five courses to be worked through, such joy to our gourmet eaters. Much to our delight they revelled in the attention given to them, especially our little blonde curly headed two, even more so Darren, with his Lord Fauntleroy locks. Andrea was in a high chair, which we felt would restrict her ability to disrupt others through fidgeting. However I doubt that would have been a problem because as long as the waitress brought us food she was prepared to sit still and eat! They all devoured every plateful put in front of them, like a plague of locusts they polished anything edible which kept them all occupied allowing us a chance to relax and enjoy the day too. Whilst they were eating we had a visit from 'Santa' who gave each child a selection box of chocolate, they were thrilled, even more to eat later in the day!

After the meal it was a time to relax, each of them had taken a couple of gifts that they had opened earlier in the day and I took a gift for each of them to open whilst they were there as a distraction should it be needed. This meant they had fifteen toys, games or books between them to keep them occupied. Between the endless runs to find the toilet, a strange fascination that all children seem to share, they occupied themselves well until it was time for the children's entertainer who would give us a chance to sit back and enjoy our flock as much as others were. The atmosphere was brilliant, each child rose to the occasion giving their best not only to us but also to each other and those around. This was to be the first of many grand occasions that we would enjoy with this family, as they were not a particularly argumentative trio. They were great supporters of each other and also to Aaron and Gareth too. My mother thoroughly enjoyed the day, and being a sociable soul would mingle and talk to others, so all of our guests behaved well that day.

The Children's entertainer was called 'Giggles the Clown', he captured the attention of the children quite quickly with his jokes and maintained it for over an hour, with his repertoire of silly tricks and collapsing wands, as much enjoyed by the adults as by all the children. He chose Jenna to help him with a trick; I held my breath ready to rescue her if necessary if she found the 'audience' element or the clown's jokes too much. She leapt to help and basked in the glory of the attention. We saw a new side to this little girl, as her infectious giggle and incessant garrulous chatter kept everyone amused. There was only one possible sticky moment when the clown asked her where her Mum and Dad were sitting. She frowned at him, and then laughed, when he asked her what was so funny she retorted "I'm not with my Mum and Dad, silly, I am with my Auntie Dani and Uncle Lawrence, and they are over there." She pointed in our direction. My mother and both Lawrence and I had tears welling in our eyes. In little more than a week we felt accepted! Surely it was our job to give them a sense of belonging, but we had not anticipated it would show itself so soon. Such a public display was indeed a gift in itself. I felt her words gave greater perspective to others around, who may have thought that we had five children aged eight and under of our own making! I had heard one or two disparaging remarks from other tables during our Christmas dinner. Such remarks were never to offend me; on the contrary I was always amused by the assumptions of others as to why we had a large family of children, and why they always thought we could not hear them discussing our situation! What mattered was that we knew, and we were comfortable with our choice. 'People watching' is a great pastime of many and can be fun. Over twenty years later I was to hear my mother recall this moment with as much clarity as the day we encountered it, the tears welled in her eyes then too!

Afternoon tea was next on the agenda, which of course meant Christmas cake and mince pies coming round, food again! Another peaceful twenty minutes or so whilst they worked through the plateful left in front of us. The afternoon was over, time to return home and enjoy the rest of the day by ourselves, our clan. I had saved a few gifts given by family and friends for them to open on our return to keep the atmosphere alive, it worked, they were all so happy to play games with each other we left them to it, only becoming involved if they invited us to, for instructions on how to play a new game, or build a model or read a book. We had all enjoyed a very special day that was to lead the way for the next few months.

Little did we know how these children were to
affect our lives in the future, how we were to become
involved in theirs, moreover how our lives would be
intertwined for a long time to come. We were to get to
know Mum and her foibles as much as we knew the
children's. Our desire to protect them was to become
immensely strong, but we were expected to walk away.
These children who entered our life so innocently and
unwittingly were to cause the community to erupt in
support of us, our friends and family to write to MP's to
countenance our decisions and decry those of the
professionals. Mum was to support us to the hilt
agreeing for them to stay with us, her view was clear,
"If I can't have them then Dani and Lawrence should."
A view reiterated by the High Court. We were to drag
ourselves through the mire almost causing a complete
family break-up when Lawrence and I came to terms with
the hopeless situation, but unfortunately at different
stages, causing a major problem between us. Perhaps
his experience of life had left him capable of accepting
major disappointments, mine had not. Being determinedly
stubborn I refused to accept the outcome set before us,
though I was not alone in this as Roger, their social worker,
was also to be disgusted, appalled and disappointed
at decisions made by one person on behalf of these
children. At this vulnerable time our own support
worker had been told by her manager she was no longer
to visit us, I believe this was purely because she too
felt the same way as Roger, though two months or
more down the line she was eventually to support us
again when common-sense reigned. During this time my
own health deteriorated, in need of surgery, barely
weighing six stones, I have no doubts that the stress

we were under from decisions made, contributed to this.

This trio of ours flourished in the coming weeks. We had taken the same decision to let Jenna join Aaron and Gareth at their school, which she adapted to extremely well. Darren and Andrea had three mornings a week at the local playschool that they loved. There was a memorable day when Lawrence had brought them home, I was upstairs as Darren ran through the house shouting "Auntie Dani, Auntie Dani," I called down to him so he knew where I was, Darren stood on the bottom step and called up to me "I need a tie and a present, quickly look!" When I asked what they were needed for he replied "'cos look, I've got a party letter!" Indeed he did have an invitation to a friend's party, the excitement was written across his face, wide eyed, grinning, rosy cheeked what a let down I was about to give him, he had a whole week to wait! Instead I took him to Gareth's room to select a tie to wear for the occasion which he could hang in his room until the day, with a promise to take him to buy a present for his friend the following day, we then ringed the date on the calendar so he could cross them off on a daily basis. We planned to do something each day, such as a visit to the park one day, shopping the next, playschool on the following day, some small everyday event that would provide a stepping stone toward D-Day so he could see for himself how close we were getting to the party. He could hardly contain his enthusiasm and excitement, the day came at last, he was one small boy at the party but I am convinced he was far more excited about the day than even the birthday boy was!

By the end of the first month their voracious appetites had increased their size phenomenally and new clothes were the order of the day. Knowing how quickly children grew I was never one for expensive clothing so I usually managed value for money and was able to buy them three or four outfits each. Jenna had been at school on the day of my shopping spree. So when I gave her the bag of new clothes I expected her to be pleased and willing to look at them. She opened the bag, peered inside, pulled out one of the tops then stuffing it back into the bag she remarked uninterestedly, "Yeah, fine." I asked her if there was something wrong, suggesting the clothes were not to her liking, maybe? Jenna bowed down her head keeping her eyes on the floor. She sniffed quietly, tears welled but refused to fall. I waited silently. Eventually she said, "Did you buy them so I would like you more than I would like my Mummy?" My timing was all wrong. Feelings had been rising in this youngster probably since day one and my gesture had brought these to a head. I reassured her as much as possible that this was not the case, that I never had plans to take Mum's place. Her position in all their lives was too important but also too fragile. The clothes were unimportant at this moment, I moved them out of the way, scooped Jenna up and hugged her, she was homesick, and missing Mum so much, but had hidden her feelings behind a veneer that told everyone around that she was ok. She cried quietly, the tears fell freely, and she talked about Mum's love of Elvis Presley and her own love of Shaking Stevens. Through her tears she talked openly about home, her own school, the difference in her life there to the life we offered. She wanted to know if I knew when they could all go back home. Why did Mummy love them but was not able to care for them? Why did I know how to cook, to wash, and to look after children, but Mummy kept forgetting? There was far too much for such a little girl to understand. She was five years old, so was Gareth, yet the difference in their little lives was enormous. His maturity came from the part he played in our children's lives, whilst hers came from the life she lead. No matter what a parent does or does not do, unconditional love abounds. The explanations I gave satisfied her need at the time, she resigned herself to the idea of being with us for the duration, accepted what was on offer with us, complied to our expectations, but both of us knew that deep down there was only one place she wanted to be and that was back with her Mum.

The younger two thrived, grew stronger and loved to play both inside and outside. When all five were riding bikes and trikes outside, negotiating my way to the washing line was worse than crossing a Motorway at peak time, my life in their hands! They all played well together, their imaginations ran riot, and there was a love of life in our home with an undercurrent of how long will this last. Each of them seemed to take it in turn to have a spurt of emotional growth as they worked through whatever was going on inside of them. There would be a little rumble of discontent in one that you could not quite put your finger on, but wait, and it would eventually come to a head to be aired and understood. One such time was when Darren went through a few days of not being the usual happy chap that we knew. Then one evening when I had the three of them in the bath all together, quite unexpectedly he began to sort of cry, well whinge loudly, we had noticed that Darren did not cry. I asked him why he was making a noise, he looked at Andrea and demanded to know why hers had already dropped off but he still had one when he was older than Andrea!

I realised he was referring to his genitals and quickly reassured him that that was because he was different, being a boy he would need his, and they never had one ever! Jenna shrieked, "Darren, you are not a girl, you are a boy, you're not the same as us, you are like Aaron and Gareth!" He cheered up immediately, smiled from ear to ear but now wanted to know that if that was true why did he have such long hair? Times they were a-changing! From this day forward Darren had a bath with the boys rather than with his siblings. We needed to work on his identity crisis and the boys were to offer their male influence. He suddenly became an expert in what girls liked or didn't as the case may be. "Us boys do this" was one of his favourite sayings. His leaning to play with the lads both at home and in the nursery setting was becoming more obvious each day. But the big let down was that head of shoulder length blonde curls and he knew it!

As foster parents we had no right to have his hair cut without permission from his mother, as this could be construed as abuse, and she was rather fond of his curls. This made it difficult for us to satisfy Darren's need to have a short hair cut like Aaron and Gareth and complete his new self-identity. Roger, in support of Darren, asked for Mum's permission to cut his hair several times, each time she would suggest he can 'have a bit off the ends'. This was not what Darren wanted to hear and he would get quite upset at the hairdresser when only the ends were trimmed. However as time went by and the prospect of starting school loomed, even we were beginning to despair. I suggested to Roger that he asked for permission more frequently so Darren could have his hair trimmed more often, this would enable

Darren to go a little shorter with each cut. It worked; Mum seemed to accept this gradual change in the length of Darren's hair and I suspect the need to control this aspect of his life became less important to her as time moved forward. I also suspect Darren nagged her on visits to her. Whatever the reason by the time Easter came he had lost the curls and now had a neat short haircut, crinkled with a slight wave in it that added to his boyish looks. Just in time to start the new school term.

*"Children need models more than they need critics."*

*Joseph Joubert*

*French Moralist and Essayist (1754 - 1824)*

# CHAPTER 8

# Laughter,
# Love and Living

Little Robert had joined us for a few days during February 1986. Andrea looked upon him with scorn initially. Perhaps she felt her position was threatened as she viewed him as competition! This did not last, as in her imitable fashion, she decided to control the situation and use him as a playmate. However Robert rather liked her toys, but Andrea became very possessive over these, so ensured she dictated terms over who played with what! As long as young Robert conformed, Andrea was content. Their arguments were of the silent type, eye contact, and facial expressions, whether frowns, scowls, smirks or smiles, each got their message over to the other and resulted in amicable play. This was short lived as all too soon Robert returned to his Mum. But the benefits of his visit were enormous in helping our trio to understand that they were not the only children to have to live with foster parents.

They gained confidence, smiled more, continued to eat well and loved to learn. Family play was what they enjoyed most of all. So time was always set aside each day, for us to be together, baking, making, constructing, drawing, painting, playing a board game, reading, anything that involved all of us playing a part, learning from each other, socialising and sharing. They were a bright bunch very keen and eager to soak up knowledge. Jenna would question the need to do something in the first place and at the end mock the result, but also showed a smile of pride at participating. She rarely had the initial idea but was great at enhancing the ideas of others. Darren was a deep thinker, saying little until he had thought out his concepts, questioned their viability and put them into practise before standing back to accept the accolade that he felt he justly deserved. Andrea would watch patiently, fingers implanted in her mouth, picking up pieces to hand to others to use or fit into place. She watched the others carefully, would answer any questions if asked by Aaron and Gareth as they tested her understanding of colours, numbers and shapes. Gareth usually initiated the type of activity we were involved in and organised who would sit where, though if the dynamics of the group dictated I would over-rule his ideas to suit everyone's needs, not just his! Aaron always made sure that rules were laid down and everyone conformed or took the consequences. He was always very polite in his attempts to get a message across to someone if he felt they were defaulting. Like Darren, he too would check out his thinking before contributing to the project in hand. We encouraged them to respect each other's suggestions or thoughts. Also to be involved in getting out and putting away anything we used, to help them to understand co-operation and working as a team, which on the whole they were pretty good at doing. There would always be the usual sibling rivalry or general disagreement that rose between them periodically, but if I nipped it in the bud immediately, they responded positively and rarely held a grudge with each other, which helped to maintain a modicum of family harmony among us.

Easter time came with the usual celebrations of egg hunts around the house and garden. Five tornadoes racing around in all directions following their own set of clues by the 'Easter Bunny', towards a basket of chocolate eggs. The older ones helping the younger ones read and decipher their little notes to enable them to find the next. This was such innocent fun, and a great way to release that pent up excitement that had built up during the previous week or two. Once their well-earned prize had been found, they would set about counting the various eggs, sorting them into colours, admiring and playing with the mini chicks that decorated the handles. Our late night Easter Saturday efforts were worth staying up for, to be rewarded by the smiles, laughter and the frustrations of this activity.

But the new school term was soon before us. Four smartly uniformed children now sat around the breakfast table chattering about their expectations of the new term. Andrea was feeling a little left out, as she wanted to know why she couldn't dress the same as the others. Gareth let her borrow Harold to look after whilst he was at school. Now Harold was his prize possession of a cuddly toy that he had chosen as a toddler from the shelves at Mothercare. No one was allowed to share Harold; he even had to go to school with Gareth when he first started to help him settle in. Gareth had thought it was terrible that Harold did not have a uniform to match his, so I made one for him out of an outgrown set. The shorts, shirt and tie had been easy to make, the blazer put my needlework skills to the test. But Andrea was as pleased about looking after Harold whilst the others were all at school, as Gareth was to know that Harold was not left alone at home.

Lawrence and I were very conscious of the need to encourage and enhance their social skills too, so to us it was essential that we had occasional family outings to the theatre, out for a meal, or that we went for a country walk of some kind. On one occasion we were visiting Nostell Priory for a battle re-enactment, we planned to have a picnic as well, and then take a stroll around the grounds particularly to take the circular route around the lake. Jenna revelled in the battle and alongside Gareth, they cheered and booed as necessary, loving every minute. The picnic was enjoyed by each of them. Their appetites had not diminished and the fresh air made them hungrier than ever. Then Lawrence suggested we had a walk. "Why?" said Jenna, with an expression of such surprise? "To give us all some exercise." he replied. "That's silly." said Jenna, "What do we need exercise for?" "Well at least we can look for things, see what we can find and explore." answered Lawrence. Jenna sighed the deepest sigh that came from the bottom of her boots at the same time shaking her head. The others were all enthusiastic ready to race away as soon as we were ready to let them. But Jenna struggled to see the reason for moving. Maybe she just enjoyed relaxing in the grounds, perhaps she was reluctant to stop what was for her a 'feel good moment,' maybe I am just making up excuses for her! Dragging her feet all the way, usually slightly behind us, she came, the reluctant walker complaining and moaning all the way around the lake. The others walked or ran ahead, only coming back to us to show us something or to ask a question. They loved it, running through the grass, picking daisies or buttercups, watching the birds fly around or ducks floating on the lake. The freedom of movement, fresh air and sun was soaked up by each of them. But Jenna could see no fun in this at all and did we know it! Her reluctance was voiced in groans and moans and sighs deeper than the lake itself. For most of the way round she held her head low refusing to have her eyes opened to the joys of nature. She stepped into a patch of wet mud that made her trainers very dirty, she was furious, even though we tried to appease her in all sorts of ways and clean off the shoes for her.

Once round the lake, the other four were thrilled that they did not have too far to walk back to the car. However having discovered we were back where we started, Jenna stood scowling indignantly with her hands on her hips, mouth wide open in shock, she was absolutely furious with us for taking them, on what she perceived as a pointless exercise. Not only had we 'made' her walk unnecessarily for 'miles and miles' but her shoes had suffered into the bargain. How stupid could we be! What was more she considered the others to be ridiculously stupid too for enjoying it! The whole concept was lost on her, no tears were shed but that look of fury was not going to fade easily. I suggested everyone might like an ice cream before going home, four eager beavers leapt at the offer looking around for the ice cream van or shop. Jenna glared in my direction not sure how to react, eventually she said "You can't bribe me like that, it won't make me feel any better or like you any more just 'cos you're giving me an ice cream." Her strength of feeling was still at boiling point. I just said, "It is not a bribe, I think we are all ready for one after our walk." Then I just walked towards the other four leaving Little Miss to lick her wounds and calm her fury. Lawrence had gone for the ices and the others had surrounded him to be given their well-earned treat. Jenna strolled up taking the ice cream a little hesitatingly from Lawrence. Then as we walked towards the car park I sensed Jenna's pace quicken at the back of me until eventually she was by my side. She continued to walk along side of me for a short distance until she summoned up the courage to reach out to slip her hand into mine. Neither of us said anything, but as she looked up for confirmation that all was ok, I looked at her and smiled giving her hand a gentle squeeze, she smiled back still saying nothing. Words were not needed we had both learned a valuable lesson.

That evening at bedtime Jenna apologised for being miserable during the afternoon. I asked her if she knew why she had felt so unhappy, she just said that she couldn't see the point of walking all that way only to be back where we started. Poor Jenna was really struggling to come to terms with certain events that took place in our family. We had one of our many endless evening chats to give her the opportunity to talk out her feelings. We began to recognise when the strength of her feelings were rising and were able to help her diffuse them, before they built up into a crescendo or were taken out on others.

This might well have been the first time that Jenna had experienced this kind of family outing. Perhaps she was just not in the mood for running around like the others or hadn't developed the sense of freedom a walk like this can give. Perhaps she was never to find pleasure in the simple things in life, we were yet to discover her real tastes. But as our holidays were usually taken in the country, either she would learn to adapt or we would have a constant struggle. We had planned a holiday in

Sussex for August, this was to be combined with a visit to Kent for a few days to see Lawrence's Mum. Lawrence had arranged for us to take our caravan to stay on a woodland site at Petworth and a farmer's field near Ashford in Kent. So before this event took place we decided to stay for a week at a more local site in the Yorkshire Dales close to Brimham Rocks, a regular favourite for us providing a natural playground environment that our children loved to explore. If anywhere was to entice Jenna into the world of nature then Brimham Rocks was the answer.

A few weeks later with the caravan and car packed we set off to the farm below the rocks where we set up to stay for the week. Aaron was well versed about his role on arrival; he would fill the water bottles from the tap in the field, determined to enrol the others in helping him on a daily basis. Our chosen site was no more than a field that took five caravans though there was a tap that gave us fresh spring water. The backdrop to the field was high sandstone rock, our own mini version of the Brimham Rocks site itself. Contained within the field, which spread a reasonable distance, gave boundaries with freedom, which the children took great delight in. Wherever they ventured we could see them comfortably. This site increased their courage to explore. They had endless games of hide and seek which Jenna seemed to take control of. The caravans were sited to give everyone their own personal space well out of the hearing of each other, a fact I was glad about with all the children we had. The van had four berths but a toddler could sleep well on the mini sofa part at the back of the van, ideal for Andrea. Darren and Jenna had the bunk beds, whilst Aaron and Gareth slept in the tent in the awning. They loved the whole experience. Clambering over the rocks, taking country walks, just sitting outside playing quietly. Even Jenna put heart and soul into the week, making us feel more confident about the trip to the South of England.

On our way back over the rocks one afternoon, our staggered troop, donned in jeans, boots and jumpers with cagoules tied around their waists, was strolling down the hill towards the van. Andrea was tired, we had walked a long way that day, and she was beginning to let us know by whining and calling out to each of us to carry her. We continued to encourage her, calling to her to follow, pointing out that we could see the van so we were almost there. She continued to whine, a drawn out "Carry meeee!". I was only a few yards in front of her in an effort to keep her motivated. One of the children took my attention away from Andrea momentarily by asking a question. I had heard Andrea cry out the 'carry' part of her repetitive phrase but it was cut off in an instance and silence followed, I turned to look at her but she wasn't there! Panic hit me! Where the hell had this little one disappeared to, there was nowhere for her to go, this was impossible. The silence was unbearable. Lawrence was well ahead with Gareth and Jenna whilst Aaron was holding Darren's hand not far in front of me. I called out for Andrea, but she did not call back though my calling had alerted Aaron who came back to me bringing Darren with him. We walked towards where I had last seen Andrea not many feet away calling her name as we did so, but not a sound from her. Nearing the spot where she was last seen I suddenly saw her peering from behind a patch of long grass and half grown ferns. Hand stuffed in her mouth watching us walking towards her, her expression of total surprise across her face as we laughed with relief at her predicament. She had slipped down the hillside, her Wellington boot had caught in a rabbit hole and she was unable to free it. I am sure she could see us all the time through the ferns even though we could not see her. Thank goodness she was safe. On future walks I would insist she always walked in front of me so that I could reduce the risk of further disappearing acts. One magician in the family was more than enough!

One memorable meal that was easy to cook in the caravan was chilli con carne. It was a beautiful evening so we chose to sit outside to eat. Everyone was tucking into their meal in their usual hungry manner, apart from Jenna, who on this occasion was pushing the food around the plate with her fork. I asked if there was anything wrong with it, she stated that she didn't like it, which rather surprised me. When Lawrence explained it was a traditional Mexican meal, Jenna responded with a shrill "Well the Mexicans can keep it!" I had actually found something that one of them would not eat!

The caravan holiday was a great success, squabbling was minimal, and usually over who was not helping with the chores! The fresh air and exercise revitalised them all. Jenna, Darren and Andrea thrived on the freedom, whilst Aaron and Gareth loved their company, sharing their time and showing off their expertise in 'rock climbing' encouraging the others to join in or at least to try and have a go. The children had lost their angst. Jenna was a wonderful chatterbox that questioned everyone and everything. Darren had a 'give it a go' attitude, not quite a dare devil, always erring on the side of safety, ideal for the rocks venue. Little Andrea fell into line with everything we did, but let us know in no uncertain terms when she was struggling to keep up. On one of the evenings Lawrence took us all into Ripon to the town square to watch the Town Crier, they were all mesmerised by his outfit and his loud "Oyez, Oyez", the ringing of his bell and the blowing of the Ripon Bugle. Their jaws almost reaching the ground as he made the necessary town announcements. The excitement of being allowed to stay up after nine o'clock, which was considered to be very late indeed! Then driving back to our field in the pitch black of the country night. There was a discussion in the car between the children about the cat's eyes reflectors in the centre of the road. Gareth commented how strange it was that the lights switched on in front of us but turned themselves off when they were behind us. Lawrence told them that there was nothing strange to this as he had total control over the lights and could switch them all off easily. They believed him, especially when momentarily he turned off his headlamps in an endeavour to endorse their belief. Aaron thwarted his father's theories by launching into educating the others with the facts that the lights were called 'cat's eyes' and were really reflectors set in the tarmac so motorists could see which side of the road they were on. Darren asked "Why are they called cat's eyes then?" Lawrence decided to come clean with the truth about the reflectors and offered a full explanation, starting with how real cats have eyes that reflect light so they can see in the dark, and how the chap who invented these lights used that concept to do so. There was a silence in the car for about five minutes. Then Gareth uttered, "Well where do all the cats go?" Lawrence, still driving, briefly looked in my direction somewhat perplexed. I looked at all the children. Aaron was smirking, the others eager to learn the answer. "Which cats?" I said. "You know, all the blind ones, when their eyes have been used," he said seriously. The whole lot of us burst into a fit of uncontrollable laughter, which continued until we got back to the farm. Lawrence did his best to convince Gareth that real cat's eyes were not used! Once back at the farm they all had fun, sitting outside the van with its soft light, just allowing them enough light to see each other and their immediate surroundings, which kept them from moving any distance away. We all sat down to have a drink of hot chocolate staring at the night sky trying to identify the constellations. Nights on holidays are for wonderful moments like these. Pleasantly tired they all drifted off to their beds leaving us wondering what the future held for each of them.

Visits had been arranged for the children to spend time with Mum. These were only short visits lasting about an hour. We had learned that Mum was very young herself, and having separated from her husband, was struggling to cope with the heavy responsibility of life with three very young children with no real support network around the family. Dad, unfortunately, was struggling to cope with his heavy drinking; the children's visits to him were few and far between. Mum's needs were great and did not involve the children at this time. She needed the support of the psychiatric services and was eventually admitted to the local psychiatric unit to be helped with her problem in an attempt to overcome it. Sadly the children were quite affected by some of these visits, they so looked forward to going, but returned forlorn, dejected and very upset. On their return to us, each one of them would be wrapped in their own world of sadness that no one else would be allowed to enter.

These times were difficult to handle, the boys found it strange to see them like this, so sad and detached, confused and bewildered. So afterwards we would be handling the fragile feelings of five little people trying to make sense of the effects of the adult world around them. Yet again the Play People were to dominate their games, as we used them for the children to focus on and act out the reality of their lives. This was often a group activity as we all surrounded the kitchen table using these miniature plastic people to represent the real adults and the children. Through this play we learned how they felt, their thoughts and fears, their hopes and sometimes their expectations, when they dared to feel hopeful enough to expect. Unknowingly they helped each other overcome some of their upsets and disappointments consequently supporting each other. This type of play let them openly voice their opinions or views on their situation for all to hear, which was clearly therapeutic in helping them to come to terms with what was happening. The other outlet for their feelings was the box of drawing paper we kept handy for any of them to use at any time. Pencils, crayons and felt tips were always available for any budding artist to use whenever the urge took them. But at the end of the day they would put their efforts back into the box in an attempt to tidy up. Through their pictures or writings they expressed so much about their emotional state, some well-chosen ones I would display on the kitchen wall, which helped them to feel accepted, warts and all!

Gradually Mum improved, and the possibility of returning home became more hopeful. Mum's world around this time was a blur and she knew she had been unable to respond to the children's needs, but without the backup of her husband she had struggled with her own helplessness. After coming out of hospital she made a greater effort to stabilise the family situation with the support of social services. The hopes of the children were raised when they returned from the access visits to Mum, their thoughts of the possibility of going home eventually strengthened. We knew this was the point where we had to focus on supporting the children to look forward to rejoining Mum, but leaving us, at the same time we had to support Aaron and Gareth to cope with the children leaving our family but remain strong enough in that loss to keep moving forward. Our five youngsters were all at different ages, different stages, all coming to the same end from different perspectives. It was to be a tough challenge to keep positive at times, but also very important to guide them through this and help our trio cross their bridge back to Mum and their own family. I simply hoped we had done enough to help these three youngsters cope and keep a reasonable balance to life. They were young; life would be serving more knocks at some time in the future, which was inevitable for all of us. But if in some small way we had helped prepare them to face those knocks and find the backbone to handle them, then we had served our purpose and the time to let go was looming.

In preparation for their return, overnight stays at home with Mum were to take place. First there was a one-night stay, home in the afternoon, stay overnight, returning to us the following morning sometime before lunch. This was an opportunity for Mum to spend quality time with them. They would have a chance to sleep in their own beds and for Mum to regain their trust. This visit was fairly successful. The girls were lively and chatty about what they had for tea and Mummy playing with them. Darren was quieter, when asked if he had enjoyed being at home, he answered with a nod but had that frightened mouse expression as he stared straight at me. He didn't want to touch the play people when the others were happy re-enacting events of the visit. He just listened but did not have a thing to say. I tried to talk to him but his demeanour made it clear he did not want to talk. I shared all this with our support worker, Emily, who suggested we just wait and see, as it may be simply because Darren needed more time to accept this change to his life. The next stage was for the trio to have a weekend visit with Mum. Darren found this hard to accept, two nights away seemed like eternity, but the girls were quite excited at the prospect. We would need to make the weekend special for Aaron and Gareth too, in an effort to not let them feel left out, also to help with their feelings about what was happening, yet at the same time not too special that our returning troop would feel that we had left them out of our plans. The balance was crucial! The planned weekend arrived, Darren was not happy and demonstrated that he would rather stay with the boys. This was the first real time we had had anything that could be construed as a tantrum from him but he was adamant. I offered him the explanation for the umpteenth time. Darren sat on a chair in the dining room near to the kitchen door. I left him there whilst I carried on with the daily happenings but deliberately kept finding reasons to go through the room to monitor what he was doing. Each time I did so Darren just sat there with his dejected expression seemingly trying to fight back the tears watching me each time I walked in or out of the room. It was like witnessing the rumblings of a volcano about to erupt. I realised then that we had yet to hear Darren cry, he had lived with us all these months, gone through so much, but never once shed a tear either through frustration or through sadness. He had struggled with his identity, coped with a new play school and then moved on to main school without crying to manifest his feelings. How much had this young fellow held inside of him? We were about to find out. Each time I walked into the room his groans became louder, he began to shake as he sat almost frozen to the chair. My gut feeling was to pick him up and hold him, but I felt if I did he would push those feelings back down from the very depths they had come from. For the moment I had to let him feel the pain that was causing so much distress. His rumbling noises became louder, his whole body shook, wailing sounds began to pour from his mouth, he tried in his way to stop them but they kept on coming. All the time he kept his eyes on me, and I kept mine on him. This continued for several minutes, eventually Darren reached his arms out towards me for help as I talked to him softly, but the wailing became totally uncontrollable. He was so frightened, and as I held him so was I. The tears began to well in his eyes that were becoming wider with each second that ticked by. He clung so hard to me in fear, and I just held on waiting for this to end. Eventually the tears began to fall, the initial release increased his fear, as this was a whole new experience for Darren. Then the tears fell like a torrent of water in a waterfall during a thunderous rainstorm. This had taken Darren by storm and was not going to pass quickly. We had a tight grip on each other; he buried his head into me, as the horrendous animal-like wailing continued. This poor little mite suddenly seemed so tiny and baby like; I really did not want to let go of him. The others had peered into the room, looked at the scene of us wrapped around each other and respected the fact that this was Darren's precious time of need. They had just gone outside to play quietly until it was all over. It felt like eternity, but eventually Darren's ear-piercing, screaming wails subsided turning into uncontrollable strong sobbing, the tears continued to fall. Every muscle in his body must have ached as the tension began to release its grip. Exhaustion was all that was left of him. He stayed with me like the proverbial toddler sitting on a mother's hip holding on tightly should he begin to fall. It was over, all that had been held in for such a long time had come out and spilled itself over the dining room floor. I sensed that Darren felt easier within himself, but anger, over the fact that one so small should have to be subjected to this, was rising in me. I carried him outside to be with the others and to bring normality back to Darren's life. Thereafter whenever Darren felt aggrieved or cross or upset he cried, but each time he did so the crying decreased in both length and volume until it began to normalise and he regained some control of his emotions.

Darren did cope with the weekend at home with Mum and his sisters surprisingly well. On his return, though quiet, he did share with us what they had done but made it quite clear he would have had a good time with Aaron and Gareth if I had let him stay with us! Well someone had to take the blame I suppose.

We were fortunate that they were able to see the term out, allowing Darren and Jenna to have the accolade of a school report. Our planned holiday down to Sussex and Kent was good; the children were now seasoned caravanners! Though Jenna has to have the final word here, as Lawrence drove out of our driveway and having travelled less than a mile away, her words of "Are we nearly there yet?" hit the air. It would be a long, long drive! They were as delighted to meet our Grannie, as she was to meet them. But we all knew that within a few days of returning home in the middle of August, the children would be going home. The photo album of their time with us was compiled so they could relive the memories to share with Mum. The leaving party organised, the inflatable castle ordered for the party of children to enjoy. All that was left was for the cake to be made. Jenna had decided on a horse riding theme, I suggested she went upstairs to the bedroom to find some of the toy model horses, from the toy farm, for me to wash to mount on the cake. Jenna ran upstairs to search for these as I heard the clip clop and the neighing of a real horse, I could not believe it, a real horse had stepped over the back wall from the field at the back of our house and had stuck it's head through our kitchen window! Jenna returned carrying the toy horses. "I've got them Auntie Dani," she said clutching the horses tightly. "But I only meant toy ones Jen" I said. "That's all I've got" she said as she walked through the kitchen to where I was standing icing the cake, Followed by a "Oh wow", as she saw the horses head peering through the open window.

The party atmosphere was good for them all to enjoy, allowing them to let off steam surrounded by friends. They had been with us almost nine months; in some ways it felt as though they had been with us forever, in some ways it was only yesterday that they came. When the party ended and farewells and good wishes had been exchanged, the children sat with Lawrence and I to open their gifts and cards of 'Good Luck' for their future. We left them to play with Aaron and Gareth before going to bed. The morning events were quietly carried out, false smiles and giggles were shared between us as we endeavoured to persuade each other that we could cope with what was about to take place, as we awaited the moment for the social worker to arrive to return the children to Mum at home, who was waiting equally nervously to receive them back into the family home. The moment arrived, we gathered up all their belongings into the car, and then strapped the children in. Hugs, kisses, and promises of 'We'll be good' all given. They left. As they did so that cavernous emptiness returned, deeper and wider than ever.

How do you define love? The form we sign on a child's arrival states that whilst they are in our care we will look after them as we would a child of our own. I love my boys unconditionally, so I make no apologies for offering that same love to any child that stays with us. Each family of children that joined our family gave us a mixture of joys and tears, but with each family we shared love. In the words of a song I was yet to learn. "If you've got some love, then give it away, 'cos you'll end up having more." If by loving all our children we helped to teach them how to love then I know I have nothing to regret.

*"The child supplies the power but
the parents have to do the steering."*

*Baby and Child Care*

*Dr. Benjamin McLane Spock*

*American Paediatrician (1903 - 1998)*

# CHAPTER 9

# A Test of Trust, Time and Tempers

Emily, our support worker, was a Mum of four and had an abundance of experience of working in the fostering and adoption area of work. She had been involved in preparing our assessment and representing us to panel for us to become foster parents. There were times when we would disagree on certain issues, but we had a mutual respect for each other and worked well together for the benefit of the children we cared for. Emily took an interest in our family and willingly gave her time to support all of us as individuals. I knew I could comfortably telephone to speak to her to gain advice over a particular issue, or to have concerns clarified. She never made us feel rushed or treated our anxieties with indifference. No matter how major or how trivial an issue was, both Lawrence and I knew we could speak to Emily and hear common sense talking. She was a pillar of strength throughout our time as foster parents, and would go to great lengths to assist us to find the right level of support to help and guide the children through any difficult issue in hand. Whenever I found it hard to accept the way of the 'system' and dug my heels in vehemently Emily would act as go-between to smooth the way forward. Foster parents were to some extent expected to tow the line and do as they were told without becoming heavily involved. Those who spoke out were not always welcomed. But I took my responsibilities as a parent very seriously and in the absence of their own parents stood up to protect the youngsters as if they were my own. (As required by the system, according to the paperwork that we were expected to sign for the children that stayed with us!) Legislation laid down is to be adhered to, but sometimes it does not allow for individual human or family idiosyncrasies. Interpretation of the legislation can be as variable as the many different people working within the system and the term 'professional abuse' was in its infancy of recognition. Emily never dictated terms to us, but would always offer suggestions and guidance to find a way to move forward when we were coping with any challenging behaviours. Our agendas were planned out in advance, so that our time mulling over these was used effectively, to find a possible workable solution for whichever child had the greatest need. Family dynamics could be as friable and flexible as the children themselves, and as in any family, a breakdown could so easily occur, to the detriment of everyone, if the cement that held them together was allowed to be chipped away.

The next family of youngsters that were to join us would need the cement putting into place before we could move forward. If our previous trio stood in a line holding hands then one held on to mine, they would be pulling forwards on me, conversely our new trio yet to come holding on in the same way would be pulling backwards. But together, I am convinced they would have supported each other, guided each other on their way forward. As individuals they had so much to offer, though in some respects pulled in different directions, but as a six-some with the addition of Aaron and Gareth as a stable force, there was a special gel that could have made it work for all of them. There were so many that agreed with us, family, friends, teachers, social workers, etc. Yet one person could not see nor believe this was so. Unfortunately she had the ultimate word that was to destroy any chance of this to be proven, whether in favour of our belief or her own. The decision was based on social work theories. But human foibles are capable of proving the exception to the rule! Although she tried to prevent any chance of us taking our own beliefs any further, the dynamics of our family foibles were to prove to be too strong, and in the fullness of time fate would work in our favour to a greater or lesser extent.

Through the years that we fostered we were lucky enough to have some very fine, supportive friends. Whatever they really thought about us the majority kept it to themselves! However one close friend was never to mince her words, would always give me her well-aired views and was frequently heard to say, "Are you bloody mad or something?" this would alternate with her other favourite sayings in the lines of, "You are absolutely bloody stupid!" But as a friend she could not have been more supportive or generous of her time or more tolerant of our children's misdemeanours and some of their difficult behaviours. Cath had one child, a daughter. We pram-pushed our youngest together. Shared our future expectations with each other, laughed and cried with each other over various situations. We were never in each other's pockets nor did we see each other on a regular basis. But we have always been able to pick up where we left off.

Her daughter would play with our children and she was to strike up a good friendship with our next little girl to join us.

About five weeks after our first trio left we were asked to take three, possibly four, more. This gap of time gave us a chance to help Aaron and Gareth cope with the loss of Jenna, Darren, and Andrea. We had a short holiday on our own, and then it was all systems go to prepare for the new school term. We had a little more warning of the arrival of these children, as final decisions had not been made. So overnight we had the opportunity to organise the bedroom, make the beds and find appropriate toys and possible clothes that would help us through those first few days if needed. We had been told that the oldest was a girl of seven, and the younger ones, both boys, were a year apart, aged almost three and four years old. There was a much younger one of a few months old who was a half sister to the others. The baby may need other arrangements as she had been in care previously, and there was a chance she could go to the same foster carers as before, which would be far better providing her with some continuity of care. We were told that the relationship between the four children was not brilliant, so the placing of the infant elsewhere should not affect the others too greatly. How right they were! Family cement was to be needed by the bucketful to forge the relationships. By the end of the day we were aware that the baby of the family would be placed in her previous foster home and therefore we were only taking the trio.

Tuesday 30th September 1986 was the last day of the month. This day was an anniversary to a variety of events that took place throughout history. Such as: -

*1399 - Henry Bolingbroke became*
*the King of England as Henry IV.*
*1861 - Chewing gum tycoon William Wrigley,*
*Jr. was born.*
*1954 - Julie Andrews made her first*
*Broadway appearance in*
*"The Boy Friend".*

But for us on this day it was the arrival of three youngsters, Danielle, Jason and James. Aged seven, almost four and almost three years respectively. The social worker and her escort carried them in. Jason resembled a little gnome; he was set down onto the kitchen chair where he crossed his legs, and sat in a very limp fashion, frighteningly pale, drawn looking, with his mouth drooling. Every so often he sniffed and flicked his lengthy dark hair back off his face. The striking thing was he made no attempt to move nor looked interested in his surroundings. The older child, the little girl, stood with her hand firmly holding on to the social worker with her head leaning on to him. She too had very dark black brown hair, fringed and lankly hanging around her sad looking face. She had vibrant blue eyes that seemed incongruous with her dark hair. But her eyes gave out the clear message of fearfulness and anxiousness. Gareth approached her trying to encourage her to go with him to find her bedroom. She pulled away from him, constantly clinging to the social worker. The youngest, James, had the scrawniest of limbs that seemed to wrap around him in a loose manner, his legs stuck out of his nappy like a pair of thin shapeless sticks. His head seemed disproportionate to his body; this was topped with a shock of lengthy blonde hair that hung over his eyes, causing him to constantly brush it to one side away from his eyes. Pale faced, blue eyed, incredibly doleful. He was the only one to really stare around at this new environment, but his expression gave away only one emotion and that like his brother was one of fear.

Bert, the social worker was a much older man, a family man who had a lot of empathy for this family. He worked as hard at supporting the parents as he did these children in our care. The family set-up was a difficult one and they held a strange but strong influence on the children even in their absence. The children's fear of their parents would eventually give us a reason to be fearful too.

The boys made noises when they tried to speak that were not discernable to us initially. Jason's constant drooling meant he was speaking with a mouthful of spittle all of the time, his words were not clear and his speech impediment caused communication difficulties in translation! James had virtually no speech at all, just sounds that emanated from his mouth in an attempt to have his needs satisfied. Danielle had a limited vocabulary much of it being regular expletives of the negative type!

Eventually we persuaded Danielle to leave the social worker's side to go with Aaron and Gareth up the stairs to have a look around. She did not speak to anyone, but every so often would interject her own silence with a short, shrill screech or giggle. Her actions were sharp edged and her jerky movements accentuated the difference between her and our boys as they made their way through the house.

When a family of children arrived we always tried to keep them together in the biggest bedroom. We could comfortably get in two standard and one small single sized bed in the room with a bedside table between the beds for each. The fitted wardrobes with sliding doors along the length of the room meant there was ample storage space for small children's clothes and toys. There was a closeness for each of them being together all in the one room. Children derive strength from knowing where their siblings are, as they need each other until they gain confidence in those around and in their new environment. We had done this with all the other children; there was no reason to believe this should be any different for our latest troop. At least not yet! The room had been laid out with a few well-chosen toys that we thought they might take an interest in.

So as their horizons were to be broadened, our experience in childcare was about to be widened! Social worker Bert explained that young James had recently been discharged from hospital having recovered from a broken leg, his second in less than a year. He was small for his age as a 'failure to thrive' toddler. "He won't give you much trouble," said a very convincing Bert. "He has yet to strengthen both his legs so doesn't walk very far, in fact hardly moves really once you put him down." And to prove his point put young James down on to the kitchen floor. The little fellow sat there, his stick like legs straight out in front of him resting his hands on the floor he leant forward and gave an "ugh" sound, still taking in his new environment with his steely eyes. Now we had two immobile small boys, Jason still had not moved except to brush back his hair from his adenoidal face, tongue resting on his lower teeth, mouth hanging open. Gareth came back in to the kitchen and passed a remark about Danielle not recognising what certain toys were, as all she had said was "What's this? What's this?" to every toy she had picked up. He was perplexed by her strange behaviours and intermittent loud giggles, as she threw her head back or exaggerated expressions of shock at everything that he and his brother had tried to show her. I looked around our new brood.

Their needs were very much the same yet all so different. Standing in the middle of all the children, and with the social worker and escort on the perimeters, one could sense the lack of togetherness between the children, a deserted feeling or the lack of a sense of belonging. After all how can you give out to others when your own needs are not being met. Bert and accomplice left leaving us with the bare minimum of information. I was later to establish that this had been done deliberately, so as not to leave us with preconceived ideas and for us to work with a blank canvas to establish as much as we could from the children. I was later to have mixed feelings about his theories, as I felt more information would have allowed us to offer the children greater help during those early days, and reduce some of the frustration we would all experience.

Bert drove away; I walked back into the house to hear Danielle running around trying to encourage Gareth to do the same. He was used to having a little girl around of a similar age to himself, but the behaviour of this little girl he was not used to! She ran around aimlessly, her clumsy jerky movements causing her to bang into furniture calling out to our boys, but ignoring her own brothers. Aaron and Gareth watched, not amused, wondering who this strange little girl was. James was not to be seen! But he doesn't move I thought. I looked towards Jason still seated on the kitchen chair unmoving apart from the occasional sweep of his hand across his head in an endeavour to keep the hair out of his eyes. "Where is

James?" I asked. Our gob-smacked duo continued to watch Danielle as they pointed to the dining room, "He went through there," they said in unison. I shot through to find James kneeling at the bottom of the stairs with his hands placed on the first step, rocking back and forth, clearly working out a way to scale those stairs. He turned his head towards me pointed a little finger upwards and announced a loud "Ugh."

I scooped him up, saying "Not yet, James", returning him back to the kitchen, en route I caught the arm of Danielle as she circuited the dining table and clamping her hand with gentle squeezes which I hoped conveyed endearment rather than dominance. Both complied immediately, no protestations, both with fear in their eyes. Their powerful stares in my direction left me feeling uncomfortable. No child that I had ever met left me feeling this way. I suggested we all had a drink and a snack around the table. I put James down on to the floor and off he semi-crawled again heading to the dining room, Gareth quickly closed the door to contain him or any other would-be escapee in the kitchen. Aaron grabbed the high chair and set it up for James. Jason still sat on the kitchen chair by the table, Gareth asked Danielle to sit down at the table too as he pulled up another chair for himself. I looked over at James, then down at Jason, two boys, same parents, oh so different, the other thought in my mind was had I misinterpreted Bert. I was convinced that he told me James does not move, but this little one was everywhere if we set him free, yet Jason had not moved since he arrived. I offered them a drink of milk and a biscuit. They played with the cups, tried to drink but the milk dribbled out of the boys mouths, and Danielle wanted to know what it was. James crumbled the biscuit everywhere but made no attempt to eat it. Jason did not even pick his biscuit up. Danielle watched Aaron and Gareth eating theirs then tried to imitate them by eating hers. None of them genuinely knew what I had offered them nor did they know what to do with their biscuit. This was the very beginning of our discovery that these children only recognised bread, chips, baked beans and juice. This limited diet had been all that they knew. Weaning them all was going to be a whole new ball game of tears and frustration, more on my part than on theirs!

Family meals with our previous trio had been interesting; in so much as they ate everything in sight with such gusto, that in many ways it was a pleasure to feed them, though challenging to help them understand that the whole day did not revolve around this activity. However with this family the whole day really did revolve around mealtimes and food they would be prepared to eat. I chose to maintain the normality we knew in providing family meals hoping they would take our lead, but if it was not bread, chip or baked bean shaped the chances of getting any food in to their mouths were unlikely. They willingly came to the table, they willingly waited for their meal to arrive, they would willingly chat away or at least make noises to each other but they were the most unwilling of all to put the food into their mouths and if they did manage to get that far they chewed and chewed but never swallowed. This frustration coupled with their endless night waking would take its toll on all of us.

Danielle's strange behaviours and low starting point in all areas meant that we could not even consider her joining Aaron and Gareth at their school, as she would need additional support within school to help her to have a chance to catch up with her education. We arranged for her to go to school at our church school where they promised to provide her with the relevant support. She was certainly to prove herself to be a challenge to their systems. This little girl lived in a world of imagination that she drew from others, as she had none of her own. Consequently her interpretation of life around her was a little misconstrued to say the least! What she saw as acceptable behaviour would be tested and tried to the limits in the form of repetition both in words and actions. Being a great believer in children picking up the cues from adults we had to be clear, concise, specific and consistent with her. We could not let our guard down at all, as she would assume that to be acceptable to recreate our behaviour at a later date. Supporting Aaron and Gareth to cope with this demeanour when they played with her was not easy as she drained their willingness to give her time, as she could not always relate to the rules of the games. We questioned autism, which was rebuked by the social services. Their explanations were that Danielle's experiences in life were so limited, and her father's dominance so strong, that she was unable to be true to herself. They insisted that all she needed were good examples around her and in time would slowly catch up with her peers, though it was accepted that she might always be at the lower end of the scale.

I had great concerns about Jason too, with his gnome like stance being ever more noticeable. He would be quite content to sit after breakfast on the same chair, cross-legged, with a pathetic expression of 'life is just too much!'; I really believe it was too! Any effort was too much to contemplate, so to fall asleep was the easy option, and Jason was capable of falling asleep in an instance if we even dared to suggest he did something. This could happen at any time, any moment throughout the day, but night times were another challenge! The art of playing was alien to him so he would switch off from life, withdraw into himself and 'sleep'. Keeping him motivated was a full time occupation requiring a great deal of one to one time to be given instantly. This little chap rarely smiled, but on those rare occasions during his early days with us when he did show a hint of recognising humour even a half smile was worth waiting for. Jason's blue eyes would suddenly sparkle momentarily from his otherwise inner dullness, that slight curvature of the sides of his mouth that tried desperately to move the muscles to form a smile proved that something on the inside was actually trying to get out. He struggled to communicate with the world, with us. His speech was extremely limited, the incessant drooling and dribbling made it difficult for him to form words and the sounds of those he did were not always considered acceptable in polite company! We questioned some of his vocabulary but hoped we were not really hearing the words we thought he might be using, time would teach us otherwise! Our initial efforts were in keeping him awake, involved and to be as tactile with him as possible. Jason did not reach out to others, I doubt he knew what he needed for himself so did not personally make demands on anyone, and found it difficult to respond to being held by anyone. He would be willing enough to be picked up, would feel limp in your arms but his only efforts were to hold onto to your sleeves rather than hold on to you, this was to prevent himself from falling. I longed to feel him respond in a warm loving way that most toddlers of his age would have done. We had yet to gain his trust, to tease that inner self of his to the surface, to teach him family ways and all this would take the greatest gift of all - TIME.

From his first day we were to be told that James did not move far and would be no trouble. "Put him down and he will stay there until you next go to him, never says much, rarely even tries to," said the illustrious Bert! Our experience of his first day with us was that either the social worker had got it wrong or we had misunderstood and we had interpreted his words wrongly. Bert could not believe what we were telling him about our little tornado who scooted everywhere on two arms and one leg dragging his second leg behind him at breakneck speed at every given opportunity of a wider space to be explored. He had a deep voice for one so young and though words were virtually non-existent, sounds he had in abundance with a volume that hit maximum on the decibel count! Like Jason and Danielle he had very little experience of the value of play, so toys were initially meaningless except of course to use as weapons, at which James was very adept. His vicious behaviour knew no boundaries, if anyone was within his reach they became a target for his practice, and the more he was to practise the more perfect his aim and technique became. He demonstrated his needs outlandishly. James filled a room with his presence, the boisterous but frenzied attitude exploded around everyone with his speed and thunderous noise. When spoken to or even approached he would freeze with a startled expression before heading off in the opposite direction. He was certainly the proverbial 'Catch me if you can' man. Once caught he never really objected to being picked up or carried and would respond with instant acceptance, slightly leaning away from his captor, making it almost impossible to be cuddled as most youngsters of his age would love to be. Out of the three children he was the only one to offer any kind of eye contact, but this was always done with an inquisitive expression of defiance or was it his way of establishing his limited boundaries. He seemed very attuned to the spoken word, but not yet prepared to yield to it, or was it just his lack of understanding? Yet underneath all of his behaviours, attitudes and misdemeanours, there squirmed the beginnings of an endearing little fellow screaming to be released.

We had a family of three, coupled with our family of four making a clan of seven. In my eyes I saw three individual, separate children plus two boys struggling to come to terms with the idiosyncrasies of the threesome. This trio would need us to work with them on their own peculiar personal traits, to be shown and guided towards the normal expectation and understanding of the world around them and how they become a part of it. But at the same time we would need to forge their relationships between each other as well as their relationships with us, our friends, their school and playschool, also the community at large. Is this any different from what every parent does? Not really, but with the exaggerated behaviours we were to witness and the incredibly low starting points of all three, could we make a difference to their lives for their futures before they would move on? Every theory I put forward to Bert was cast aside, simplified, treated with contempt, but yet truth of their experiences was not forthcoming. So for the first few weeks we had so little to work on. We had been told that James had not been out of hospital long following treatment for failing to thrive and having a broken leg. When I commented that Jason had a scar in his hairline that indicated stitches, the response was simply, "Yes we know how that happened." But we were not told nor could Jason tell us. When I commented that Danielle constantly asked me to cut her long hair to look like mine I was told categorically "Well, that could cause a problem, so I wouldn't advise that you do."

Visits to the parents were organised on a weekly basis, they were to spend an hour with Mum and Dad to keep up a relationship, or so I thought. Unfortunately these visits would take a week for them to get over as these caused them such distress. From the moment that they knew of the impending visit their anxiety levels were raised phenomenally, none of us would sleep the night before or the night after as they refused to sleep, using any tactic possible to keep us in or near their room. On their return they would be bearing the gifts given to them during the visits, these were always in the form of plastic weaponry, guns, knives, bows and arrows and handcuffs. Gareth thought this was wonderful as they were forbidden toys in our household. I had the difficulty in showing any kind of enthusiasm as I did not want to destroy what seemed like the only thread of positive parental behaviour, that is the ability to give your child a gift even if that gift is considered to be unsuitable by others. Likewise in banning such toys from our own toy box I did not want these regularly re-occurring items to be seen as acceptable to Aaron or Gareth. Our different family standards were not easy to handle to the satisfaction of everyone. The other situation that put Danielle under an awful lot of pressure was being asked by her father what had been said to her by either Bert or us about why they were in care. He also offered her endless threats as to what would happen if she told us anything at all. This came out one teatime when Danielle was deliberately breaking the toys she had been given by her parents. I suggested she put them down whilst we ate tea, instead she threw them across the room shouting, "You don't like them, I don't bloody want them, I hate them." The unexpected outburst came as retaliation with a force of turbulent emotion that flawed everyone in the room. She began to shake, as tears raced down her red cheeks. Danielle's eyes stared at me uncertain of how I would react, this feeling of expression had come from the very depths within her and may have been the first time ever in her life that she had put forward her own opinion. Now she was frightened of retribution. So scared of what to expect, Danielle froze, but rising inside of her was an uncontrollable strength of mixed emotions ready to fire in any direction. The boys watched and waited, not daring to move either. This was to be the first time that I had witnessed any kind of togetherness in this family trio, joined by fear that painfully gripped them. What the hell had they been through! I was even more determined to pin Bert down with his manager to demand further explanations. A meeting was needed to review the situation.

As I stood up to walk towards Danielle hoping to diffuse and remove the unnecessary fear in our kitchen, I saw her eyes widen even more so, as she pressed herself backwards on the chair pushing against the wall in an attempt to move further away from me. "Come on Danielle, let's go for a chat," I said, bending down to lift her up and take her away from the unwilling audience around the table. It was like lifting an iron block, still frozen with fear; I felt the racing of her heartbeat as she reluctantly pressed against me. Leaving Lawrence with the other four to continue with tea I took Danielle into the sitting room so we could talk.

Slowly as I spoke gently to her about what had happened and how I would need her to talk to me about how she felt, the fear began to drain away. Danielle began to relax, she spoke of hating the visits to Mum and Dad, as she didn't know when they were going to hit her but she was convinced that they would, even if neither Lawrence nor I did. I asked her why she felt that we should, she replied by explaining that that is what mums and dads do. She knew she shouldn't have shouted or thrown the toys but she explained that she also knew I did not like her having that kind of toy, as I would not let Gareth play with them so they must be bad. Then she blurted, "Dad said you don't love me and you will tell Bert when we are naughty and bad, Bert will tell Dad and he will have to be the one to bash us when we are." One sentence spoken with stoked up fear and anxiety explained so much. Adults play games with children, but to play with their emotions to gain an unbelievable level of control that could destroy them to the core meant war in my book, but this was not my war to fight, as at some point these children may have to return to their parents to function more positively as a family unit. In front of Danielle I had to contain my views, feelings and thoughts on the situation and just pour reassurance on her. "Are you Mum three?" she asked in a calm manner. I questioned this "How do you mean?" "Well Kathleen is Mum one, and Helen is Mum two, so you must be

Mum three!" she exclaimed. I reiterated that we were Auntie Dani and Uncle Lawrence, that it was not our intention to take Mum and Dad's place but we would do all the things that any mum or dad would need to do to look after children properly. "So will you bash us when we are naugh'y or bad?" she asked. I soldiered on explaining that this would include letting them know when they were doing things they shouldn't, that it would not be necessary to hit them or 'bash' them, but I would expect them to learn from our 'telling' so as not to make the same mistakes again and again. She had given me eye contact throughout, she had listened, and there had been a two-way conversation. We had a revelation! My ecstasy was to be short lived and I had to learn to hang on to this moment in time to keep my own sanity! Danielle was to put my words on trial; she was to test our sanity, our physical and mental energies to the limit. She was determined to prove that I could not have meant it, nor could I sustain it, and I was equally determined to prove my innocence and disprove her theories of parenthood. For this moment only though, I sensed a breakthrough, we had a foundation to build on. The building blocks would occasionally be razed to the ground but we would start again many, many times not just during the two years they spent with us, but throughout their years into adulthood as their need for explanations of this time would rise in search of answers.

We had many gaps to fill in their lives, and realistically it felt like mission impossible, but in the short term we had an opportunity to offer them a different life style, a chance to grow physically, emotionally, mentally and to gain positive life experiences, what they did with this after they left us would be up to them, but at least they had a chance to live a different way of life which would allow them to choose the way to go when independence came their way.

*"What a child doesn't receive*
*he can seldom later give."*

P.D. James

*English Crime Novelist*

# CHAPTER 10

## Working Solutions

Mealtimes were no longer enjoyable. But we refused to allow them to become battlegrounds. No child ever starved itself, I told myself, though these children seemed to be hell-bent on working very hard to do so. Food might go into their mouths and be chewed but swallowing seemed impossible. Simple basic family mealtime rules were hard to adhere to. It seems the idea of sitting around a table was a new experience and one they found difficult to accept. James sat in the high chair, which was pulled up to the table, partly to help contain this tornado as he spent more time leaving the table to hide under it or race to the other side of the kitchen. Danielle considered it to be her right to follow anyone who had a need to stand up or clear the table. When no one was doing that she constantly dropped cutlery or her serviette for an excuse to get down from the table to retrieve the item. Another ploy would be to spill her drink deliberately then have an excuse to get a cloth to mop it up. She would find or make up any excuse to move. Jason just sat in his gnome-like stance making very little effort to eat, to feed, and on some occasions keeping him awake throughout a meal was virtually impossible. James in his highchair played with his food, making very little effort to eat but used a great deal of concentration in picking up the food with his hands, feeling it, squeezing it, watching the squashed contents of his palm dribble to the table before smearing it anywhere and everywhere that he could reach, including his own face, hair and legs. He was very reluctant to be fed by anyone else, but Gareth would spend endless time making up different games to encourage him to accept the spoonful of food he was determined to get inside James. One spoonful of food in James would make Gareth put one spoonful in his own mouth then he would encourage James to chew by making 'mmm' noises to emphasise his enjoyment and James would imitate. Then with an exaggerated swallowing sound persuaded James to swallow, which eventually he did. This slow process progressed to Gareth persuading James to use a spoon and feed himself. Aaron would spend time talking to Jason to help him to stay awake, suggesting he looked out of the window to spot things in the garden or to search with his eyes for items in the kitchen, if Jason spotted the item Aaron rewarded him with a mouthful of food and endless praise. We tried any tactic to keep the children focussed, awake, fed and moving towards more enjoyable mealtimes.

Between Lawrence and I we had Danielle to persuade to sit and eat and be sociable. She would take heed of what Aaron and Gareth were doing with the younger boys and make some effort to emulate their actions, but when a mouthful went in she could chew forever and never swallow. Consequently the meal also seemed to go on forever. The whole experience was incredibly painful. No amount of coaxing, cajoling or distraction could speed up her eating. She rarely conveyed her distaste of food, on the contrary would enthuse ecstatically about how much she was loving something but this made no difference to the length of time she would take to eat. Part of me felt she had little control over this, part of me felt she did this deliberately as a sort of dominance or hold over us.

Eventually, I accepted that this was learned behaviour which she felt was normal, it did give her an element of control but, there were days when she would be keen and eager to go back to play a game that had been interrupted by a mealtime and then would eat far quicker even though her fast was still slower than anyone else's slow!

Realising that these children had missed out on the all-important weaning process in their early years we decided to trial this, encouraging all three to play their part in identification and recognition of different foods. We had 'guess the food' games, 'food handling, cutting and slicing' sessions, 'texture and tasting' games, sometimes this would be done blindfold as confidence grew. The textures of some foods, especially meat, were difficult for any of our trio to eat as the act and art of chewing was not what they were used to doing, so I did what I would have done for any weaning baby, I minced it initially gradually progressing to finely chopped meat, until they were able to cope. The children were involved in baking sessions and I would make a batch of play dough on a weekly basis where all five could pummel away and use their imaginations constructively to create play foods. This activity was also great for increasing their concentration levels, for expelling fears and aggression and for experience in parallel play. But amazingly it also encouraged them all to sit around the table in a sociable manner and be pleasant to each other. Gradually we were taking slow but certain steps back towards our normality!

Out of the three children, only Danielle spoke in full sentences of a kind, unfortunately her vocabulary included some strong, and unacceptable expletives, which she used with regular monotony. She was not doing this to gain attention or for bravado, this was her normal everyday speech learned within the family home. Aaron and Gareth were shocked the first time they heard such language used and I am sure they tried it out between them but quickly realised this was not acceptable. Gareth could be heard to call out, "Mum she said it again" on a regular basis, and a confused Danielle wondering what it was she was supposed to have done, would be looking at me. Jason had very little vocabulary; his sentences were short and succinct but frequently involved the same expletives. However he also had a speech impediment and his 's' sounds were always pronounced as 'sh' sounds. This gave rise to some confusion at times when he would tell the others he was going to 'the shitting room'. The reason being, as we were to discover, that this was their family terminology for the toilet, but poor little Jason was actually meaning he was going to the sitting room! Inevitably either Aaron or Gareth would be heard to call out those words. "Mum, he's swearing again!" The hardest part of this was our reluctance to take them out or even go to church, containing their behaviour was difficult enough, but the added language usage was unpredictable and therefore not easy to handle in front of other parents. I was told that Danielle was very quiet in school so it had rarely shown itself to be a problem, but of course as soon as she started to find her confidence this trait did rear itself. Eventually this problem subsided as their vocabulary increased and the examples around them were of a different nature, but in moments of stress or anger both Jason and Danielle were to resort to falling back on their store of colourful but unacceptable language usage.

The review meeting was to take place about five weeks after their arrival. Besides our support worker, and us, there was Bert with his manager along with the head teacher from Danielle's school. We had yet to settle Jason in a Nursery, as we did not feel he was ready to cope and the playschool we had previously turned to had no further placements as they were closing down. We were to establish that both of James' legs had been broken, one more recently than the other. It was thought his father had caused the injuries but this had not been proven at this time. His father had also thrown Jason against a brick wall causing his head to split open, which now explained the scar in his hairline. We also learned that Danielle was considered to be the favourite within the family, but that did not sit comfortably with me as she had started to talk about some of the angry behaviour she had endured from her father, this had stemmed from her insistence on having her hair cut like mine. Washing her hair had produced awful screaming sessions that were taking its toll on both of us as we both began to dread her hair-wash day. Dad was a very dominant character who had grown up in the care system from the age of two; he had other children from a previous relationship that he no longer saw. On the other hand Mum was a very quiet unassuming person who did not have the courage to express herself confidently, her own poor family history had not provided her with the mothering skills she would need to protect her children adequately. Dad had taken a girlfriend who became pregnant; this resulted in Mum and James moving out so girlfriend and child could move in. But Mum and James visited on a regular basis until eventually they moved back in. This explained Mum one and two! The children's diet had been very limited and the family did not have a table, which is why sitting around the table for meals had seemed so strange to them. On numerous occasions the children had been left alone locked in the house for several hours at a time in the evenings, without electricity. This explained their evening and night-time fears, and their need to know we were still there. Their whole family situation was unstable, exceptionally fragile, the parents lack of understanding and poor parenting skills explained so many of the disruptive behaviours they projected. To his credit, Bert was still determined to try to work with the family to look for a positive way forward. For our part we would continue to care and support the trio, but in doing so we also felt that we were putting Aaron and Gareth's lives on hold when they came home from school as so much effort by all of us was invested in the children in an endeavour to surge forward with any progress achievable.

The safer each of the children began to feel living in our home and the more confident they became in trusting us not to leave them alone, the more outlandish their expression of behaviour became. Exaggerations in their demeanour or reactions to given situations actually became the norm! Keeping a perspective on all of this was difficult when all around just seemed in turmoil, and there was so little sleep time available to us to recover in time to cope again the next day, and the next! We went from child to child picking up the pieces, praising where we could but trying to give clear messages of right and wrong, even when, allowing for their early poor experiences, we sometimes lost sight of this ourselves. They needed intensive parenting in supporting their family unit as siblings to love and care for each other. But when your youngest brother constantly knocks the hell out of you with any form of weapon that he can find, and toys make wonderful ammunition, then it becomes very difficult to even be benevolent towards them. James' noises were gradually becoming word shaped, but we needed him to have our use of the English language not that of his brother and sister! Gaining control of his destructive behaviour was paramount, so keeping James involved in constructive activity was vital not only to his own survival but also for the survival of everyone else, especially Jason. Jason continued to shut himself off into a world of his own, actually allowing his rogue brother to hit him regularly rather than retaliate or move out of the way. So efforts were made to keep Jason on the move, away from James at such times, and teach him to say no, as strongly as possible, whilst at the same time encouraging the boys to play together as positively as possible. Meanwhile Danielle would struggle to accept this new way of living purely because it was so far removed from anything she knew. She only had the role models of the boys to fall back on within the home, so I was pleased when my friend's daughter invited her to play at her home where I felt she had an opportunity for 'girl play', and on occasions when they played at our house, Danielle had a chance to see the friendship and relationship between her friend and our boys which she would try to imitate. Building and maintaining relationships were not easy for Danielle and she had a tendency to behave in an obviously false manner in an effort to mimic others.

Hair washing for Danielle continued to be a challenge. We had tried doing it in different ways, whilst she was in the bath, over the bath, over the washbasin, in the shower, using a cup to pour water over her hair, using a jug, tipping her head backwards, having her head forwards. You name it, we had tried it, but every time we attempted to do it Danielle went wild, screaming and shouting, ranting and raving with such strength of emotion that it was imperative to find a way around the difficulty. I had discussed the situation many times with Danielle to try to understand how she felt and what thoughts went around in her head at the time the water touched her. Each time she would feel confident to cope, that she could control the fear and anxiety within her, she insisted she wasn't frightened of me washing her hair, but rarely a day went by when she didn't ask if she could have short hair instead of her very long thick hair. Her parents were told how she felt but refused to allow us to have it cut. We dissected the issue stage by stage to establish from Danielle how she would like me to wash her hair, as she felt unable to do it herself. She was reluctant to even brush it. Step by step I wrote down her own suggestions of how she felt she could cope. She preferred to have it washed over the washbasin downstairs using the shower head from the adjacent shower, she chose the shampoo she wanted me to use, she tested the water before we started to be certain of the water being just the right temperature. She chose the towel to be used. We were both ready, armed with our list, towel wrapped around her, showerhead and pipe stretched across to the washbasin. Danielle put her head forwards over the basin but the moment the water touched her head she screamed, I moved the showerhead away, tried to calm her down and waited till she felt ready to start again. Did we have progress? She had screamed but kept her head down and continued to hold on to the sides of the basin. I tentatively started again, this time she screamed louder and shook her head from side to side, her wet hair spitting water around. Once again I managed to calm her before we progressed. Then in one almighty surge of emotional energy, screaming loudly and waving her head in all directions, she kicked onto the door causing it to close, as she did this she knocked the shower head and pipe with her outstretched arms out of my hands and therefore out of control. She continued with her loud wailing screams, flailing in all directions, whilst the showerhead and pipe had a life and control of it's own writhing and squirming all over still pouring water in all directions. I slipped on the wet floor of the smallest room of our house, there was hardly enough room for one in this room never mind two of us and a live water fountain spraying everywhere. Danielle was screaming and wailing unable to hear anything I said, clinging to me yet at the same time pushing me away, we were both on the floor soaked through. I tried to catch the showerhead to tame it and direct the water into the washbasin but every time I came close to catching it Danielle would pull away from or kick me again making it impossible, nor, because of the lack of space in the room, could I reach into the shower cubicle to turn the water off. To add to all this commotion Lawrence tried to come to our rescue but as Danielle was pushing against the door he was unable to open it and his banging on the door was only fuelling Danielle's fears and perpetuating her behaviour. Whilst water kept pouring all over the two of us I was in no position to calm her or get the door open for either of us to escape. I bellowed to Lawrence to turn the water off at the mains, eventually he heard me and carried this out. We both sat on the wet floor, her wailing lessened, as it did so she reached out to me, I put my arms around her and held her to me as she sobbed and sobbed, apologising for what had happened. Eventually I was able to lift Danielle up and carry her out of the drenched room with dripping walls, ceiling and window with a puddle of water all over the floor. The deep wrenching sobbing lingered on for a considerable time. Lawrence brought us clean towels and as we dried ourselves she began to talk.

Having planned the hair washing exercise totally around her own expectations hoping she would be able to cope, so she knew what would be happening at each stage, I had in fact unknowingly recreated the scenario in which Danielle previously lived. This poor girl had relived the painful emotional thoughts and a feeling attached to the experience but in doing so now was able to verbalise her anxieties and express her fears. It seems that more often than not Dad washed her hair and used the length of it to grab hold to manoeuvre her head around. She talked about him banging her head against the sink or the taps still grasping her hair, "and if I screamed or cried he dragged me by the hair to sit me on the high window sill until I stopped. It was very high and I couldn't get down" she then added "That's why I want it cut short like yours, 'cos then no one can do that to me, and you can't either." Once again I reassured her that this was something neither Lawrence nor I would ever dream of doing whether her hair was long or short! She hugged me for a few minutes gripping with dear life itself before asking, "Will you have to tell Bert? 'Cos I don't want him to tell Dad." I explained that it might be necessary to explain all of today's events to Bert but I would not expect him to tell her father. Danielle endured hair washing as something that needed to be done, but she was able to prepare herself better without the drama and consequences of this day. She only became more comfortable once she was in a position to have her hair shortened.

Sibling groups held a strength of their own that could sometimes over-rule ours if we allowed it to, but this trio did not achieve this with a united front, more so with a division of diversity, that left us struggling to bring them together in unison to support each other. Therefore family outings were restricted, especially when I had all five on my own. Attempting the school run could be fraught with nipping, biting arguments that would result in having to stop the car to regain order at least twice before I reached the first school all of a mile away from home. But eventually we were able to consider well-planned short outings involving all five children. We tried the local country park which was only a five minute drive or a fifteen minute walk through the fields, this gave each of them a sense of freedom and space, an opportunity to laugh and play together without antagonising each other. They could play and enjoy simple games of hide and seek around the trees; jumping in or over puddles; search for insects; paddling in the stream etc., but most of all they would enjoy each others company and master the simple challenges in life that such a walk would offer. They would briefly meet up with other people in passing, and though initially I would hold my breath hoping that none of our trio would throw out an expletive in the hearing of a passer-by, we quickly learned how to distract them to prevent this from occurring! They also needed the experience of playing in the playground and on playground equipment. We had been told of Danielle's reluctance to play with other children at school, instead she would choose to cling to the playtime assistant. But here we could encourage her to watch the others and emulate their behaviour and gain the pleasure that others derived from such play. This was never easy for Danielle and she would often be seen wanting to go on some climbing frame but then freeze and scream to get down when the fear kicked in. But once we had talked her through the 'how's and where fore's' of what to do and encouraged Aaron or Gareth to show her, she would eventually overcome the screaming 'habdabs' to master the art and then become obsessive about that particular piece of equipment. Through these walks and other similar outings more acceptable behaviour and social skills were creeping back in to our family life.

With all the fun and frivolity of the Christmas season behind us and the celebration of a new year, 1987, in front of us the children were getting into the swing of their newfound routine. Going back to school after the holiday was more looked forward to by Danielle, though, lacking in imagination, she found schoolwork quite a chore. I was frequently called in to discuss some aspect of her work or behaviour in an effort to support both the school and Danielle in their working relationship. But on one occasion I felt she showed all of us that she did indeed share an imagination, but perhaps the teacher did not appreciate it. I was shown a piece of her work that clearly depicted two stripey animals and at the side of them a huge square shape that had hastily been coloured heavily in black. "Well what do you make of that Mrs. Valdis?" The confused teacher asked me. I asked what the remit had been, and was told the class were working from work cards, that Danielle had done well with the first two or three. Then she was given the card that asked her to draw seven tigers and this drawing had been the result, but what did it mean and how on earth did Danielle reach the conclusion that she had in answering the question? The teacher was desperate to understand. "Have you asked her?" I answered, yes indeed she had but Danielle could not understand why her teacher did not recognise this. Danielle was running around in the playground with her brothers, I called her inside and explained that her teacher was showing me some of her excellent work and I was so proud of her, she beamed the biggest smile. I suggested that she might like to tell me what she had had to do. Danielle was delighted and an enthusiastic explanation of the work cards and her drawings was given. Then we came to the last work card. "So what did this card ask you to do for this picture?" I questioned, "I know." she said running off to get the work card. She read it to me. "Here is a tiger, draw seven tigers." I continued to look between the work card and her drawing. I started to count her stripey tigers, "One, two, oh where are all the others?" I asked. "Silly, they are in the cage of course, don't you know tigers are dangerous animals?" She answered pointing to the black box in the picture. I tried to hold back the stifled smile as I asked her how many were in the box, she counted on her fingers, "Five, can I go back outside now?" Maths concept confirmed, one up to Danielle! In the car on the way home she admitted that she got bored with all the drawing and colouring she was expected to do which is why she really put the tigers in the box! I was secretly delighted her hidden depths were surfacing along with her imaginative ideas. Sadly as with all things that Danielle did she would eventually take this new skill to extremes that frequently caused problems as much for herself as for others in her struggle to connect with acceptable boundaries.

Jason was a deeply affected, insular child who seemed to go through life lacking the survival instinct that usually exists within most toddlers. He was unknown to demand or expect attention. He seemed to have been totally rejected by his natural family, the little attention around was shared between his older sister and younger brother. He displayed 'middle man syndrome' to the full. Any attention, good or not so good, shown to him was brushed away with indifference. Jason would often be found in a position of quietly sobbing whilst younger brother happily enjoyed beating him with various toys. But then I realised that the more we 'rescued' him from such behaviour the more he put himself back into that position. Ha! He clearly communicated his needs now! The equation was - 'I get hurt = they give me time!' We spent endless time showing this young man how to move away from being a target without having to use similar aggression. Initially we were rebuffed or not even offered a response no matter how we tried. He had still been using nappies at night-times when he arrived but after a few weeks I felt it was time to start trying without. Our reasonable, quiet little unresponsive chap became grossly upset, refusing to settle in bed for fear of wetting it. He expressed that if he did his father would find out and beat him so he would get out of bed to wet the carpet instead! Eventually with endless reassurance we persuaded him that the occasional 'accident in bed' didn't matter as we had protective sheets on the mattress so we genuinely would not mind, nor would his father get to know, as we had no intention of telling him. After having had occasional wet beds and nothing being mentioned during access visits, Jason slowly began to believe us. But he still needed proof of the former! One wet bed a night rapidly became several a night over the next few weeks. Each time a smiling Jason would present himself to our sleeping selves saying he needed a change of pyjamas and his bed to be dry. A clean pair of pyjamas and all the love and reassurance that we could muster, given the circumstances, would accompany each dry sheet put on the bed. Then came the day I could take no more! I put our little friend to bed one evening in the usual routine way, but this time with the addition of a few dry sheets and pyjamas neatly stacked on the floor. I explained to him that he knew I didn't mind if the bed got wet, however I really was tired, and would prefer it if he didn't wake me up as I needed to sleep, after all he now knew how to make a bed as he had watched me often enough. He replied rather sadly, "Does that mean you won't be coming to be with me tonight?" I explained that that was exactly what I meant, because then I could be with him all day wide awake and ready to play. That night he was continent and wet beds were infrequent thereafter.

This little fellow had found a way of securing a very special period of time with us that he could enjoy all to himself. Having had a taste of it through his own insecurities, he wanted more, and successfully engineered it. By refusing to give him that time during the night, though proving our word that we would not be cross if he wet the bed, he became more devious by day as he devised new ways of gaining our constant attention. No one had really given Jason time consequently his responses were abnormally exaggerated. I'm happy to say he was able to redress the balance during the following year or so.

Spring arrived and we were making headway in helping Jason accept that he would be joining the school nursery after Easter. He and James had attended the playschool for almost a term and as long as James' need to hurl his weapons at others was kept under control, and Jason was kept away from James with his attention held in constructive play, they both showed signs of positive physical and emotional growth. Though in honesty their access visits to parents did nothing to enhance this. Both boys were unhappy about having to go and demonstrated this with their regression and silence beforehand, and their abrasiveness on their return. Danielle was also unhappy about the visits but was better able to verbalise her feelings through our play people games, so found it easier to work through her thoughts and experiences and share these with us. Bert had spoken with the parents to suggest more acceptable gifts for the children so gradually there were slow improvements.

About this time we were told that our previous trio, Jenna, Darren and Andrea had been brought back into care and were hoping to return to us. Lawrence and I gave it a great deal of thought and discussion to weigh up the pros and cons before offering them a chance to rejoin our clan. We were advised that it was not considered to be in their best interest or in those of our current children's. However as the weeks went by the message was clear, the children were 'working their ticket' away from their temporary short-term placement and almost demanding to come back to us. We were asked if they could visit us to help them understand why they would be unable to live with us but also that such a visit might help them settle better in their current placement. This was agreed and arranged for them to be brought by their social worker to have tea with us after school one evening. Aaron and Gareth were thrilled to have a chance to see them all again, our latest foster children were indifferent as they appeared to accept them as friends of the family, which of course they were. Roger, their social worker was to stay throughout. We had a wonderful party atmosphere during that teatime, not one child put a foot out of place! They just gelled in a most unexpected way; our guests fell back into our routine immediately. Jenna took Danielle under her wing and with Andrea tagging along brought out the girly side of Danielle, which she loved. Darren also worked magic with Jason and James taking the lead in their game encouraging them to play better together, they were mesmerised by his cheerfulness and ease. That left Aaron and Gareth to join in where they felt comfortable, Gareth of course was the same age as the two older girls so he joined their company whilst Aaron watched over the boys offering suggestions to enhance their game. Amazing! Looking after eight was easier than five! Roger was fascinated and admitted he could not believe how at ease they all were in each other's company, even when they all went outside together to play. He asked how keen we were to have this as a permanent situation. We insisted we could manage. But after a great deal of discourse with his manager and the fostering department it was not to be, but Roger stuck out on behalf of his trio, finally getting an agreement for the children to visit us one day a week, on Saturdays from nine in the morning until seven in the evening. Lawrence volunteered to do the journey of sixty miles to collect and return them to their foster home. This arrangement lasted for almost nine months during which I hoped we could prove the benefits of such visits, but most importantly convince the powers that be that these children belonged with us if Mum was unable to look after them.

The family dynamics were changing; those Saturdays were so well looked forward to by all of us. There was almost a feeling of the clan being incomplete from Sunday to Friday, but on Saturday everything fell into place. Our home just buzzed, if we went out and about we just filled two cars! The children were so involved with each other they had no time to argue and all the positive attitudes and leadership qualities of Jenna and Darren were pulling power to our current trio. Having more girls around the home gave Danielle good examples of behaviour and being so comfortable in our home meant that neither Jenna nor Andrea stood on ceremony, they simply adhered to household rules offering Danielle boundaries to work and play within. Darren and Jason would swap notes about their respective schools and took great delight in sharing time together. If one of our brood had an issue they were working through the others all pulled round to help, sometimes this meant they gave space allowing that child to have special one to one time with either Lawrence or me, and we would be left alone undisturbed to give it. Before they were taken back to their foster home we would prepare them for bed and wind the day down by being all together drawing or playing a game around the kitchen table, or sometimes watching a programme. I still treasure those moments watching and listening to them whilst they were occupied. We kept a box full of scrap paper for general usage; this was kept on the trolley in the dining room for any of them to help them selves to at any time. At the end of the day I would tidy this box, throw away those drawings or scribbles I hoped would not be needed but kept their masterpieces to adorn the kitchen walls or retain for the care reviews. This box of paper was another place where the children would express their feelings, leaving clear messages about their expectations. Sometimes I would be left questioning some of these 'messages' as they poured out in pictures or in words some of the negativity of their lives. Jenna left a drawing of our house and garden with all of the children depicted as stick men, all named, Lawrence and I were also pictured holding hands. Underneath she had written - 'Our happy home, why can't I live here all the time forever?' Danielle had attempted to copy this; her version was 'This is my happy house.' Feelings of the moment maybe and of course I am practical enough to realise that seven days a week of having eight children would make for a busy household, a great deal of cooking and a huge mountain of washing. But weighing up the benefits I felt we had it made and we could make it work. I spoke to Roger again, as well as Emily our support worker; they were both prepared to support us in our quest, which would last for the rest of the year, and in some respects for eternity.

*"Feelings of worth can flourish only in
an atmosphere where individual differences
are appreciated, mistakes are tolerated,
communication is open, and rules are
flexible — the kind of atmosphere that is
found in a nurturing family."*

*Virginia Satir*

*American Psychologist and Educator
(1916 - 1988)*

# CHAPTER 11

## Moving On

Many meetings were to take place in trying to achieve our hopes and intentions. But the answer was always the same, 'Not in everyone's best interests.' We were to dispute this in so many different ways. The community support we had was astounding, our friends thought we were crazy but never the less gave us their full support. Supportive letters were flying from many parts of the country landing on the desk of both the fostering department and our Member of Parliament of the time. The decision was made by one person who considered that one family were not able to meet the needs of all the children especially as the two family groups were likely to be under different 'umbrellas.' By this she meant that one family was working towards adoption whilst the other was likely to be in long term fostering. Titles, names, circumstances, the future may have to be considered! We had not made the decision lightly, nor looked at the situation through rose-coloured glasses, the decision was based on the reality we were living with, those that could witness it had insight, hence gave the support we were fortunate enough to receive. We had worked extremely hard with both families, and to some extent we were beginning to realise that we needed to keep moving forward for Aaron's and Gareth's benefit. Throughout this period letters would arrive on our doorstep from the department regularly, but never during the week when we could question them or respond immediately. These letters consistently arrived on a Saturday morning which only served to fuel my fire and culminated in a fury born of frustration that sometimes proved difficult to contain, though at times like this the garden benefited in an effort to redirect my anger.

During 1987, the children in our care continued to make strides, some days these strides would be huge and there would be a personal developmental breakthrough for one or the other, on occasions for all three at once! The greatest change came when Dad was finally held in custody for James' injuries and those of another child. Though visits to Mum continued until the middle of the year. These visits were more enjoyable to the trio now that the strongest influence was no longer around, hence relieving the fear embedded in the children. Their behaviour had improved but now lingering doubts for their future were hovering over them. We continued our ongoing debate with the department to provide a family home for all six children because this worked for us! There had to be a way around it and we were determined to find it for the sake of all of them. In time we received a letter to the effect that we could be considered for one group but not the other, we had received the letter from the department explaining the 'reasons,' however the lengthy letter actually contradicted their view and could be our evidence to their futile excuses. One family group was to have their case presented in the High Court, where the judge ruled that arrangements should be made for the children to live with our family in the long term. This had been based on statements and evidence from many people and included our letter from the department, which had been taken in by Lawrence. The court held on to this until the case was finalised, then all correspondence was sent back to the department for distribution to the owners, we were never to receive that letter no matter how many times we asked for it. But then the family involved were never going to be allowed to come either, even though their social worker had rung me after the court hearing to give me the 'good news' as declared by the judge! His recommendation being that the children should live with the Valdis family and this would be on High Court paper so the children will be yours! Not so, the department had other ideas. We were completely shattered as a family, there seemed to be no way forward for any of us, and yet we had to hold it together for everyone. We still had five children living with us, and three children visiting on a weekly basis. We had to go on. They were caught up in the middle of it all. But now we had to prepare all of them to move on which would take several months in all. Life seemed so bloody cruel at this stage of our family life. We both began to wonder what we were working towards. We had heard all of the arguments, we were determined to work to the benefit of each child but though there were no plans for their futures at this time as nothing better was actually on offer and new homes would have to be found for both families, the whole situation was ludicrous. Both support workers were as dumbfounded as we were but this was as much out of their control as it was ours. It was now our turn to lose faith, trust and total understanding. The only thing that gave me any focus at this time was the children and their need to be prepared for what lay ahead, this included Aaron and Gareth, what effect would it have on those two? I felt the system had let them all down so badly, we couldn't, nor wouldn't do the same. Lawrence turned to his work for consolation and solace.

Fortunately our support worker was magnificent in recognising that although we were close to breaking point we would not let it affect our care of the children or our determination to maintain the equilibrium within our household. We had to stay as positive as possible at least on the surface, but it was a grief we both held within.

Towards the end of the year we were advised that we could have one further visit by our Saturday trio, we were to explain that because they would be moving to a new family shortly they would need to concentrate on that move and therefore coming to visit us would not be possible anymore. This visit was to take place in the middle of December, we requested that they allowed their visits to continue until after Christmas, was two more weeks going to make that much difference? Apparently so! The date was set for us, take it or leave it. The date chosen was the same day as James' birthday, the day before Jason's birthday! Was there no end to this pressure? Poor Jason was struggling to handle the fact that his younger brother dared to celebrate his birthday before he was allowed to! Now, with birthday parties on consecutive days, to have to incorporate a leaving party too was unbelievable, especially two weeks before Christmas. Emotions were heightened at this time of the year as a matter of course, how much more so this year. The day chosen was a Sunday rather than the Saturday and I was determined it would be a day to remember. Our neighbours loaned us a video camera so we could film as much as we were able for our own records. That footage of film was to help me to cope with losing them all, but oddly enough we were asked if the department could borrow it to present the children to new parents as an introduction to the children. Such irony.

The day was amazing, from getting up helping James to enjoy his birthday, to Lawrence collecting the children, to returning them and putting those with us to bed. Today we could have one last day of this united clan spending time together and we would enjoy and savour every moment. I had planned our Christmas biscuit making session, so that each child could have their own biscuits. What you can do with one child you could do with eight; we just needed a bigger batch of dough! Whilst they pummelled, shaped and cut the Christmas shapes they chattered on about their previous Christmas's celebrated as well as their expectations for this Christmas. The atmosphere was alive with the thrill of them all being together, I had to keep repressing the thought that this was to be the last day of this kind for these children. As each of them finished making their biscuits and putting them into the oven they ran outside to play. Apart from Andrea and James who both stayed in to play with the play boot and play people. Whilst I was clearing away after the baking session and preparing Sunday lunch I listened to Andrea telling me about her 'house'. She explained that the play boot was her own house and only special people were allowed to go there. I asked her who else lived there with her in this special house. She told me, "Well Mummy does sometimes, but really I live in this top part on my own, but you live here as well, 'cos you have your own room." "What about everyone else?" I suggested." She looked at me coyly with her fingers in her mouth smiling. Then she moved a few of the play people about and said "All of the other people live near so they just visit me sometimes." Now it was James' time to interject. "Which room is mine?" He had been a bit of a nuisance to Andrea moving her people about and although she had frowned and tut-tutted she hadn't said a thing to him, so now she had the opportunity. She leaned forward across the table to him and said, "Well, James you are just a big pest so you will have to build your own house." This was said with firmness and certainty leaving James a little non-plussed. James frowned back to her; they were locked in an eye-to-eye stare. Then James retorted, "I know I'll build it next door to yours so we can still see each other." They both smiled before breaking into fits of giggles and getting on with the game. I have often thought of that moment as they were both so close together they could have knocked each other off their chairs, being strong determined children, they could both have gone for the jugular, instead they resolved their differences amicably and to the satisfaction of both of them. Yet they had also conveyed the closeness they had and needed. They were good together, and good for each other. But above all else James had convinced me he had the capacity of mutual agreement without having to always fight his corner. Another giant step forward in his small world.

There were thirteen of us for Sunday lunch that day. Our friends and their daughter joined us, which added to the party atmosphere. During the meal whilst I was cutting food up on one or two of the youngster's plates, among the buzz of chatter between everyone, I could hear one of them repeating, "Mum, Mum, Mum." The words were barely audible, deliberately spoken in low tones, When I looked to see which child was doing this I realised it was little Darren, he was looking straight at me, continually repeating the word Mum in such a way as not to draw attention from the others to himself. I walked around to him, stood at the back of him to lean over to cut his food, as I did so I whispered in his ear, "I think you mean Auntie Dani." He looked at me, smiled and said, "But you are mum here." I was left wondering how to take his remark.

Late that afternoon was the Christingle service in our church. Our children loved this service as much as I did. I wondered if our friends would join us and was delighted when they agreed to come too. When there were so many of us it was easier to sit in two pews, with a few trusted children of ours sitting in front of us, whilst we sat behind, in easy reach of all, with those that might need restraining. This service holds a special magic every year for young and old alike. The church would always be packed with all generations sharing the meaning of Christmas. When the lights went down and the candles were lit and all you could see were the expectant, delighted faces of the young under the watchful eyes of their elders a glow of warmth spread throughout the church surrounding everyone. I looked down at our motley crew; they were singing "Away in a manger" in hushed gentle tones holding their candles with their cherubic faces lit by the incandescent light. They appeared so angelic and innocent it was enough to make me want to check to see if they had wings on their backs! I felt emotionally overwhelmed knowing that in a very short time I would be trying to explain to three of the children that they would not see us for a long time to come, and in the foreseeable future the other three would be moving on too. But for now I had to smile and enjoy the moment. A few moments later we were to sing 'Give me oil in my lamp keep me burning,' I heard giggles as those in front were looking behind, I stared down our row to see my errant son Gareth giving another performance as he sang with gusto emulating a falsetto singer, this time I smiled along with him whilst giving him the meaningful look that conveys everything without the use of words. He smiled back, kept up the facial exaggerations but lowered his tone to an acceptable level hence he continued to entertain with less embarrassment. The others turned around to face the front but every so often one or the other would half turn to look and smile at Gareth as he kept up his act. This service should have been the beginning of our Christmas celebrations; instead it was the end of an era and the shattering of our illusions.

A birthday tea for James was next on the agenda. My friend's husband had to go home, but Cath and her daughter stayed to join us. Aaron leapt to our assistance to prepare the party food. For the next two hours Christmas was set aside to make way for the birthday festivities. The clan excelled themselves finding new energy to keep up the momentum of the day. They all made a fuss of James, the tornado, as his excitement rose, realising he was now the celebrity of the day. Blowing out his four candles he remarked that he was like Jesus and God as he had four candles on his orange world! Surprisingly he had absorbed something of the meaning of the Christingle after all.

The day was nearly over, there was little left to do but allow the children to enjoy each others company in whichever way they chose, we played some Christmas music whilst they all danced about, free to express their own spirits, to dance and just be silly. An enormous part of the days events had been filmed, we were to turn to this whenever we needed to feel close to the children, to remind ourselves of what life could have been. The problem with this was that in our mind's eye these children were never to grow any older.

Before Jenna, Darren and Andrea left us that day I explained that decisions had been made about their future, and there were plans for them to move on from their temporary foster placement. I reminded them that we would always love them, but as I had often said before that love was like elastic, it could stretch and reach anywhere in the world, so we would never be far away, really. I commented that they would be very busy getting to know new people, that it was important to try to enjoy the fun in finding out about their new lives, though it might be a long time before we saw them again, we would always be here. The exuberance of the day had a hold over them; they hugged and kissed everyone, still bubbling with excitement. They must have been exhausted with the day's events and I wondered at which point my words would have penetrated their understanding. But tears were not allowed, as Lawrence drove away to take them back to their current foster home I ushered the remaining five back into the house to calm down their excitability before going to bed!

There was school in the morning and another birthday to celebrate. We had given Jason a bicycle as he had just mastered the art of riding one without stabilisers; before it was even full daylight he went outside to ride it around in circles. The serious look of concentration was a delight to witness. His pride in this achievement was great.

I called out to him "Jason do you know how to use the brakes to stop?" Maintaining his concentration and without looking my way he called back as he squeezed the brakes. "Yes, I do." As he said the words, the bike stopped instantly and Jason fell over sideways. Gareth called out, "That's one way Jason!" In direct contrast the day was a much calmer day, far more relaxing and at an easier pace for everyone. But on looking back these two consecutive days served to reflect the two diverse characters of the birthday boys, hurricane James with his crazy, madcap ways dashing around like an eternal whirlwind on one side and laid back, easy going quiet Jason, the calm that came after the storm on this occasion!

Christmas 1987 was to be a quieter affair, pleasant in it's own way, as it was Danielle, Jason and James' second Christmas with us, so they had a memory of a previous Christmas to fall back on. With the change in their everyday language and the virtual disappearance of their previously regular expletives we were able to go to church comfortably without fear of judgement and prejudice, well that is except from those who didn't know us and would look us up and down with our entourage of five as we paraded into the building. They obviously questioned our need to have so many children, I've often wondered if those same people saw us with all eight and would hear any one of the children at any time call us Mum or Dad as they frequently did! It was not uncommon for onlookers to question among themselves how many sets of twins or triplets we had. In the New Year we would have to start preparing this trio to transfer their affections to the idea of a 'new Mummy and Daddy'.

During January and February 1988 the search was on in earnest to find suitable parents, I found it very hard to accept the 'marketing' techniques to showcase available children for adoption. To some extent the absence of the former trio actually made it slightly easier for these children to gain insight into their need to have new parents and a new home. Of course we were also living on a knife-edge not knowing how much longer they would be with us. It was impossible to plan too far ahead, especially family events, as we never knew when the phone call would arrive that would reduce our family even further. Our attempts to slowly introduce the new parents idea to Danielle, Jason and James initially fell on deaf ears as they focused on their daily lives with us. The whole concept of having to move on was considered by them to be ridiculous, unless it included Aaron and Gareth. Danielle's interpretation was that the five of them were staying and it was Lawrence and I that were actually moving on! Wishful thinking perhaps! Generally the introduction of the subject was brought in to conversation as a direct result of something one of them would be talking about or in their games with the play people as they acted out through the figures their own thoughts and feelings. Eventually it was possible to include their own thoughts and desires and expectations for their future lives. We would choose appropriate books for them to read that focused on reasons for needing a new house and having a different garden to play in, finding new friends and things to do. Their existence was based on routine, with these children it was difficult to have a spur of the moment idea, being impulsive would throw them out of kilter and they would be totally unsure of how to react or cope. This could result in regressive behaviour to a lesser or greater degree that could affect anyone and everyone, the recovery period could often be as variable as the responses endured. I felt the need for a wall of protection around them whilst we took the tentative steps forward.

During the case review in January the idea of compiling together a booklet for each child depicting its own life story was introduced. The idea behind this was to help each child work through their understanding and hopefully make the satisfactory adjustment to past events. The support worker for the children would normally do the bulk of this work. But I was very concerned about the possible outcome of the very nature of it and the disruptions it would cause. The children were so emotionally and physically stronger than they had ever been, but this inner strength was exceptionally fragile, so easily damaged or destroyed. They had so little experience to fall back on and all too often in times of stress would still resort to the behaviour they had arrived with. We were about to find out just how thin eggshells really were! It was also accepted and recognised that our relationships with the department remained fraught, so in our case the decision was for us to do the Life Story Work with the children and their worker to liaise with the natural family to obtain information and photographs. During the monthly visits he made to the children the worker would spend time with each child and their growing books to review their understanding and progression. The main support for this work was allocated to our own support worker who would regularly visit to work with me for the benefit of the children and our family as a whole. We were also informed at the meeting that a Guardian Ad Item had been appointed for the children and would be contacting us shortly to spend time with the children in order to compile her reports for the court. This is a totally independent person whose role is to appoint a solicitor for the children to act on their behalf in the court. They ascertain the views and the opinions of the children, which would be presented to the court so a decision to free them for adoption could take place.

For the children at this time there was very little talk of past events, but their fears of meeting or returning to live with their natural parents indicated that they would have some confused, unresolved feelings about past events. Receiving Birthday and Christmas cards from their natural parents had aroused those unresolved feelings. In spite of all the recent difficulties, it was recognised and stated in the reports that all three children had continued to make significant social and educational progress. That they were aware of the plan to leave the foster home at some point, although their understanding, acceptance and emotional preparation for such a move was variable.

The discussion of the meeting then turned to prospective parents for the children. There had only been three put forward for choice and two had been dismissed as not suitable for our brood, leaving only one more to be followed up. The moment of reality was sitting round this table with us. In the not too distant future we would be saying our farewells to them. There was little time left for us to give them the experiences we so wanted them to have, and how were we to do this and expect them to come to terms with their past ready to face their future. Which part of this were we to focus on first? Where did we begin? What if decisions were made and taken quicker than the children could focus on and adjust to? We also had to consider and work with Aaron and Garth to adjust to yet another change in our family dynamics, they were not even at the beginning point of accepting the loss of our previous children. I felt my anger rising to the surface, then realised this was not going to be helpful. At the end of the day the nature of the work had to be time limited and the quicker the children moved on perhaps the sooner they would adjust to their new lives. The case manager talked about attachment disorder but felt that, given the children's experience in gaining a positive attachment to us, there was an improved chance of them transferring their affections to the prospective parents. There was further work to be achieved before the identified couple would be presented to the panel as prospective adopters for these children. Only then would arrangements be made for the relevant introductions to take place. I asked if they lived in the area, but was told that they lived in the South of England so there would be geographical difficulties to overcome too. However it was reinforced that they were 'only prospective parents' and the work still to be done would decide whether they would be put forward as a match for our trio.

We were still in limbo, suspended in time with unknown boundaries. My protective walls around our fragile trio just became thicker.

Visits to Mum had been stopped in October 1987, and she had challenged the decision to terminate access to her three children. The final visit to her had gone well as their support worker had arranged for time to be spent in a small park and he remained present throughout to supervise and monitor. He had also taken photographs that we could include in their Life Story book.

I was yet to be convinced of the benefits of the Life Story work. To work through the events of their young lives at a time when their immaturity was so delicate and brittle. How would we portray the information involved, to include all the facts yet detract from the negativity that had been a big part of their little lives? To give them understanding, and hopefully gain acceptance to move forward, whilst still keeping strong. I knew there would be moments of regression resulting in some challenging behaviours and trying times ahead of us, but somehow we had to focus on the positives, pick up the fragmented emotions along the way, to enable our three individual characters to gain a sense and need to belong to another family, without losing the love and respect we had shown them and without feelings of rejection that would hamper their willingness to move.

That great gift of time was to prove to us the true therapeutic value of Life Story Work, which is only undervalued by those unfortunate enough not to have been involved with such work. Acquiring the skills isn't always easy and we learn by our mistakes, as there is no greater teacher than a child! Our initial attempts were uncertain and naive. There was so little literature available to consult and even fewer people with first hand experience available to speak to. Some saw it as no more than a glorified photograph album when in fact it is an incredible tool that these and future children were to use to remind themselves of their roots, the reasons behind their experiences of life, and providing themselves with pride and an identity to be the adults they were to become. Interpretations of instances in life are different among siblings and even more so between generations. The chances are one would be closer to a situation than the other, age and the level of maturity of those concerned might reflect the diversity of opinions. The differences in personalities would bring out distinct feelings in those involved. This was certainly the case between our trio and often initiated open discussion on a valid point as they desperately tried to piece together their lives.

Putting a life story together for someone could not be done by another without involving the lead character! It can only become acceptable and believable when the child has focused on, recalled and worked through arising events of the touchstones of their life. I found we could only turn the page to work on the next stage when they were comfortable to move on. They loved to add their own personal touches, through drawings, photographs; their own words sometimes even in their own handwriting. All were valuable and important steps of ownership and acceptance. However the book is really only a bi-product of the main work. First and foremost it is documented evidence of the work completed, providing a point of reference for the future to reflect on their roots whilst offering reasons for the present. Through such positive work a closer bond naturally forms between foster/adoptive parent and child, this helps to build a trusting relationship as each accepts the other. The adult's understanding of the child is greater which spills over into other areas of life. Likewise the child is offering his innermost thoughts and feelings, good and not so good, he sees the adult accepting these, which surely means that he is accepted. Acceptance is the key to so much, especially when they tend to carry the effects of so much rejection, blame and guilt.

Secondly, from the child's viewpoint this whole exercise must be a positive experience even when handling the negatives of life. For once they can begin to share their views and feelings, examine them and sort them out. They begin to understand some areas of their lives are not so different from any other child's life, or even that of the adult involved as experiences of childhood are shared. This is the foundation for common ground between the two! Eventually a sense of identity is gained, they begin to accept the past without forgetting it, so become ready to face the future with greater confidence. But the book provides concrete evidence of the child's existence, a medium they can use to share their life with others. A common remark at this time about children in care was that their relationships were shallow, but how could they be anything else, for some moving on was the only constant factor in their lives. I was to discover that Life Story Work gave an opportunity to offer real depth to a child's character and being, thus helping them to become whole.

Communication is a lifeline. No less important is the lifeline of a child. Many seem to think that food, warmth and protection are their lifelines. All are essential to life, but more is required. Human beings are far more complex than this. Children deserve understanding in a caring, sharing, loving environment, thereby filling their emotional tank. The opportunity to reach their full potential will also increase their inner sense of well-being. Simply put, a child's lifeline is a dependency on other people; the ability of communication is a two-way affair. It is the responsibility of parents and those acting in 'loco parentis' to keep the channels of communication between them open. This can be rather difficult, (as those of us with telephones know!) when there is interference on the line causing a distortion of messages received!! During the ensuing months we were to work through a few distortions the children held on to.

Danielle loved doing her book, took great pride in her life and recent achievements, and was less keen about the idea of moving away, but that we could work on! Whenever Bert visited she would show him her special book and the latest pages she had worked on, telling him all about her family, the reasons for coming to us, things she had done and all the certificates she had achieved. With very few photographs of when she was little to use, we sourced other ways of depicting her baby and toddling stages, which she adored. We included a picture of the hospital where she was born and photocopied her birth certificate for inclusion. Bert asked her "And what is this page all about?" Danielle replied, "Oh that is the ticket they gave me when I was born." Priceless, but if this was her view who was I to change it!

Jason would also enjoy sharing his book as it slowly developed. He was always so serious and intense about the area we would be covering, and then would lovingly hold on to the page taking it with him wherever he went until he reached the stage of feeling ready to include it in his file. Whenever divulging information about his birth family he would become lifeless, start to drool again, his shoulders would droop and his eyes looked downcast. Conversely whenever he talked about more recent events he would sit up straight, grin and talk non-stop as he made his decisions about what to include and what to leave out. If I tried to touch on future events such as moving on to new parents, he would make it clear that although he was listening he was not accepting any of it.I made up a story of a little boy who had similar experiences to him going in a similar direction in life to help him focus on the events he found hard to face. The ending was always left open for him to finish and his answers would give me insight as to how far his understanding was prepared to go and his own wishes for his future. We often used the play people to play out the story, there would be two houses in the scene, ours and the new parents, he would continue the story giving the boy a little adventure with the new parents but always coming home for tea! I asked him why the little boy felt he could not perhaps sleep at the new parents home. Jason leaned forward towards me staring me in the eye and very seriously said, "Because he lives at home!" That was me told in no uncertain terms!

James just loved to talk about things he did, and places he had visited as well as all of his favourite things in life, but try to touch on life before us and he would put his hand over my mouth to stop me from talking telling me "No, we don' say tha'." James's speech had improved considerably but he still continued to clip off the endings to all of his words which could make it difficult to understand when he had a lot to say. Every time I broached the new parent subject James would say "No than' you James no' nee' new mummy or new daddy I go' one alweddy." We plodded on building their books together, in doing so building the jigsaw of life together, aiming towards that moment when we would know which parents had been chosen to take over their young lives, warts and all.

*"Children are unpredictable.*
*You never know what inconsistency*
*they're going to catch you in next."*

*Henry Ward Beecher*

*U.S. Clergyman (1813 - 1887)*

## CHAPTER 12

# Questioning Trust

During early March we were told that a couple not dissimilar to ourselves had been found for the children and it was time to plan for introductions so that we could move towards visits by the prospective adopters. This would mean speeding up the preparations a little as leaving time for our brood was imminent.

More conversations about having new parents and how they would feel crept into our daily lives. The three of them would listen avidly to the explanations, but as it was not happening straight away, and at this stage we could not offer a time scale, they inevitably snubbed the idea. The more play people games we acted out, the more their figures came back to our 'house.' Fear of the unknown was a huge factor. I suggested to Lawrence that we would need tangible evidence for the children to relate to each day, that they would understand that the reality of the move was really going to take place. This set him the challenge of producing a large 3D model of our house, one that could be wall mounted, and of course the doors and windows would have to open and close. Behind the windows would be photographs of the children, "I suppose you even want a real light in it that they can switch on and off!" He said sarcastically. "Of course!" I replied in the same tone. And it did!

Arrangements were made for the couple to have an overnight stay in the area so they would have an opportunity to meet the children's support worker, and also ourselves, to allow us to explain some of the difficulties as well as some of the highlights in caring for this trio. We were asked not to put them off the task ahead but to give them enough information to understand the magnitude of their undertaking. Striking the right balance was not going to be easy! Lawrence and I both felt that they had to face this full on, be realistic, and feel comfortable about the challenge ahead. The children's difficulties of two years before could rise again and may even manifest themselves through different behaviours. They would need a strong constitution and a determined commitment.

Our first meeting with the couple was to take place in the evening in our home but not until after the children had been put to bed. Then they were to spend the following day with us as family friends, stay for lunch and join us on an outing so they could witness variable behaviours or responses to different situations to give themselves 'a fly on the wall' view of the trio.

During the course of the evening the four of us began to relax as we discussed the children's histories, subsequent difficulties, those overcome and those still being worked on and through. We had asked the children if we could share their Life Story Books with our visitors, they were delighted about this and were more than willing to leave their treasured books in our hands to show off. These helped the couple to gain even further insight of the long road the trio had travelled but also how long that road they journeyed on just might be! Any questions asked were answered as honestly as possible on both sides. The thought of handing over three very vulnerable small people frightened me. We had attempted to forge relationships between the threesome, but as a family group they presented as tolerating each other rather than wanting to be with each other. I knew we had never overcome that intrinsic stance that rubbed between the three, which is why we were so successful with Gareth and Aaron's presence as they provided the 'glue' that held them all together. This couple would not have that advantage. But maybe they held the key to open the youngster's imaginations and initiate a spark of something that we hadn't managed. To finish our evening we crept upstairs to our sleeping beauties so the couple could peek at the reality of their own dreams, a family of their own. Their warmth and determination and openness was reassuring to us, helping us to feel more confident that this had a chance to work. The thought provoking evening left all of us with a great deal to contemplate.

Our guests arrived in time for lunch the following day and were introduced to all the children as our 'old family friends.' We may have convinced Danielle, even Jason and James, but both Aaron and Gareth were quick to question us, as they had never heard of these people before! Aaron took me to one side to comment on the couple's fascination with the children and asked straight out if they were perhaps going to be the new 'Mummy and Daddy' I had talked about for so long! The game was up we were caught out! I took him to one side to confirm his suspicions and put trust in him not to say anything. Rather proud at being given this trust he stood in his 'protective brother's shoes' determined not to let the children or us down. He actively encouraged them to interact with the couple standing back to allow them their limelight. We chose to have a walk to the Country Park and Danielle was to give some of her best behaviour but also display her well practised attention-seeking type too. But I was really delighted when she brought herself back into line very quickly when reminded that she was stepping over the mark. On our walk back through the field, they talked generally about needing new parents, especially Jason who was making it clear he did not need new parents as he already had some, totally unaware of our guests' future role in their lives. But again this had the positive effect of allowing the couple an inkling of their fears and apprehensions about their future beyond our family.

This time was also a reality check for us, after almost two years of being together and all that we had been through to achieve our aim; we would be losing that final link, and be left wondering what price to our family. Boosting the boys' morale about their part in the lives of the children would be of no consequence compared to the grief they would share with us after the youngsters had left. They were to feel desolated, losing confidence in us too, on a huge scale. What kind of parents were we to give children away? Would we give them away too? What had seemed such a wonderful thing to do suddenly came at a hefty price, my own children's trust and confidence.

The couple left us to return home to have some very serious thoughts about their own future. They had gained insight into the challenges of having three children who each came with their own 'metaphorical' suitcase of hang-ups, difficulties and experiences that had shaped and misshaped their personalities. Based on their short introductory visit to us they were left to make their own decisions about whether to commit to our threesome for the rest of their lives. The magnitude of such an undertaking must have seemed frightening and overwhelming as much for this couple as for our children in their quest and need to have new parents. Within a few days, we were to be told, that after some prevarication, they had concluded that parents who give birth have no choice in the resulting child and whilst ours did not come with a full instruction manual at least a basic handbook had been written! Now it was all systems go to work towards the smooth transition of three children, to transfer their affections to this willing couple, to live not in our home but theirs. Could we do it?

We had planted the seed in the children's heads, now we were to encourage it to grow and become accepting of the situation that lay in front of them. Bert and Emily both visited us for a meeting so we could formulate a plan of expectation with clear roles in an endeavour to support the children as comfortably as possible. Bert was to spend time explaining to each of the children who the couple had been, offering them more details of their background, helping the trio to start their own thinking processes on moving away in the not too distant future, also to ascertain their understanding as they worked towards the transfer. Emily was to support us with some of the backlash that would surely come our way, and guide us as necessary as well as liaise with the new parents. Lawrence and I had our own thoughts on how this should be done to minimise the disruption and regression that would definitely be encountered.

Photographs between our two families were exchanged. Those we received were mounted and put on the kitchen wall to kick start reality and begin to make the whole thing more tangible to the youngsters. The kitchen became a display area for all of them. Aaron and Gareth were involved in helping us to mount, collage and display all that came from the new parents to be. Because of the couple's own work commitments, there was to be a time lapse of a few weeks before the first visit would take place. The couple had given us their Life Story Book to share with the children, which they keenly read, and re-read. We asked for photographs of the interior and exterior of their home, in particular the children's bedrooms to be, bathroom, cloakroom, living room and dining room, but also the garden where they would play. I had wanted to show the similarities between the two separate homes to familiarise them with the reality when they finally visited. A different area of our kitchen walls would be dedicated to each individual child, portraying photograph's of their bedroom taken from different angles, to help them understand the concept of having their own space not only in their new home but also emotionally, mentally and physically to enable them to come to terms within themselves all that was needed. These displays also helped them from the moment they got up in a morning to touch base with the daily reality and help each child to become familiar with the new surroundings they would soon encounter. During the following weeks, we also produced road map diagrams of the new vicinity to explain the geographical positions of how school, church and the park might be.

Eventually a date was set for us to take the children for an overnight stay with the prospective parents. If the couple had lived nearer to us, the children would have spent a day, an overnight stay would be arranged, followed by a weekend visit. Assuming that all went well, the permanent move would then take place fairly quickly afterwards. However the long distances between our households meant adopting an alternative plan. Emily had spent time with the couple, photographs had been exchanged and we had also encouraged an exchange of letters to keep up a healthy contact between children and adults. Then came time for the visit. Lawrence and I were to take the children South, spend part of the day with everyone to help settle the children then leave them there, we would then return the next day to collect the children and bring them back to our home. This gave the couple hands on experience of caring for 'their' three children in their own home and an opportunity for the children to face the true reality in facing their future move, no longer to be living with us. We had made the trip as exciting as possible for the three youngsters, though obviously delighted about a night away, there was also the high anxiety levels resulting from fear of the unknown.

Our car journey seemed endlessly long with three rather impatient passengers constantly asking the proverbial "Are we nearly there yet?", which started almost before we left our own driveway. But eventually we did arrive and found ourselves knocking on the couple's door. We now had three very apprehensive children. Following the introductions to the house and gardens we let the 'rein' off the trio for them to go on a tour of discovery around their new home. They took enormous delight in recognising various rooms from the photos on our kitchen wall. So the familiarity exercise had worked, they were able to relate to this new home almost instantly and see the many like for like settings as in our home. Though theirs was more sprawling with long corridors and two staircases, which fascinated the youngsters. Once they felt settled we left them with a promise to return the following day, we waved this family group goodbye feeling confident that all augured well. The emptiness we felt was exceptionally deep as we drove off to spend time with Lawrence's Mum who lived a two-hour drive away. What message had we just given to the children? I felt it was in the lines of 'Even though we love you so much we are still prepared to give you away.' Suddenly I did not like what we were doing even though in the very depth of me I knew we had no alternative, Lawrence's silence as he drove confirmed that he too had similar feelings.

Returning for the trio the following day, we kept the visit short, this seemed the right thing to do so that their memory of the weekend was their time with the couple and not the time that involved us. Our giddy brood talked of the events of the weekend. They were excited about having their own room, and were generally feeling more relaxed about the possibility of eventually moving there. Danielle and James enjoyed all things new, and having a 'new Mummy and Daddy' was quite exciting, but Jason was different, he liked his life to be the same and he still refused to accept that a move was necessary, unless of course our family could all go with him! He would throw looks of exasperation and sheer annoyance at his brother and sister whenever they passed a positive comment about moving. He had his own agenda on this matter and refused to be moved, in all senses of the word! His conversion was to prove to be quite difficult over the coming weeks.

We had a rule for the children for when they felt upset over anything and perhaps could not sleep. If they felt ill they were allowed to wake us for help, but if they just could not sleep, usually through anxiety, they were allowed to come to our bedroom bringing their duvet and a pillow to find a spot on the floor to bed down on. No one was allowed in the bed, they could climb on the bed with us in the morning for stories or to chat, but not to get into the bed, sensible rule of safety! Up until now there would only be the occasional morning when on awakening there would be a sleeping body, usually Gareth, somewhere on our bedroom floor. However on the lead up to the children's leaving date we were to awaken to several children camping on our floor. Sometimes trying to negotiate my route out of the room without treading on a child was like mastering an obstacle course. But this behaviour and need to join us just highlighted their insecurities and vulnerability.

Discussions and decisions with the powers that be, culminated in arranging the couple to spend a week living close by, actually at the far end of our garden in a caravan, to give them personal space with the children. If this went well they would return South taking the youngsters with them to their 'forever home.' This would mark the end of an era for us and the beginning of a new era for their family. Half term week school holiday was chosen.

I suppose on reflection this was not to be an easy week, the children would look for the best of both worlds, if admonished by the new parents they would turn to us for comfort, equally if they did not like what we were saying they ran to the couple. We devised a strategy between us to manage this behaviour, after all a united front between us would provide the wall of security that was needed. Jason did rise to the attention of having four adults and our boys around, it seemed the ideal solution to it all for him! James raced around in his inimitable fashion emulating a mini tornado backwards and forwards between new Mum and Dad and old Mum and Dad, which is how he now told us apart! Danielle occasionally regaled that now she had a new 'Mummy and Daddy' she no longer had to take notice of us! She was soon reminded that indeed she would. One day during that week Danielle opted to come shopping with me leaving the boys with the couple. Sitting in the back of the car she opened a conversation about events in her life, which was unusual for her to do. I drove, occasionally nodding, or briefly answering her in an attempt to acknowledge whatever she said. Then as I drove up the drive she blurted out, "So if my birth Daddy hadn't hit me then I would never have known you, would I?" Of course she was right, but her forthright explanation left me squirming with discomfort as I nodded in agreement, as these were the facts. We then sat in the car for quite a lengthy time mulling over past, present and possible future events that would influence her life and those of her brothers. I reiterated how much we all loved them, and it did not matter where they went in the world we would always love them, and this love would stretch like elastic to wherever they were. We would miss them but we knew how important it was for them to start a new life, in a new home in a new area well away from where there had been so much hurt. Danielle had never felt happy walking down certain streets in the neighbouring town as she was frightened of meeting her birth parents, on one occasion the parents had turned up outside the school they now attended, this had not only unnerved all three children but also me as they were standing not too far away from my car, on the hill overlooking the school. This was the prime position to see every child leaving the school premises; we had all felt very threatened. My own fear had given me further insight into the children's responses too.

The week in the caravan must have been a huge strain on the couple as well as us, and handling fragile emotions belonging to all five children was far from easy. But planning the inevitable leaving party gave us something to focus on especially for our own boys who were having a very rough half term holiday. They needed to have a soul-lifting event to cope with all that was going on around them and though there was the sadness of the children leaving looming in front, an excuse for inviting friends and making merry on a bouncy castle was good news. They all invited their close friends, many families popped in to say their farewells and to offer gifts and cards, the party was a wonderful end to this era, memories of the arrival of this doleful trio and all that we had encountered during the past two years drifted through my mind. I knew they still had a long way to go, but for them to get this far, to see the animated expressions of sheer joy on their faces, their ability to accept what was about to happen and to be in a position to face their next era was a credit to them all. The road in front of them would not be smooth, the bumps and potholes of life would shake their foundations, but I hoped eventually they would understand why they had to leave us, and the area, and try to leave some of their fears behind to enjoy a brighter future. Both Lawrence and I had sensed the shaky foundations in Aaron and Gareth, we would have to repair the damage caused.

Was their trust in us as thin as we felt it seemed? Aaron would talk out the way he felt, but Gareth held it in choosing not to share the depth of his feeling. In doing so we often felt punished by him for helping children to move on in life. For now, at least until the children left within the next twenty four hours, our concentration would have to be on emphasising the positives for their benefit, to keep their spirits high and focus on their need for their new parents. Aaron and Gareth were more than able to play their part to keep up appearances but, once removed from that situation, we knew their emotions would collapse in the crater of emptiness that was always left behind.

And so the last day arrived, a rather subdued trio came down for breakfast that morning and ate in silence. Their new parents held back from joining us until mid morning to give everyone time to pack and prepare. We tried desperately to lift the sprits of all the children, but Gareth was unable to hide his feelings, saying goodbye was never easy, but each time we had to say it to another family it just got so much harder. We all sat around the kitchen table to have a mid morning drink together, the children chattered quietly about the events of the past week in particular about the party. They talked of the many gifts they had received and their new home and family. We gave them each a parting gift to remember us by, not toys, they had more than enough, but something I hoped would prove to be of more significance the older they became, something I hoped they would appreciate. We had bought three silver napkin rings and had them engraved with their names on. They loved them; Jason immediately wrapped his up very carefully and came to give me the biggest hug imaginable. Our own boys used theirs that they had received as christening gifts, but I had used little wooden mouse shaped ones with leather ears for our trio. They also gave Aaron and Gareth gifts. Aaron had attempted to lighten the mood by trying to guess what his was which only served to encourage James to tell him! But Gareth broke down, it was all too much for him, he left his gift unwrapped at the table and ran off. I ached for him. We gave him a few moments to himself, and then I went to talk with him. He just sobbed, admitted he loved children coming to us, but hated it when it was time for them to go. I asked him to try to put on a brave face at least until they left then we would talk some more. His young years understood this need, I returned to the kitchen only to meet Jason on his way to look for me, he clung to my legs, I bent down to him and he whispered in my ear, "Do I really have to go?" I reminded him that yes he did, because a new life and a new beginning would help him grow stronger and grow up to be a good man. I reiterated our love for him would not change, but now he also had the love of more people, not just his new parents but also their families who would now be his family. Whilst this was happening the new Mum had spent time with Gareth helping him to overcome his feelings and encouraging him to open his gift. The children's bedroom was devoid of all their belongings, the silence in there echoed around the room. Their car was packed to the gunnels; all that was left was to strap the children into their positions in the car. Final hugs and kisses given, they climbed into their seats so Dad could buckle their straps. We all waved furiously to each other shouting our goodbyes as their car disappeared down the drive. They were gone.

Aaron was the first to speak, "Now it's back to just us Mum." He said quietly as we walked back into the house. He had spoken the truth but I could have choked on those words as he said them. Tears welled in all our eyes, Gareth let his fall but he said very little. Adjusting would prove difficult. I tried to accept that the time we had invested in this trio had been beneficial, though I agonised over the effects of the last two years. Our efforts to conjoin three families had finally been dissolved; all six had left today not just the threesome.

Our pact of raising each other's spirits had also been erased as both Lawrence and I were at our lowest point ever. Again he turned to his work to redirect his energy; mine was put into supporting the boys when they were not in school, and re-decorating the house when they were.

Yet again we would deliberate on whether we should continue to foster. But there was room in both our home and our hearts and when the need was so great, especially for family groups, it was far too difficult to say no. But could we rise above the hurt we all felt, and the loss we had endured to start all over again? I was yet to be convinced.

We were approached by our support worker who suggested that we made a visit to see the family about six weeks later to see that they had settled into their new home. She felt it was essential for us to feel more confident about the move and also very helpful for the children to understand that we did still exist and care about them. That 'out of sight, out of mind' was not reality.

Over the next few years we were to realise that fate had a strange way of working. All of the children had touched our lives, influenced the people we were and helped us to rethink different approaches to different problems and challenges that we faced. Between them they had taught us so much. We felt we had lost them, in actual fact they continued to pop up at the most unexpected moments when they needed help or advice, or just required to be supported temporarily to enable them to move on to the next step in their lives. Sometimes these contacts were wonderful, they could be short lived, open ended, sometimes devastating and at times damaging. There would be times when they expected answers to questions they were afraid to ask, occasionally they just needed to touch base, say hello, and know that we were still there for them. Sometimes we would have to go to extraordinary lengths to prove we still loved and cared for them, sometimes it would be necessary to put strong boundaries around their expectations of us, in order for us to keep some element of control when they were quite definitely out of control when deep in the teenage turmoil of confusion. Many people who knew us thought we were mad, stupid, and utterly ridiculous for what we put ourselves through. I genuinely did not care what they thought or felt, what mattered was how we felt.

We only have one chance of life; so the more you pack into it surely the more you get out of it? The next family of children to join us all too quickly taught us the meaning of love through a song that they learned in school.

*"If you've got some love then give it away, give it away, give it away,*

*If you've got some love then give it away, 'cos you'll end up having more."*

They frequently sang this during their early days with us, and believe me those words were really vital to them as a family

> *"To lose a child ... was something*
> *that could end one's world. One could*
> *never get back to how it was before.*
> *The stars went out. The moon*
> *disappeared. The birds became silent."*

(The No 1 Ladies Detective Agency)

*Alexander McCall Smith*

# CHAPTER 13

# So Now We Have Four

From June until September there were just the four of us. Initially it seemed so strange and weirdly manageable! Everything seemed so straightforward apart from coping with the huge emptiness of the void within each of us. On a daily basis its existence was noticeable, we functioned, but only on a practical level. I think each of us felt so emotionally and physically drained we had little left to give each other. There were so many unanswered questions left behind, and whenever I ever found myself facing these questions it only served to fill me with anger and a fury so strong that it was difficult to contain.

But time teaches each of us how to step over the craters of life, and during the next three months I was determined that the crazy system, that claimed to act in the best interests of children, would not bring us down any further. After all when you are at rock bottom is there any further to fall? Instead our focus was on the boys, helping them to express the way they felt, gain insight into their understanding and instead of asking for their time for others, giving them time instead. We planned a week in the caravan at our favourite place in the Dales, Brimham Rocks, where we could be in touch through our memories with all the children as we recalled some of their antics enjoyed there. We also planned a week in Scotland, which despite the rain, nay the flooding in the field, was great fun! I also had to overcome my health problem for which I had needed surgery three times during the previous year.

So it was that for the foreseeable future there were only the four of us, we guided the boys through their summer term, made the most of the school holidays, when anger or tears from our experiences arose within us, we used that adrenalin boosted surge on the garden. This way something beautiful would be born out of sheer damned frustration and pure anger. Gradually we started to piece our lives back together again, but what was our life without the aim we had started out with? We still had that inkling to help and support youngsters; we still lived in a house with a garden that could accommodate those children, what was more we still had the love, the time and the need to give. Yet again we weighed up the pros and cons, agonised over the 'should we or shouldn't we.' We listened to friends and relatives who were now convinced that we were totally insane to even contemplate fostering again after what we had gone through. Some even threatening to 'wash their hands of us,' I could understand how they felt; they had lived through our nightmare with us, but not in it. What they did not grasp was that our frustration and anger was aimed at the department, not at the children, and there were many, many children who needed help with fewer and fewer families being available for them. If we gave up something we so desperately believed in what would that actually achieve? Making a decision is always the hardest part, when made - you move forward! Once I had accepted my own position, understood the possible consequences, I was ready to move forward but only if Lawrence and the boys felt they were ready as well.

Lawrence's senior years left him balancing on the edge wondering how fair we were. But the boys were determined; of course we are having more children that is what we do! Their message resounded loudly and clearly, and Lawrence was dragged off the edge to the centre of our universe, we agonised over this no longer! I rang Emily on our return from Scotland in August 1988 to inform her we were ready to start again.

Within a week of the boys returning to school for the new term in September, the phone call came. We were being asked to look after a family of four, though there were actually five children involved. One child was living with his father, but only those with Mum would be coming into care as she had requested voluntary placements because she was struggling to cope.

So now four or at some stage even all five could appear, I had to bite my lip to stop myself from commenting on our previous situation. But then this was a family group and their placement was only a temporary one, not expected to be long term. We had been asked to take this group, as at the time there was no one else to take care of them unless the group was divided. There were three girls, aged eight and five years old and the younger one was fifteen months, the little boy was only eleven weeks. Mum was stressed, and in a relationship with the father of the youngest. This was not an unusual occurrence for this Mum to request for her children to go into care. History was repeating itself, as she had been taken into care as a child, along with her sisters when her own mother had left the family, leaving Dad to cope alone. Unfortunately he didn't cope. This Mum was not to return to the family home until she was aged fifteen when her father requested her return. Care Services had been her 'family', and as a parent she now resorted to them for her own support.

I wanted to ask Lawrence first and talk to the boys but they were not immediately available. I had to make a decision, and before I knew it I had agreed to take them. My understanding was that the placement was unlikely to be for very long, based on previous history they usually went back to Mum fairly quickly.

I set about preparing for the onslaught, bedrooms to get ready, a cot or two to set up, a meal to prepare and of course baby feeding and sterilising equipment to find. We had one cot in the attic, I rang Lawrence at work, and he came home in his lunch break to get it down so that I could wash it. I sorted all my baby linen out, washed, dried and aired it as this had been in store since Gareth had used it! I assumed the baby would arrive with bottles and food, but no such luck. My neighbour of the time had a toddler; aged two and a baby of about nine months old, both were boys. I hastily rang her and she came round with two baby bottles and a few clothes. Lawrence was reminded to get me disposable nappies a pack for each of the younger children. Cath, my pram-pushing friend of days gone by happened to ring me, I explained what was about to take place. She made her view of my decision succinctly clear. She was far from pleased, but recognising my inherent insaneness rallied around bringing me baby clothes from her daughter's doll. She also brought some additional bedding. She reiterated my stupidity in no uncertain terms, constantly reminding me of the previous two years and all that we had been through as a family, so demanded to know why were we doing this all over again? I listened, I had no choice, I tried to explain that this was not the same, and before long the children would be back with Mum, our role to support the children would be time limited! At the time Cath only lived five minutes away, so she insisted I was to ring her when the children arrived. I duly accepted the reprimand, thanked her for everything and went to collect the boys from school.

They were 'over the moon' with the news, Aaron insisting the baby would have to sleep in his room so that he was near our bedroom insisting that any crying would not disturb his own sleep. He was right, Aaron slept like a log every night. This left all three girls to sleep in the big bedroom. Their excitement could not be hidden, anyone would have thought I was about to give birth to quads. It was the happiest I had seen either of them since the trio left us. They busied about sorting toys and games that would be suitable for the girls to play with. They searched for baby rattles, and the bouncer chair. Between them they would continually bob up and down to look out of the window to see if there was any sign of the social worker's car.

Shortly after five o'clock two cars came up the drive, bringing our 'new' family group. The two older girls walked in looking pale and forlorn, they had long but very untidy hair, the two younger ones were carried in. I noticed the toddler first with her enormous saucer like eyes; this was Laura who remained unsmiling with a fixed stare, clearly frightened. She had rich auburn hair, was able to toddle quite well and was an exceptionally independent soul who listened to no one! The baby, Andrew, had a rough skin the texture of leather that was badly peeling; his scalp had the worst cradle cap I had ever seen, thick layers of an orange grey mosaic mass that lay across his scalp, with his thin wispy blonde hair struggling to grow through. His tiny hands were so tightly clenched, that it was to take a few days before we had him relaxed enough to let us see the cuts to his palms caused by his extraordinary long finger nails, that I doubt had been cut since his birth. He was incredibly tense, his whole body was stiff with fear or anxiety or both. The older girls were unusually chatty, especially the five year old, Penny, who spoke with a high pitched monotonous raised voice that was later to be described as being pitched to create maximum irritation. The volume alone was off the decibel scale and she was not even talking to anyone in particular! She clucked away in the background talking to herself, I struggled to make sense of anything she said at this time among all the confusion. Her pixie like appearance emphasised her short stature, and her scrawny limbs seemed out of proportion to her body. I immediately wondered if she had a growth hormone problem. The older sibling, Jenny, divided her time between holding on to the baby, getting annoyed with Penny and cooing to the toddler. I guessed that she had taken on a great deal of responsibility for all of them. At eight years old she had been 'Mum' to the children, I believed Andrew owed his survival to her. He was certainly her real live doll, and I was going to have to tread very carefully to gain full care of the little chap without upsetting her. Our peace was shattered, chaos surrounded us. Poor Lawrence walked in on all of this and he was initially shocked at the scene set before him. We certainly had our hands full!

Feeding the baby was a priority, but when we opened the tin that came with him there was barely enough to make half a bottle! But then, half a bottle was better than no bottle! I asked Lawrence to buy more from the village before the shops closed, he disappeared to his car, and I suspect glad to be away from the bedlam that had taken us over. Now I had a problem, I had never ever in my life had the need to make up a baby's bottle of milk! I hastily read the instructions during which time Jenny came over to show me what to do! Between us we succeeded in producing a bottle that would help to abate this poor baby's cravings. Aaron happily took over this part and was thrilled when baby Andrew gulped hungrily on the teat. He then very adeptly changed the baby's nappy; I was very impressed with his 'parenting' skill. The social worker sat down to fill me in with some of the information that she had, but agreed to call the following day when hopefully the children would feel a little more settled. Then it was roundup time, settling everyone else around the table to eat. Mealtimes always provided the necessary focus to calm a situation and though everyone would be together, they could also have their own personal space whilst being sociable. Mealtimes gave them that initial sense of belonging, even though they were only around the table. We would all be together; they would have their own identified place at the table, their own plateful of food to eat (this was quite a new experience to some children that joined us). Today was no exception. The highchair came out of it's hiding cupboard to be used again this time to provide a safe seat for little Laura, to reduce her fidgeting and give her space of her own close to the table. So we ate our first meal together, and as we ate I looked around the table and wondered what joys, hurt and disappointments were in store for us. Though there were smiles and giggles and an awful lot of noise, especially emanating from Laura, I had an underlying suspicion that whatever was to reveal itself was slightly uncomfortable. I just could not put my finger on the situation.

One of the greatest benefits of the older two girls was that they knew how to play and occupy themselves. Though they were easily distracted and could be very fractious, particularly with each other, they were reasonably pliable youngsters who wanted to please the adults around. A visit to the local church school was organised to arrange a starting date for the girls. I wondered how they would manage with Penny's high-pitched tones all day, but then her attendance there would give our ears a bit of a rest! Penny also found it very hard to talk directly to either Lawrence or myself, constantly talking to us through Jenny. She would ask her to "Tell that lady and mister that I don't like eating peas", even though we might well be sitting right next to her. This was very difficult to adjust to as she behaved as though we had no presence, as though she knew we existed but could not be seen, and certainly not spoken to. I was all the more determined to aim conversation directly towards her, but gaining eye-to-eye contact was virtually impossible. She had a strange attitude towards Lawrence which I put down to her own father leaving her Mum, and new men entering Penny's life but not staying around too long. Unless we were all to go around wearing earplugs to protect ourselves from her endless high-pitched squawking that now invaded our days, we knew it was essential to find a way to calm her down and bring her off her pedestal. She had an elevated view of herself and considered herself better and far more important than anyone else. If we had visitors she would talk constantly, usually to herself, dominating and invading everyone else's space at the same time. It was a skill I loathed and despised, and one we would have to find a coping strategy for.

But there had to be an underlying reason for such behaviour, it was so energy consuming, hers and ours!

In direct contrast Jenny was a rather quiet girl, but there ran an unpleasant streak through her, especially towards her five-year-old sister. She was a mother hen towards the younger two, and as long as they were responsive to her she tolerated them both well. But any adverse behaviour from them and she walked away and left them to their own devices. But towards Penny, she was wickedness itself. If anything went wrong Jenny would surely blame Penny, even though she was not responsible. Any opportunity to get Penny into bother or trouble Jenny revelled in. She would engineer situations for her sister to be caught in, then when Penny was seen to be admonished, Jenny would laugh and point her finger at her younger sister, almost taking delight in the child's downfall. Relationships seemed strong between them, but not necessarily for the right reasons. I also noticed that they rarely spoke of their brother who was living with Dad, but when they did it was with true sadness as they felt he should be with them. On the surface we seemed to have a workable family unit who may have had some strong positive experiences in their lives, but that undercurrent of uncertainty had an even stronger pull, that led us to believe that all that stood in front of us was not really what lay ahead of us! Gut feeling was uncomfortable at the best of times, but this gut feeling about this particular sibling group encouraged us to be patient. Whatever was lurking would surface, but would inevitably take time to do so.

Having a young baby around the house once again felt good, he provided innocence; he was a real charmer that absorbed all the activity that went on around him. Once he began to relax and respond more appropriately, he smiled more, which made the others smile too. Jenny began to relax, trusting me to take care of him, so letting down her guard as well as letting go of the responsibility of Andrew's care. One of the strongest concerns I had for this baby was his reaction when carried downstairs or down steps. Going down from any high point such as the top of the stairway caused him to be filled with fear, he seemed literally gripped by terror with a stiffness of body as he gasped for breath, this would take several minutes for him to relax and the aftermath was always a very quiet unsmiling baby. But normally Andrew would chirrup away in the background smiling and gurgling providing a reminder to all of them of their own origins and also unknowingly providing each of them an understanding of how a baby should be looked after! Aaron and Gareth particularly enjoyed his presence in the family, as they had not been involved in the day-to-day care of a baby. So between all of us there was always someone willing to give Andrew the attention he needed, and in his turn he provided a focus that distracted his siblings from concentrating on the hurt in their young lives. The hurt we were yet to discover.

The abrasiveness that existed between Jenny and Penny rattled on causing Penny to escalate the tone in her high pitched squealing whenever she spoke, which was usually to herself. This was very wearing on all of us, as this background monotonous 'sing-song' drone would start when she awoke and not rest until she went to bed. It was frequently accompanied by hyperactive behaviour, which became far more noticeable whenever visitors called. We were not certain whether her behaviour was attention seeking or attention diversion, but whatever had caused the problem between these girls had to be sliced, dissected, demolished, and attempts to rebuild relationships made. However we were also aware of how protective Jenny could be towards Penny and also how responsive Penny could be towards her sister in moments of stress or uncertainty of how to cope in given situations. The dynamics of their relationship increased the doubts in my mind of what was really going on in this family.

Then there was Laura, a very pretty little girl with those huge 'saucer like' eyes that were always on the alert, staring as she frowned, watching, waiting, as though she was on the lookout. Most toddlers of her age would crave to be held, cuddled and love to put their arms around others. But not Laura, there was a coldness of attitude if any one tried to pick her up or carry her. She froze in your arms holding her body away from those holding her. Her eyes exuded mistrust; the dour facial expression spoke volumes but yet said nothing. She seemed to live in her own little bubble chattering away, but her lack of interaction with others was very disconcerting. Even more strange was when I put Laura to bed in her cot she lay down instantly, never complained, never moved, never tried to get out. This was not normal. What were we missing? What were we not seeing? Why could I not see what was in front of me?

Lawrence and I would share our views of the children's behaviours, but we could never conclude the reasons for such adverse reactions. We talked with both our support worker and the children's in the hope that someone could throw light on their situation. I felt we had many jigsaw pieces spread out in front of us, but very few of those pieces joined together, and the gaps were too big to give a clear picture at all. In general, on the surface, their behaviour could collectively be as normal as the next child but move in closer and then the diverse strangeness they each displayed glared before you. Lisa, their worker, offered an explanation. Mum appeared to love her children very much, but since separating from the older children's father had felt very alone and vulnerable. Her new husband was older, did not really live in the family home, he preferred to live in his caravan. Their relationship seemed to be a strange one, very turbulent, and stemming from Mum's own needs for her husband to be around, and his stemming from only having the children around him when it suited. This often left Mum unable to fulfil her own needs so was totally unable to see those of her children. The more children she had the harder she struggled to cope. She seemed unable to respond to either of the boys in any way at all, to the point of ignoring their existence, resulting in total neglect. She saw the older two as one child, having wanted to call them by the same name. Laura had been a twin, her sibling died 'in utero'. Mum had recently had another miscarriage that she was getting over. Putting all these facts together certainly helped us to gain insight into why the girls behaved the way they did. We were later to discover that during the previous fifteen months, the whole of Laura's life, there had been no less than fifteen different moves in their lives, and those were only the ones that were known about. Those moves included previous fostering placements, hostels, family or friends, the caravan site.

Schooling had been very disruptive. Now we were getting to the bones of the matter!

We noticed that the girls hardly spoke of their own father unless it was in terms of their brother, whom of course had been sent to live with him a week or two earlier, as Mum really could not control or cope with his behaviour, and we were also told that this small boy had difficulties in school, well behind his peers with his education. Though nor did they speak very well of Mum's current husband, Jenny spoke in almost whispered tones whenever speaking of him, whilst Penny raised her voice another octave if she talked about him. Sometimes their conversations or manner of speech about their home situation left the listener feeling cold and uncomfortable, and yet there would be nothing in the content of their conversation that ought to have that effect.

On a daily basis we just got on with the everyday caring for the four of them, encouraging them to play, interact with each other, enjoy friendships and generally fit into our expectation of family life. To maintain a contact with Mum I encouraged Jenny to write her a letter, with which we sent some photographs of the children. Both the older girls were drawn to our box of paper and spent endless hours drawing pictures and colouring. This was when we realised how limited they both were. Penny had little control over her pencil, her colouring was not as defined as expected for her age, and indeed she had no colour recognition at all. Jenny was very careful with her pictures, they were usually very tiny, almost insignificant and coloured in very faintly. We also discovered their number skills were virtually non-existent, though Jenny could count comfortably from one to twenty, she was easily confused by the actual numbers, Penny was unable to recognise any number or retain the information when taught. We had to filter in as many learning opportunities into our day, which they responded to very well indeed. We would play counting games in the car, around the table, count the stairs as we mounted them, in fact we would do anything that introduced numbers, colours and letters into their lives.

I was getting accustomed to little Andrew's routine and the inevitable slight changes to his routine that his growing produced. Even coping with his night-time waking for a bottle was no problem. I did not bottle feed either of our boys, so discovering that I could share this responsibility with Lawrence was great, he usually did the late night feed, leaving me to manage the middle of the night, when it was necessary. Andrew was certainly a joy to have around and so easy to look after, well certainly at this stage! In contrast, young Laura was not so easy, held inside her own protective bubble that no one was allowed to enter, she kept all of us and even outsiders clearly at arms length. She never objected to being picked up but nor did she respond in a natural way, she still just slumped like a stiff bag of coal not sure of what to do, she did nothing but stare. But the moment she was put down she ran off to find her own little world again, chirruping away to herself like a bird set free. We also noticed how, instead of copying or relating to the older two girls, she would emulate the baby, she was fascinated by his toys, but would also pick up his baby bottle to drink the moment I put it down, or she would climb into the Moses basket the moment I took him out. She would just lie in it not moving. We took the assumption that, as she was only a year older than Andrew, she had possibly been pushed to one side to make room for the baby. But yet we knew the girls took priority over the boys. Things did not add up, they just made no sense at all. But whilst trying to analyse the 'why's and where fore's' in front of us we still needed to care for the four of them to the best of our ability. So with the dynamics between six children to consider we plodded on in our well rehearsed manner, the characters were different, the needs similar, the expectation high, we now needed to 'raise the bar' by pushing out our own boundaries of family life to incorporate each individual whilst helping them all to have positive, loving, sibling relationships. Better known in our house as a parental challenge!

We tried not to have 'problems' in our house, my theory was that if you called a glitch in life a problem, it weighed you down, so would in time bring you down. But call it a challenge and you would look for a solution and more often than not, you would find one! Equally, we rarely referred to something as being good or bad, but instead chose to refer to a situation or issue as being good or not so good, this helped us to find a glimmer of positivity even in our most difficult times. This attitude has helped the children enormously to accept their part to play, without feeling totally negative about some of those not so good moments, of which there were quite a few! On really difficult days we would encourage the youngsters to understand that the issue in question was totally unacceptable, but tomorrow was another day, and they could have another chance to prove to us that they understood where they had gone wrong and put it right! Sometimes they would just push their luck too far expecting too many chances to start all over again. On reflection many of these were their test to us, to push us to the brink of our own sanity, to knock us down and see if we would stand by them yet again. For far too many of the children that lived with our family a feeling of rejection sat under the surface of their character. Consequently that awful feeling could so easily overtake them, lowering their self-esteem, resulting in taking many steps backwards. This would be detrimental to one child, but in sibling groups you could feel the domino effect, when one had a difficulty it gradually affected the whole group, the only difference would be the resulting behaviours would manifest in different ways according to their ages and stages of life and their own individual experiences. This meant that as we helped or guided one child through an issue another would be crumbling and needing help, this certainly took its toll on Lawrence and me and of course on occasions also on Aaron and Gareth too.

An access visit was arranged for the children to spend time with Mum and her husband. I was asked if I was prepared to go along with the children to help the social worker, not only with the transporting of the four but also with the supervision in case any of the children had difficulty coping. We arrived at their own home to be welcomed by a young boy, Nathan, their brother, and a very tired drawn looking woman who thanked me so much for looking after the children. In the corner of the room sat an older man, her husband, who greeted the children by reaching his arms out to them one by one as he asked each one of the girls if they were ok. They did not reply. Lisa and I were invited to sit down. I still held Andrew, as I tried to hand him to Mum she simply said "In a minute", then went on to talk to the girls. The children seemed pleased to see their brother and also Mum, but as they all moved about in the centre of the small room they gave only a fraction of time to the man and there was no eye contact at all with him. He must have realised this as he moved forward to pick up Laura to sit her on his lap, she froze with that stare looking at the floor, not at him, he cupped her chin to turn her head towards him, she had no choice but to look at him, both Lisa and I were watching and feeling uncomfortable, he then smiled at Laura and said he missed her. Jenny went over to where they were sitting to hold Laura's hand and gently pulled her, telling her to dance with her and Penny. Laura responded by getting off his knee to join her sisters. Penny was singing louder than all the rest as they played around quite noisily, and though the man called each child none of them went near him or looked in his direction. We tried again to get Mum to hold Andrew, this time she took him but held him away from her as I explained how he had progressed. She smiled, nodded, and thanked me again, then gave Andrew to Lisa. Then Mum got out a carrier bag and asked the children to sit down to see what she had for them. She gave each one something out of the bag, explaining that their gift was for each of them to remind them of home. They were asked to take their gift to show the man, as each went towards him he leaned forward cupped their chins pulled each child nearer to him giving him direct eye contact, he told them how lucky they were, that it would not be long before they were back home and they would have fun together again. There was an instant calming down in the room; even Penny and Nathan were quiet and they had been the noisiest of all. Nathan was asking if he could come back with us, saying it wasn't fair if he was on his own. After an hour it was time for us to leave, I went out of the door first holding on to Laura, the man stood by the door holding a forlorn Nathan by the wrist, he systematically took back each gift given to the children saying he would look after them until they came again. Not one child questioned this until they were in the car. I tried desperately to offer an acceptable excuse for what he had done, then Jenny spoke out, "He never really gives us nowt, 'cos he always takes it back." Penny added, "He gives us sweets!" Jenny pulled a face at her sister, "You mean he gives you goodies." Those words were spoken wrapped in venom. We travelled back home in silence.

On our return home the girls quietly disappeared into the sitting room to watch television with the boys, whilst Lawrence took the younger two to get them organised for bed. Lisa and I stayed in the kitchen to talk. Both of us had felt uncomfortable about the gift retrieving and how dejected the children had felt. We shared our views on Mum's reluctance to hold the baby, and how neither of them particularly gave him time. But what had really unnerved us was the strong dominance that man had held over all the children simply by cupping their chins to draw them towards him. We both had similar distasteful feelings, we both sensed the anxiety in all the children, and their smiles had not been the warm, glad to be at home type. The children's walking around in the middle of the room constantly on the move had left us wondering what was going on, why had they seemed afraid of settling down. Lisa was not certain whether Nathan was living at the house or just visiting because the children were also visiting, and felt that needed looking into. Our combined concerns were ringing warning bells but not loud enough for anyone to hear or answer.

About ten days later a review was held to discuss the placement and the criteria required within the family home before the department was prepared to let the children return home. Our views and thoughts were raised and listened to, the many moves the youngsters had experienced was an influencing factor also. Lisa had approached the schools for the reports for the girls and Nathan, which indicated deep problems. We now discovered a possible reason for Andrew's fear of heights, the police had been called out to a report of a woman who was threatening to drop the baby she was holding over a motorway bridge, whilst telling a group of children she would throw them over too, one by one. These children were that group, and Andrew was that baby. Mum had been totally out of control and a question mark hung over a diagnosis of post-natal depression. The decision was taken to make it clear to the parents that there would be no more voluntary care, the children needed stability and care orders would be necessary in the future to offer the children greater protection. "It seems Nathan is living back with Mum, if Mum requests to have the children home soon, but a breakdown in the family occurs again, how would you feel about having them all back including him?" Enquired the care manager. Well, we had managed the four what difference could one more make? Both Lawrence and I agreed that in that event we would be prepared to take them all, of course it would mean Gareth being open to the idea of sharing a bedroom with Nathan.

Little more than a week later whilst the girls were at school and I was playing with the tots, we had a phone call to say Mum felt ready to take the children back, that same day, could I get everyone ready for about five that afternoon as transport had been arranged to pick them up. I tried to be stoical and sensible as I packed up their few belongings and rehearsed in my head how I would tell them all the news. There would be precious little time from school pick-up to leaving us, so an early tea was organised.

Lawrence collected the children from school that afternoon; I explained to the girls what was about to happen and how Lisa would arrive shortly to take them back to Mum. "Why?" asked Penny, this time she actually looked at me and spoke to me, not through Jenny, as she was prone to doing. They were not impressed, and though they ate, their appetites had plummeted along with their mood. I kept up an act of all things being positive, telling them that Mum was really looking forward to having them back, that they would be going back into their own schools, meeting up with their own friends, anything to instil confidence into them to help them cope and adjust yet again. Lisa and a colleague arrived whilst they were finishing tea, as each child left the table they were donned in coats, shoes put on, another round of hugs and kisses given, then they were taken to the waiting cars to be taken back. We waved as they craned their necks to see us out of the rear window, their sad faces looking at us. What a shock to their system this had seemed, they were not ready to go back, but Mum considered she was ready to have them back. I hoped and prayed that she really was for the sake of those little ones.

I hugged our boys, and once again we talked as positively as possible about our expectations for the children when they got home. We both reiterated what fantastic lads they had been in helping the children with their learning of all things, but most of all with the way they shared their lives, their home and their crazy, mad-cap parents so willingly. We got out a family game to play together and have a laugh together, to remind ourselves we were a family, and we were strong enough to cope with all of this because in comparison to what the children had to put up with our lot was not so bad after all. I just cannot remember who won the game!

*Home is the place where boys and
girls first learn how to limit their wishes,
abide by rules, and consider
the rights and needs of others.*

*Sidonie Matsner Gruenberg*

*Child-study Expert (1881 - 1974)*

# CHAPTER 14

## And Now Five

Part of me did not want to believe that the children's return home would collapse again, but then their history did not fill me with confidence either. We had agreed to take all five should it become necessary, but how long did I put our family on hold? I decided to carry on with the decorating of Gareth's bedroom. During the middle of the second week of our freedom Lisa rang to see if our intention to have the children back was still a possibility. She explained that the situation was not good and would I be prepared, just in case of a breakdown within the family.

There I was standing on the top of a ladder painting walls! Never has a paintbrush moved so swiftly to get the room finished, as quickly as possible, and return the furniture with the addition of an extra bed to accommodate Nathan.

It seems that when the children returned home the stepfather had been imprisoned for a month but was due to be released a few days later. Lisa's visits to the home revealed that the children were very unhappy, the younger two were subdued, Jenny was slamming doors and going to bed the moment she came in from school, Penny was pleading with Lisa to go with her, and Nathan switched from hiding in a corner to running wildly. The couple's endless arguments were affecting the children badly too. Care proceedings had commenced.

Then events took a different turn, Jenny and Nathan had been sent around to the house of a Grandma figure in their lives to take something or collect something, but sadly had discovered that Grandma was dead. This caused the whole family to reel and crumble, as she had been their strongest support. Mum called for voluntary care again and given the circumstances this was accepted putting the care proceedings on hold for a week. Consequently I was asked to meet the social worker at their house to collect the children. The girls were to travel in my car whilst the boys were to be in Lisa's.

I arrived minutes after Lisa, Mum thanked me for taking them, I looked around the room, and never have I seen five children look so shell-shocked. Even Penny was quiet, very pale and frightened beyond belief. She asked if she could come back to my house, I told her she could; she nodded and held on to my hand. Jenny was standing against the door that led to the kitchen, staring at the floor, I walked over to her and put my arm around her shoulder, she gave no response. "You want to come too?" I asked. She nodded. I gestured a nod towards the front door. It was then I saw Andrew in the pushchair, I could have wept, that beautiful lively baby I had returned home was lifeless, so thin, and his skin, especially his scalp, was as bad as ever. Laura, with her huge eyes, sat on the floor motionless, totally unresponsive. Young Nathan was the only one talking, asking what was going on, could he go with the girls. He was garrulous, his speech almost incomprehensible, his face looked rubber like, no real muscle tone, which made clear speech difficult to achieve. I gathered the girls as Lisa took the boys, we tried to encourage the older ones to say their farewells to Mum, but they barely looked at her. Laura slowly soaked in the familiarity of the car interior, she chirruped, only once on the whole of the half hour journey. Jenny remained silent all the way back. Penny actually talked to me, still high pitched; she was shaking with every muscle of her body tense and taut. Over and over in my mind I kept asking myself what on earth had caused them to be in this state, they were so weary, exhausted and emotionally drained.

I reached our house minutes before Lisa so had just got in as she drove up to bring in the boys. Their collective response as we walked into the kitchen was unbelievable and almost heartbreaking. Relief hit them all simultaneously as four of them stood in the centre of the kitchen looking around, though it was Nathan's first time in our home he obviously felt the relief of his sisters, again he was the only one to speak, asking endless questions. In contrast the girls held hands in silence, their eyes searching around the room checking that everything was as they remembered it two weeks earlier. I watched them physically and emotionally melting before me, I felt sick with anger that they were reduced to being physical wrecks in only two weeks. Why? How? Little Laura repeated her behaviour of slowly soaking in the environment; a small smile appeared on her face it was as though inside she had a 'deja vu' feeling and then to confirm it she went to the toy cupboard in the kitchen, she then positively beamed when she saw the familiar toys, she chirruped again, but her smile was for herself, not to be shared, she had made that protective wall around herself even thicker, she needed no one save Jenny or Penny and even they were held at a distance. Her warmth had gone, she was emotionally frozen from within. Lisa gave Andrew to me, he had no muscle tone at all, lifeless and expressionless and clearly undernourished. He was only nineteen weeks old, just how far back does one so young regress? I looked around at this forlorn group. It was then I noticed another problem, oh no, not this, not today of all days. I gestured to Lisa to look at Nathan's head; she frowned, not understanding what was wrong. I put my hands on his shoulders so the back of his head was facing Lisa, as her eyes came out on stalks I knew she now had seen the same as me. We glanced at the heads of the girls, only to confirm the extent of the problem I now faced. We had an infestation of head lice, not the odd nit or two, but between them more of a city community! Their heads shimmered with the movement of the little beggars. Nathan's hair literally had a life and movement of it's own. The older girls long hair would be a nightmare to clear. This put a whole new meaning to feeling 'lousy!' These poor souls were in a state of shock, coping with the loss of their home and parents, a death, general neglect and now the indignity of hosting the worst ever infestation. Just which part of them did we attend to first?

Lunch! Feed the soul! Bring that sense of belonging to them, and increase their confidence by providing the routine they knew from their previous stay, at the same time laying down a foundation for Nathan to build on. Lisa chose to leave, she had unfinished work at the parents home and had promised to return there. I gathered the brood around the table to eat, though the girls ate little, Nathan more than made up for them. Penny and Laura were so weary I suggested a quiet lie down in bed. Surprisingly Penny agreed, her tenseness had not diminished and as she left the table she ran to the bathroom and vomited profusely. I put this down to her emotional state even more convinced of the benefit of sleep for her. In a short time I had the three younger ones asleep in their beds. This gave me time to sit with Jenny and Nathan, one quietly ruminating over her situation, the other becoming more exuberant and excitable about his new home wanting to discover everything all at once, though he was seven years old, his behaviour was more akin to that of a two to three year old.

I phoned Lawrence suggesting he called at the chemist to collect a shipping load of head lice shampoo! Suddenly Jenny leapt off the sofa and ran to the bathroom, she too vomited violently, and her emotions had caught up with her also. Afterwards she curled up on the sofa with me and wept as I held her, she said absolutely nothing, but silently sobbed. Just how cruel could life be?

Witnessing all of this had a profound effect on me, I felt responsible for being a part of all this hurt and pain even though I knew otherwise. But I had helped them into the cars that took them home. More so I had set them up to believe that all would be well. While we had laughed, played and lived in our house, they had cried and inwardly 'died' in theirs. We had given them six weeks of good living but did that only set them up for a greater fall on their return? Guilt hung heavily, but I was not going to take that on my shoulders alone, the department that made the decisions would be made to share that guilt. I needed to know that all that could have been done had been done, that every attempt to protect them had been taken. I knew we were only mere foster parents, minions in the scheme of things, but at the end of the day we were left picking up the pieces of fragile emotions, shattered lives, and the consequences thereafter, at least until they moved on.

The rest of that day passed by in a rather subdued manner coping with the fragility of both youth and human nature. When the boys returned from school they were surprised and delighted to see the children, but overwhelmed by the heavy atmosphere of such sadness. The feeling of melancholy literally hung in the air so strongly you could touch it. I was glad when bath time came and I could get them all ready for bed, it would help them to relax before settling down for the night, and hopefully after their bedtime stories, they would fall into a deep sleep and wake up feeling more refreshed and hopeful of a better day ahead. Under more normal circumstances each child would be given his or her own story time befitting their age and interest, but tonight they were all functioning at a very low level, tonight they would have a shared story time. They seemed to need to be in each other's company. Dynamics between the family group had changed, the pecking order now included Nathan and his appearance was another piece in the jigsaw completing another part of the picture. By the time they were all asleep in their beds I felt confident we could manage or at least cope with this brood, we had even stemmed the head lice situation. We just needed to get Nathan adjusted to the ground rules of our household, or adjust ourselves to having Nathan in the household! Another family challenge!

But as I reflected on the day, something else niggled me that was not within my boundaries of normal living with children. All children sported bruises, we were used to that. Sometimes they would have some quite hefty looking ones that you felt sure they must know how they received them, but if you asked them they never knew as they acquired them with the rough and tumble of life. But at bath time I had noticed bruising in unusual places on three of them. I searched my mind for possible scenarios of these occurring but could not come up with anything that made sense. I was to agonise at length over these bruises until I had a chance to share the facts with Lisa. Her reaction proved to me that I was right to be concerned. She explained that the children had shown trust in our family and to be aware of anything they might say that gave insight into what may have happened at their home.

One would have expected that the disruption that these children had experienced over the past year alone should have resulted in more bizarre behaviours being displayed, but yet again on the surface they desperately tried to behave 'normally,' but the underlying telling behaviours were rising, but what were they actually telling us? During the review, two weeks after their return, it was recognised that the short return home had had a detrimental effect on the children and it would take time for their confidence and trust to grow within the stability afforded to them by us.

Penny had needed an enormous amount of attention especially during the first forty-eight hours of rejoining our family. She was calling out in her sleep constantly as she was so emotionally distraught. On waking she would be exhausted but have no memory of the night-time events. This crying and calling out was so distressing and also so disturbing to the other girls in the room we decided to have her in our room in a makeshift bed to let the others sleep, but we would get very little sleep. We had also had to take them for the usual health and dental checks that highlighted that Penny needed a general anaesthetic to have four teeth removed, more trips to the dental hospital. Along with her siblings, Penny needed to get her immunisation programme up to date as this had been ignored in the past but was another source of stress to her. Jenny also required some dental treatment, but we decided to wait until she gained more confidence, she was also showing signs of stress during her sleep hours. Sleepwalking was to become a big issue, along with her safety and that of her siblings. There would be no indication of when this would happen, and ransacking the clothes drawers was a big part of her night-time adventure sleepwalks. She refused to believe that she was responsible for the mess in the bedroom in the morning and instead blamed her sisters even though Penny was with us and Laura was in a cot.

Nathan was at a disadvantage, as he had yet to learn the house rules, which he could not remember from day to day. He was a boy of routine, so we had to have a strict routine for him to live within to be able to cope. It was so difficult to see the world through his eyes, incredibly hyperactive, considered to be educationally subnormal, he loved to have an interaction with us but only from behind the thick imaginary 'brick wall' he had built around himself. He was to make our waking days and eventually that of his schools a living hell, with his testing and trying behaviours as he struggled to accept the basic rules in life that allowed everyone else to survive. But the rejection from birth that he had experienced had resulted in an admission to hospital by the time he was little more than a year old, his serious condition was the direct result of the physical neglect he lived through, or in reality almost died of. All the signs were that history was repeating itself for Andrew. But not anymore, young Andrew was with us, and I longed to keep it that way. I had missed him so very much during the two-week return to his family home. Andrew had returned a pathetic dull and lifeless scrap of humanity. The sparkle in his eye had been replaced by a glazed look and an unresponsive withdrawn baby. His skin condition had deteriorated. The severe eczema affected every area of his body. His tiny bottom looked as though it had been burned, the skin was so red and raised. The dry scaly skin fell about him like a dust cloud every time he was moved. There was no tone to his body, and for the first forty-eight hours he barely moved when put down in his cot. Jenny had told me that she had fed him because Mummy wouldn't. Then added, but sometimes as they didn't always have baby milk she gave him ordinary milk or just water.

Jenny and Penny were to return to the local church school where they were welcomed with open arms. Nathan needed a school but was to see the educational psychologist to establish the right place for him. His endless new placements in so many schools, and his poor attendance, had resulted in very poor progress; his behaviour in school had been horrendous. Initially we kept him at home and I taught him on a one to one basis helping him to recognise shapes, numbers, the alphabet, colours etc. By the time he had an appointment to see the psychologist, Nathan was more relaxed, relatively happy though still hyperactive, he was able to show off his progress in his new learning, so the decision was made for him to attend the nearest special school to support his obvious needs. Another challenge for us!

Initially Nathan tried hard to please everyone, going on the small school bus with about ten other children.

Unfortunately he was one of the first to be picked up which meant he would be travelling for an hour and a half whereas a car journey was only about fifteen minutes. Poor Nathan struggled to cope with the school environment as much as the school struggled to cope with him. We offered to take Nathan into school but we were firmly told that would not be possible as all the children were collected by bus or taxi. To us this was ridiculous, so we challenged the school but they stuck to their principals insisting that he was to be transported by bus. Naturally Nathan rebelled. The fuss and furore we endured was a daily challenge, and each day took more time to persuade him to conform, to be ready on time and be prepared to go to school each day. The bus arrived at ten minutes past seven, this meant getting him up, dressed and breakfasted in time. Our morning would start at about five, he struggled to wash and dress himself, was usually not awake enough to eat breakfast, but as soon as he heard that bus come up the drive Nathan revved into his own fifth gear, racing around, talking or shouting to us or to no one in particular about why he was not going on the bus. The doors would be unlocked and we would be encouraging him to enter, but Nathan fought, flailed, kicked and swore. This behaviour was repeated daily. We were told to persevere, that eventually he would accept going to school more easily. They did not know Nathan! Coming home was even more of a challenge. The bus drew up, the driver waited until I was near the door before opening it, then out leapt Nathan, flinging his bag anywhere, cussing and moaning about that "Horrible school, not going there again, I hate it, why do you send me there? I'm not going again" Every word was spat out of his mouth with utter contempt and hatred as he squirmed and flailed, inevitably throwing himself onto the floor to avoid being caught by us. We had tried letting him run loose but when he was out of control he could not handle the freedom given to him, open spaces were huge voids that filled him with fear and anxiety that heightened his reactions and prolonged the behaviour. What he needed was to be held whilst throwing out his uncontrollable feelings, and though he fought back when anyone tried to hold him, he also recovered much more quickly even though these sessions went on for lengthy periods. Most days I would have helped Nathan recover and he would be settled and playing happily by the time our boys came home from school. On one such day, when Nathan was struggling to control and manage his pent up feelings, I was equally struggling to contain his flailing arms and kicking legs, it was like catching an octopus in the kitchen doorway. Suddenly Aaron and Gareth arrived home, both boys took a great stride over the top of Nathan and me without batting an eyelid at the sight set before them, as they did so they said in unison "Hi Mum, hi Nathan." They proceeded to make themselves a drink; I was in shock as I looked at them. This rather strange behaviour of Mum and small boy grappling on the floor was accepted as the norm in our house! I could not believe it. Furthermore there was no progress made in the school, Nathan had stopped learning, in fact he had gone backwards. Time to state our case. At the next review we insisted that an alternative school was considered, we were told we had not given him a chance to settle and adapt. All I could see was that in real terms Nathan's negative behaviour was shouting his intentions, disrupting everyone, there were no positive values to even look at. Back to the educational psychologist! We explained that we felt Nathan was yet again segregated from his sisters, to him a form of rejection, at a time when he really needed to be with them for a sense of safety, identity and strength. Eventually we had to go one step further and put his placement with us on the line. Our message was clear, move him to another school, preferably to be with his sisters and receiving the support he desperately needed, or find him a new home. These people were making decisions for him but not dealing with the consequences, now we were asking them to. Losing Nathan was not what we wanted to do, we knew that would not be fair, but nor could he, or any of us, continue living with the daily battle we were expected to endure, it was far too destructive to everyone, as every day started and ended with dread and fear. Nathan was given a chance to start afresh at his sisters' school, the problems did not entirely go away, they just evolved and changed. Most teachers coped with his bizarre behaviours using a form of rejection; maybe he was just too much to handle given the needs of all the other children. One headmaster at one of the many schools he attended told us to forget about him, as he had been damaged beyond belief, forget about him and deal with the others if they still have a chance. I challenged the social worker again, I was livid, and how dare this man of education tell us to give up on him, a child aged seven! Whenever a school could not cope, which was most days, we would be contacted to remove him from the school for that day, however this could happen several times a week. Once home Nathan would be fine. How can you sit in a classroom to learn if your wits are on high alert because your safety is threatened?

Family life with seven children was full, entertaining, plenty of laughs and at times great fun, conversely it could also be, hectic, frustrating, tearful, demanding and a never ending roller coaster of emotions. Every day always had plenty to offer, not always what we expected, sometimes it did not reach our expectations; whilst at other times it exceeded them. Life was a constant juggling act to accommodate their endless activities both in and out of school. Travelling was always in convoy; twice the petrol usage was the price we paid for separating the sibling rivalry when it occurred, at least until we reached our destination and they met up again! But on the whole they did get on well together, they shared the trials and tribulations in life, encouraged each other to succeed, but most of all supported each other when the chips were down. There was only one way when they could not do that and that was if one of our famous five was locked in their own personal distress relating to their past. There had to be a key to it all.

Through all of this, certain behaviours surfaced that left doubt in our minds about what had happened in their own family. Whenever I went through the box of paper with all their drawings and colourings I would find a picture that did not quite make sense. Their schoolteachers were also discovering similar behaviour. Penny in particular could not verbalise her feelings but was constantly drawing pictures of her family or herself. On one occasion in school she drew a picture of our family, all nine of us were clearly depicted. We were each drawn as a stick man with a separate rectangle drawn around us. There was a circle drawn around all nine rectangles enclosing them, and then on the edge of one side of the circle was a dark and prominent splodge.

Her teacher asked me what I thought she was saying as Penny had refused to speak when asked. So I asked her, she carefully explained that we were all safe in our own beds; the circle was our house keeping us safe. The splodge? Penny looked frightened, leant towards me and in a low voice so 'Miss' didn't hear said "That is the lock on the door, so no one can get in." I asked her how we could get out, perhaps to go to school or go shopping, she relaxed a little, "Oh that's alright, 'cos you have the key in your pocket see?" she said pointing to the picture of me, I was the only one with a small pencil mark sticking out of my side, the key. Why was there such an emphasis on feeling safe? This was even more exaggerated than our other foster children and was reiterated by her siblings in different ways. Other pictures that she drew included those of all five children on one side of the page, whilst Mum was on the other side; stepfather was depicted away from everyone. This one was explained by Penny as being 'everyone is where they need to be,' so when I asked what she meant she replied, "Well all the children are together and safe, Mum is over there, she is not with the children any more, and he is not going to be with anyone, 'cos he has a big stick." She was telling me something but I just couldn't grasp it. Then I found another drawing of hers. It was the head and shoulders of a girl wearing a hat with a flower on a stalk sticking out of the top, the mouth was stretched wide with big pointed teeth. The face had been coloured in a deep red, the teeth were black, green and brown, and she had crayoned the eyes blue and orange. The hat was striped, each section a different colour. She must have used an incredible amount of effort to colour the whole picture and worn down every crayon as she had pressed on so harshly throughout the picture. It was ugly. I could not imagine what was going through her head for her to even think about such a gross drawing. Then whilst I was studying it she came over to stand at the side of me. "What are you looking at?" She quavered in a soft voice. "This" I said, "Who is it?" I was hoping it was a character from a story she had heard at school, Penny paled, tears welled, the words stuck fast in the back of her throat, then she quietly shook out the answer, "Me." I reached out to her circling my arm around her shoulder, "But you don't look like that do you?" Penny let the tears fall, I stood up to get a small mirror from the drawer, "See Pens, you are much prettier than that, it can't be you, can it?" Penny nodded, "It is me when I am at my Mummy's house and he is there, 'cos I am always angry, angry, angry." She lowered her head; silent tears flowed, but no anger. I asked her what sort of thing happens at Mum's house to make her so angry. Penny tried to tell me in her own words, I felt certain I understood what she was saying, but she was five years old, her vocabulary was limited to that of the average three year old. I just did not want to believe my own interpretation of what she said.

Each child was enveloped by it's own sadness, but if the flap of an envelope was lifted unspoken vibes would escape and cause one of the others to lift a flap to their own, to let some of their unhappiness escape.

As I put Nathan to bed one evening, he talked about living with his Dad and Dad's girlfriend. Most of it was positive, but he explained how much he had missed his sisters and wanted to be back with his Mum to be with them, especially after that night when Dad was at work and the girlfriend had a boy friend in. He tried to explain, but kept repeating that he did not know what happened only that it really hurt. He clearly felt better that he had talked about the strange events, but I was left filling the gaps and I did not like the filling provided.

And so the reverberations between them crept on. Silently, deadly, determined to destroy every scrap of trust built between us. Neither knew what each had said, nor shared with their siblings. But those capable of speech more than understood what they had been told by the perpetrator in the event that they told anyone. I knew I had to tell the support worker, I was also aware that I risked losing the children's trust in us for doing so.

I shared all with the social workers involved. It was just before Christmas. Arrangements were made for medicals to take place, and enough evidence was discovered to warrant police involvement for action to be taken. We tried to rise above it all, to create normality, to bring order to the fold. This was far from easy.

The atmosphere in our house left you unable to breathe. I didn't care if it was the middle of winter, I needed every window open, for we could still not breathe. The air was a dense, heavy blackness that filled our home, in every crevice, hanging lankly from ceiling to floor.

Walls of trust and confidence are fragile when first made, time strengthens them, but doubt can destroy the structure so easily. When a child has reasons to mistrust, walls crumble quickly as the cement does not get time to dry. And so they did. As fast as we rebuilt them, the children's doubts, fears and anxieties would erode our every effort.

After the police and social worker left that evening I just wanted all of us to get out of the house, we needed to change the mood of everyone. At this stage Aaron and Gareth were unaware of why our home was so unhappy.

They were confused and bewildered. Lawrence and I fluctuated from being 'OTT' angry to being fiercely protective; neither of these responses was appropriate for any of our children. We took them all out for a late tea to the local 'Happy Eater' restaurant a short drive away to give us the space we needed and to be in touch with a more positive world other than the one we now existed in.

But did we now know everything, or had we only dealt with the tip of the iceberg? Again only time would tell.

A long winter was in front of us but Christmas provided the focus we all needed, to put the ugliness to one side and remind ourselves that life could also offer and provide good times. With their initial relief from the release of their locked in experiences, the children enjoyed a happy Christmas with us, but some of that peace stemmed from uncertainty and anxiety. There were no parental access visits over this time, so they could relax and distance themselves from any retribution that might come their way from letting out the secret.

After the festivities were over, periodic visits to Mum continued, that is when she turned up, but those to Step Dad were discontinued. The children were physically sick before and after virtually every visit, they dreaded going, it was suggested that I stayed for the duration of the visit but in another room, so if any of the children could not cope they could be filtered through to me. The biggest problem was Mum's insistence in talking about her husband to the youngsters. We suspected this was either her infatuation with him, or her way of reminding them all that he was still very much on the scene, or perhaps a combination of the two. The disturbed behaviour displayed after every visit, was more than evident whether Mum arrived for the visit or failed to turn up. Why was everyone so surprised at how little they could learn or absorb when all the time they were being subjected to continual stress?

During the late springtime we squeezed in a holiday to our beloved Brimham, an escape from the everyday trials, from schools, and judgemental people. Joke! The older ones coped admirably, Laura's whole disposition changed. Endless wailing, crying, at times screaming, refusing to eat, to smile, to be her! It was so pitiful and at the same time exasperating to witness. She remained in this morose state until we came home, then with one quick look around the house, knowing she was home once again made her smile, and settle down a little, but the protective bubble of hers was wrapped around her once more, and would last for about three weeks before she began to truly relax again. Talking to the social worker we realised that we had taken her away from her safe haven and recreated the environment, i.e. the caravan, where her initial abuse had taken place, reviving the painful memories that she held deep within her.

Eventually the care orders were obtained and the need to consider their future was imperative. Adoption was the route of choice, so visits to their Mum were terminated. Meetings were held to discuss the situation and the way forward. Planning ahead meant being prepared. Once more I found myself engulfed and immersed in Life Story Work with the children. My main aim was to help them to come to terms with their young lives, help them to be proud of whom they were, to cope with the recent events without it being allowed to ruin the rest of their lives. This was only the beginning of rebuilding their characters, their confidence, their self worth and the greatest need for all, their trust. Eventually they would need to step out into the world to do it for themselves, but that was a long way off.

*"Trouble is part of your life, and if you don't share it, you don't give the person who loves you enough chance to love you enough."*

*Dinah Shore*

*U.S. singer and television host (1917 - 1994)*

# CHAPTER 15

## Home search

So many to deal with, so much to do. Some days we surged forward, made progress, other days we moved backwards. Then there were the 'treading through treacle' days when life just seemed an uphill struggle for everyone. Nathan was constantly creating problems in school, and therefore we were regularly requested to bring him home, so most afternoons were spent helping him to gain understanding into his behaviour and the triggers that occurred. This was time consuming along with all the other time consuming necessaries. Moreover we were exhausted by Penny's ongoing nightmares, calling out, crying and screaming. Baby Andrew was now on the move, crawling around, and we were dealing with Laura's dark moods and frozen watchfulness, she trusted no one. Setbacks for one or the other could easily arise and were as much initiated by the small changes in life, as being affected by the bigger issues in their lives. The unpredictable behaviours had to be faced head on, in an effort to reduce the rumble factor and the domino effect between the siblings. I was reaching the end of my tether finding myself asking how much more could one family take?

Their original social worker, Lisa, had changed jobs, and was replaced by another, June. She was of a different calibre, and I did not feel she had the strength of character to get to grips with the difficulties of the children; it was as though it was too much to face, which I expect it was. She had yet to gain the trust of our five. They felt dejected at losing Lisa who had been with them for quite a while and knew their background history. Nathan blamed himself and his behaviour for Lisa's decision to leave; convincing him otherwise was a marathon task. Now they were being told it was time for them to move on, which loosened their foundations, causing ructions at every twist and turn in life, by day and by night. Lawrence and I worried about the lack of progress with Nathan, at times the disruptions he caused and the subsequent effect on the others was soul destroying. We questioned how long we should or could continue with him at the expense of the others. After yet another not so good day at school, Nathan had been brought home mid afternoon. He was fine by teatime, the only one that was! Displaying his hyperactive, exuberant demeanour, talking ten to the dozen whilst all the rest were morose and miserable. Suddenly he asked what was wrong with everyone, why were they all unhappy! I flipped; I lost it, total loss of control. We had been sensitive to their situation; we had handled all that came along, this needed a different approach but not quite what came out of me!

Voice raised, temper surfacing, I glared at Nathan. "They are feeling miserable because of the way you behave and upset everyone every single day. Don't you see that?" I bawled at him. The rest stared at me, stopped eating and waited for the next move. "Well, what would they do if that man and Mum came knocking on your door?" He shouted back. The others again waited in silence, but both Penny and Jenny looked at me wanting to hear the answer. What would I do? Control now flew out of the window. Wrapped in anger at the very thought of those people knocking on my door, I silently walked across the kitchen to the knife block whereupon I withdrew the longest bladed knife that I owned. I turned back to the seven children sitting around the table. Their eyes on stalks, mouths wide open. Then I launched into just exactly what I would do! "I would use this knife to cut them into tiny pieces, they would be strawberry jam on my doorstep, I would tell them to go away and never come back." I couldn't stop myself, but I realised that the older three were smiling, they were enjoying watching and hearing my anger and my 'actions' of retribution were what they needed to hear. At which point the telephone rang. I was trying to deal with my children. I did not need this interruption right now. I grabbed the telephone, "Yes?" I spat down the receiver. "Oh have I rung at the wrong time?" said a quietly spoken June. I roared on, "Actually, yes, you have, I am just brandishing the biggest knife I possess over all the children." "Oh alright, I'll ring you back in the morning." She quietly replied. I put down the receiver; the call had acted as an icebreaker. I then turned back towards the table to see seven pairs of eyes fixed on me; all were waiting for me to finish what I had started. I came to my senses and realised what I was doing. I lowered my voice and the knife, saying as I did so, "Only I wouldn't really do that, that is how I might feel, but if I did it I would be as bad as they were and I would have to go to prison and then where would you all be? Who would look after you? You would have to go into care wouldn't you?" Their open mouths dissolved into smiles then fits of raucous laughter. My drama had stated the obvious, as Gareth acted as spokesman, "But Mum, five of us are already in care." His words gave the perspective that the children needed to hear. They then got on with their tea chatting among themselves. But a chill ran up and down my spine. What had I just done? What effect would such stupid behaviour have on the children, how would they interpret my actions and intentions? Even worse, what of June? I waited expecting to hear sirens sounding, cars flying up our drive, fear hit me what if all the children were taken from me, including my boys. God, just what had I done?

But nothing happened. This was as worrying as if something had. No June, no sirens, no taking of any children. Whilst putting Penny to bed she put her arms around me and said as she screwed her face up shaking her head from side to side, "I know you wouldn't really hurt them, but someone should. They should be in a prison with the door locked." We sat quietly hugging, gaining reassurance from each other. She then added, "I want to go to the prison and look through the window to make sure he is there, but I don't want him to see me." This child was five; I detested those responsible that had caused her to talk this way.

True to her word, the following day, June did ring up and arranged to call in later that morning. She seemed unperturbed by the previous evenings conversation over the phone. I asked her how she felt about what I had said. She simply said, "I trusted you, to me there wasn't a problem." I pointed out that everyone has a breaking point, and I felt I had reached mine at that moment. She laughed, told me not to beat myself up over it because from what she could see it was of no consequence to the children. However I was asked if I wanted some support to cope with any of the sensitive negative issues we were handling. This was also shared with our support worker and arrangements were made for me to meet up with a professional who could talk out some of the difficulties. The most profound thing he said was that sometimes actions speak louder than words. They most certainly did that day!

The appointed Guardian Ad Litem visited during March 1989, and though the visit and talks with the children caused them to be wary and guarded, they were relieved at the thought of not having to ever return to their previous home. It was about this time that we were asked if we had any interest in continuing to care for the children on a permanent basis. We clearly stated that given all the inherent problems and the numbers involved, we would consider offering a long term fostering placement, as we felt that through life, the children would need ongoing support above and beyond the help that we would be able to offer. Our offer was not considered to be sufficient or in the children's best interest by the panel. They concluded that the best route for the family group would be for them to be adopted, even if this meant separating the children.

We went through a reasonable phase when the children began to gain trust and believe in us once more. I gradually introduced the idea to all of them that their future involved new parents. Nathan's response was simply, "Which shop do you go to for new mum's and dad's then?" We were moving forward, small achievements, responding to education and learning, family teamwork. Just having fun! As parents we were beginning to relax and actually enjoy having all the children. There were still the occasional setbacks, more on the health side; such as childhood ailments, three had German measles, two had measles, coughs, colds and having the children in four different schools and two nurseries meant that we had our fair share of peer shared tummy bugs and head lice!

Whilst clearing out the head lice on one particular occasion, with all the children around the table, I was combing and checking their hair; we talked among us about the life cycle of the head louse. I had shown them the leaflet about the head louse; they held a fascination about the insect recalling their infestation on their arrival to us. Two of them were looking at the fallout from Nathan's head using a magnifying glass. When I mentioned the egg being the actual nit, Penny, looking oh so knowledgeable, piped up with, "Well of course we would get nits now you know, and I expect everyone has them." All heads turned to her and in one voice said "Why?" Looking extremely serious believing her own words completely she passed on her insight and knowledge. "Well it is Easter, and of course everyone gets eggs at Easter don't they?" One of the older children passed a comment that she must be the biggest nit of all if she believed that!

During the summer of '89 we decided to go back to the Dales and risk the caravan holiday again. We were desperate for Laura to feel happy and comfortable there. So we decided to spend the full six weeks of the school holiday living in the caravan and our tents. Lawrence would spend the first week with us, and thereafter would visit midweek and weekends. He would bring the weekly shopping and clean clothes, taking back the washing to be done when he returned for work. When he came to stay I would be able to come home over night, bringing whichever children might cause a problem for him, depending on the dynamics of relationships of the week! This gave me an opportunity to do some of the washing and ironing, as well as keeping things in order at home. It worked, within a couple of weeks Laura began to relax and enjoy the caravan experience in our usual field. Without television and given the freedom of the field to explore, we watched them all grow, mature a little and gain confidence in themselves and their new skills. We arranged for tuition in canoeing, rock climbing and abseiling, horse riding and general exploring and mini caving. Success comes in many guises and raising yourself, with a little help, on the self-esteem scale has to be beneficial. Our famous five did just that. Gareth's dare devil antics and risk taking behaviours only served to encourage them to do so (even though my heart was in my mouth watching him on the rocks at times). Whilst Aaron's sensible approach offered the 'do it with caution' attitude needed. Above all else they had time with each other, away from the usual trials, tribulations and routines of life, which helped them to get to know each other better. They were to discover each other's weaknesses and strengths that helped to bridge gaps and forge relationships. They had their daily duties and chores, which gave them a responsibility to rise to! We had separate tents for the girls and the boys, so they were expected to sweep out their own environment, keep clothes and belongings tidy and renew the water supplies. The farm dog was a great bonus and kept them amused endlessly bringing back the balls or Frisbees they threw. Each day really was a new adventure of discovery. We had various large boxes of construction toys such as Lego, Constri, Quadro and Kinex, if I set a couple of these out on the picnic blanket outside they would construct and play for hours quite contentedly. Andrew took his first tentative walking steps in Pateley Bridge Play Park during this holiday. Long walks, fresh air and plenty of exercise did all of us good, calm evenings spent star gazing, playing board games and family quizzes gave us a combination of a good laugh, some sibling rivalry, but also led to some nightmare free nights as they slept so well. At the end of the holiday we were ready to come home and start afresh, a new term for school and the possibility of further working towards a new home for our fivesome.

School term commenced and with it a return of some of the negative behaviours, especially in school. Two of them really struggled to cope with being away from our home, saying that they did not feel safe. There were times when I felt it was an excuse to not go to school as they found it very hard work! But each and everyday they did go, we might get a phone call asking us to collect one or another earlier than usual but each day was another day to prove they could achieve, and when they did we praised them to the hilt! If we succeeded in keeping Nathan in school all week that was a mega achievement and would be celebrated in some small way. Once again they would see the example that our boys set which helped, especially as they had homework to do most evenings. Homework rapidly became very interesting, as each child preferred the work set for another, instead of doing its own. This became a pooled resource that was quite effective as a learning aid.

I was called into school to discuss Nathan's disruptive behaviour yet again; this was the end of another very long week of not so good school reports and threats of suspension. It felt like 'blame the parents' time. That evening Nathan shared with us how hard it was going to school, carrying the feeling that he would have to keep on the lookout through the window in case his natural parents turned up and took him away. We tried to reason with him, to offer him our trust in him to do the right thing and behave as others did. To prove this Lawrence took him to Cub Scouts, which he usually enjoyed, but his disruptions surfaced and spoilt the evening. We settled Nathan in bed. He knew we were disappointed and displeased with his behaviour, having said goodnight we left him to think things over but it seems tiredness, and sleep, got the better of him. He was soundly sleeping in minutes.

I stood over him, almost resenting the peace he had found whilst we were still left reeling in the wake of his outbursts. It ran through my mind perhaps we were not the right family for him after all. Perhaps we did not offer what this lad needed to keep him on the right track. Maybe we were holding on to Nathan for the wrong reasons. "Why, Nathan, why do you do it, why do you behave the way you do?" I said out loudly as I stood over him, exhausted and believing my own turmoiled thoughts. I then went downstairs to ring our support worker, asking her to call in the following day to discuss Nathan as I felt we had come to the end of the line with him. I went back to his room. Standing over him I cried hating myself for what I was about to do, but what option did I have? I had to think of everyone's progress, didn't I? Then I heard a sleeping Gareth shuffling in his bed, only he wasn't asleep! He had shuffled to the end of his high bed looking over the end peering down at me, he sniffed, then quietly and oh so knowledgeably said, "He just needs more time Mum, he hasn't lived with us long enough yet." The wisdom of a child! He was right of course restoring perspective to our situation. I smiled and nodded, "Yes you are probably right." Out of all our children Gareth had the most cause to complain about Nathan's existence in his life, but he never did. He shared his bedroom, his toys, books and games, which were frequently just taken without permission, that Nathan regularly broke or destroyed. I rang Emily again, apologising, and explained that he would not be leaving this family, but perhaps we could talk coping strategies instead.

But background rumbles entered their lives, as the department advised that if a family could not be found for all five together, then they would be searching for two if not three families to adopt them. Our long term fostering offer would keep them all together, but would not provide them with the long-term stability and legal safety framework that they needed, or so we were told. Arrangements were in hand for a family photograph to be professionally taken for the relevant magazine for prospective adopters. There was talk of Mum and Step Dad making an appeal to the decision, if this happened the Guardian Ad Litem would have to make further visits. Heaven forbid.

Enough was enough! Members of the adoption panel had listened to our reasons for long term fostering but they were unmoveable. Adopt the children or they will have to move. Our clan had now lived together for over a year, it would be several months before they would move on, their future was uncertain, but so was their past. Young Andrew only knew us as parents, what damage would we cause if he left us. Laura was gradually thawing out, albeit slowly, but occasionally we would move forward, make strides, and though she could so easily inwardly withdraw, she was also beginning to reach out to others. Penny was quietening down, at times, though she was a past master at circular conversations or as we called it 'hole in my bucket' syndrome. She could be as changeable as the British climate, but one area of her life that remained constant was her strength of feeling for wanting to remain with us. Nathan would always have a world of turmoil, but he no longer tied up the trees or the chairs with his ball of string as he used to! Jenny was beginning to show signs of maturing, making good friends and catching up with her peers. If these children meant so much to us why were we not accepting the terms and explanations given to us? Perhaps fear of the future with all seven played a part. For Lawrence it was the responsibility of so many. I struggled with their loss of identity at the point of adoption and really found that hard to come to terms with. But deep down the idea of separating these children, whose foundations were so easily rocked, kept us both awake at night. We had forged relationships between them as well as with our family. We had seen the dysfunctional element when Nathan was not with his siblings. Then we realised how angry or upset we could be when we objected to some of the decisions made by the department. Bite the bullet and take whatever is ahead of us! At the end of the day isn't that what every parent has to do? We agreed to adopt all five, panel agreed in late December to allow us to.

As a family unit, our clan had other challenges! Christmas was on the horizon; there were parts for concerts to be learned and we had yet to fathom out how two of us could attend three events in three different schools all taking place at the same time! Whilst making tea I would be coaching children to learn their parts for their concert or play. We had quite a good routine going, and they were all doing so well. Then the evening before Penny was to do her recitation we practised once again, Aaron, Gareth and Jenny had no problem, but Penny could not seem to get started with hers, I prompted her, she tried, but the words were not coming back to her. I gave her the first line, she looked at me almost crying, and the words meant nothing to her. I was stirring the gravy and trying to keep my patience with her, whatever was wrong? She had done so well, almost word perfect the previous evening. "Come on Penny. Let's try again from the beginning." I sighed. I gave her the first line. Penny quietly repeated it but then looked totally blank. However Nathan had come into the room, hearing the prompted first line he went on to finish the whole piece. I praised him and asked how he had remembered all of it, "'Cos it is mine to say in the school play, why are you making Penny learn it?" I am not sure whose relief was greater Penny's or mine. With the right piece in front of us Penny now excelled herself and succeeded in reciting her part for her play. Lesson for me indeed!

Christmas was special; it had to be, for they were about to become ours. We made it a musical Christmas, various musical instruments as gifts, Jenny was learning to play the flute, she had tried the trumpet but she found the flute so much easier. Aaron played piano or electronic keyboard. Gareth was taking guitar lessons. Nathan wanted to learn how to play the drums; we were not quite ready for that! Together with a little help they produced their own family concert, making programmes to give out to anyone prepared to watch. We borrowed our friend's video camera so they could watch themselves afterwards. On the whole, Christmas was very special indeed. In the last year they had faced such a lot and done their best to overcome so many negatives in their lives. The New Year had to be kind to all of us, surely?

Life Story Work continued, and our boys wanted to know why we had not done any for them, so we included those two in our time allotment. On a weekly basis, each child had its own special evening set aside to piece together the jigsaw of its life. Consequently emotions could run high or low dependent on whose evening it was or what area of life we had reached. The speed of the roller coaster varied from day to day and could be difficult to keep up with.

The department's expectation of an appeal by Mum and Step Dad became reality. Hell was to begin again, initiated by the Guardian Ad Litem's visit. The youngsters had readily accepted that they would not be returning home, they were aware that they would be staying with us. However their understanding of the Guardian's visit was that they would need to see Mum again. This stirred fearful anxiety deep within the older four and we had a return of the endless nightmares, screaming out, sleepwalking, and disturbances in school. Another period of regression took over the household. The feeling of being safe was compromised and all trust in us dissolved. We found ourselves back in the fog. One day ran into another as we met ourselves coming down the stairs in a morning as we went up the stairs at night. Sleep was virtually unknown. Life Story Work came to a halt. Their vulnerability was awakened by the grip held by the perpetrator. I knew this but I was not expecting what came next.

Looking back our family life exploded. We reached the stage of not knowing where to turn, which way to go.

The fear of going to their family home or meeting up with birth parents was deeply ingrained. Each child was reliving its own painful past experiences every night, leaving them exhausted and drained by day.

I was asked to collect Penny from school. She rested then sat with me to talk, I asked if she would like to draw a picture of anything she wanted to. She drew three, each one very graphically disclosing the appalling abuse she had endured. This was far, far more than anything she had said before, I dare not show my feelings or my repulsion that she might so easily misunderstand. I had no choice but to tell her social worker. Penny's stirred emotions reverberated on Nathan and the strength of his feeling was expressed in minute detail. His disclosure was recalled clearly and concisely, his face showing the pain, releasing the agony and the disgust with hate and despair. I sat up with him virtually all night as he sobbed, no child could tell this unless he had lived it. Now he was frightened 'they' would find out he had told.

Jenny must have felt the cold heavily laden atmosphere; her mood matched it, so I knew it would not be long before she divulged her thoughts. Eventually she asked me how I would feel about them going back to Mum and Step Dad? I reassured her that would never happen, reminding her that the appeal was an attempt to stop their adoption but not for them to return to her former family. She was aware that her Mum was expecting another baby and this stirred up frenzied behaviour and a distressed attitude. She needed proof that the baby would be taken away from Mum. She explained that she did not want to ever grow up, nor did she want to leave us because she was so frightened. I asked her why. She spent the rest of the evening telling me.

It could not be stressed enough that any angry, disruptive and manipulative behaviour expressed by the children since the Guardian's visit in March in no way compared with any other previous pattern of behaviour. The damage to these children's feelings of security unfortunately far outweighed any benefits gained in releasing the disclosures. The strong feelings of insecurity and mistrust were manifested in their present attitude towards those trying to offer the greatest level of support. I carried their anger, their hatred and their despair for a very long time to come, but I had to put this to one side to cope with the daily grind of life living in the shadows cast by their former family.

When they were in our home, there was a sense of safety, rare moments of normality, but anything at any time could trigger a behaviour pattern that was completely unexpected and consume their confidence, their trust and belief in us. Testing and trying behaviours could be extreme, they were certainly challenging and they would be utterly exhausting. Any one of the four out of the five could, and would, disrupt at any given moment. Were we not the only parents around, and hadn't we raised the alarm that caused the police involvement again? How could they, or should they trust us? So hurt and afraid of reprisal none of the children could find strength of character. None of them truly felt safe anywhere unless they were all together. Then their individual needs were so great they could not tolerate each other or the idiosyncrasies of each other's demonstration of feeling that only reflected their own.

They brought their anger and their mistrust, as well as their tears to us, this alternated with their need to belong, to be loved and wanted, to be good, acceptable and to have self-worth. I constantly reminded both Lawrence and myself that a child does need more love when he least deserves it. But finding the right balance of holding on with love, or offering tough love, to teach a lesson, was like treading on the fragments of egg shells which matched their emotions.

Lawrence and I learned the art of time out! Not for the children but for ourselves! If he walked in looking more refreshed than I felt, I would leave the house for an hour or two. Sometimes I would walk to the country park, or just have a drive out. Occasionally I would visit friends or have a cup of tea with my neighbour. I just needed to be in touch with the real unspoilt world away from our own bedlam to regain perspective and understanding before going back to cope again. Lawrence could at least escape to work! We learned to change the dynamics among the children, as these altered whenever just one child had an event to go to, so taking that one out of the equation for a short time. These could be invites to friends, or specially engineered events such as adventure holidays or weekends away. This gave everyone a break of sorts. Their friends were regularly invited for tea, so enhancing their social skills, as they tried to impress our young visitors, whilst giving them an opportunity to enjoy the companionship of their peers or chosen friend in their own environment.

Winter turned to spring and was rapidly heading towards summer. We needed to help our youngsters focus on a future with us. No one knew when the adoption might take place, but we needed a really special event to show our unity and for the sake of our sanity, the sooner the better.

I had explained to each of the older ones that they could if they wished change their name or names at the point of adoption, this gave them something to think about and practise using alternative names, which provided a focus of fun as we would all offer suggestions which included some rather silly names. I tried to encourage Penny and Jenny to consider changing their first name or switching their first and second names around to reduce the aggravation and annoyance factor that they shared, having similar names, but neither would give way. In the end, the older two girls chose to keep their names but Nathan was desperate to alter his middle name, and we chose to give the younger two an alternative middle name too.

During the past months, we had received a great deal of support from members of our church where the children went to Sunday school. We had been considering having the younger two baptised, but when we were unable to trace any proof of Penny being baptised, we were advised that we could have a conditional baptism for her also. Lawrence and I were concerned that Jenny and Nathan would view this as something very special for the younger ones but might lead to those two feeling left out. We shared this with the extremely understanding vicar who suggested that they renew their vows, but how would that leave Aaron and Gareth? "Then why don't you go the whole hog and all of you renew your vows, make it a family affair." He jested. But he was right, that is exactly what we needed. The adoption was a situation foisted upon us by circumstances, this would be our choice, something they could all relate to, understand, and would create the family unity so badly needed. This occasion was to become the main focus of our year.

Every child revelled in the preparations, choosing of Godparents, hymns, practising the words and understanding the true meaning to each as an individual and to us as a family. Planned with the same precision, as a family wedding would be, it was the event of the year. The church was full, friends, relatives, and all those who had supported us were there to offer their unconditional love and a source of much needed strength to all of us. Seven children, seven sets of Godparents; this was a real symbol of not only our commitment to the children but also that of others around them. Everyone was invited back to our home for a buffet lunch. Although it was July, the weather was wet and wild, so all plans to spend time in the garden were abandoned. The boys had organised entertainment for any children that arrived. Gareth had set up the garage as a staged affair giving his audience a full range of seating. He had made a sign claiming that he, Aaron and Nathan were the "Boogie Box Baptism Brothers." Music and games to suit all ages had been planned and executed. I was not aware of how much they had put into it, or what was going on in the garage until I saw the video footage filmed by our friends. I was so proud of their combined efforts and how they kept Nathan under control by giving him responsibilities to rise to. The garage must have had about twenty or more children all having a thoroughly good time, no problems or stupidity, no arguments, just pure fun. The only adults in there were the fleeting onlookers checking on the proceedings and their own child's behaviour. The house was bulging with people even using the stairway for seating! Our guests had come from near and far and on that day, I doubt that any of them could have guessed the difficulties we had been surmounting during the previous months. All of our children excelled themselves. They were a family to be proud of and Lawrence reiterated this in his speech that day. A relative had made us a beautiful cake, which included the name of every child and our title of Mum and Dad, as part of the decoration. The message on it said 'Our Family, Nought But God Can Sever.' A guest book was laid out for all who came, to sign and leave their personal messages to us, a true treasure trove of their love. The weather may have been poor, but the day was as bright as any day could possibly be, it was a real celebration, and to our children a symbol of what they meant to us.

That proved to be the turning point for all of the children, from that moment a sense of belonging crept back into our lives. This was so evident by their need to call us Mum and Dad; at least by Nathan, Penny and Laura, Andrew quickly caught on and followed the others. But Jenny stuck to the original Auntie and Uncle titles for us. The others challenged her and she sulked. Realising that as the older one of the five she would naturally find it harder to change our titles, I waited until we were alone to explain that it didn't really matter what she called us, as long as she was not rude! Expecting a smile from her, I was surprised at how wary and uncertain she seemed, so I asked her why she found it so hard to call us Mum and Dad as Auntie and Uncle took longer to say. Still unsmiling she looked me up and down and retorted, "How do I know that if I call you Mum and Dad you won't do the same as they did?" The impact hit me like a hard slap on the face. I sat down, tried to hide my feelings and replied, "Have I ever given you reason to believe that I would?" "No." She said with her head bowed down. "But when I say it I think of them not you." She quietly quivered. I hugged her, kissed the top of her head and reassured her that all we had ever done was to protect them all, and that we would go on to do that so what had happened at their previous home would never happen here. And anyway it didn't really matter what she called us. She continued to use the comfortable titles of Auntie and Uncle but when we were alone she would try out the Mum and Dad version. Eventually with so many using those terms around us she automatically became used to using them too.

During the following month, which was during the school holiday, we had threats made to our family. Their birth family and associates were making it quite clear they were still around and trying to unsettle the youngsters. Their aim would be towards the weakest and most vulnerable, Nathan. We had to take advice from Social Services to implement the coping strategies for all of us. We also had to take legal advice as the adoption had not yet taken place. We stood firmly, the children were now part of our family and their past would no longer be allowed to undermine this unity. On the day of the baptism, Aaron had read out a poem that meant so much to all of us.

*Our Family*
*Our family is a blessing*
*it means so many things.*
*Words can never really tell*
*the joy our family brings.*
*Our family has mutual love,*
*the love of Dad and Mother*
*Showing children how to love*
*and care for one another.*

*Our family is heartfelt pride,*
*a feeling deep and strong,*
*That makes us glad to take*
*a part and know that we belong.*
*Our family is always home*
*a place where we can share*
*Our joys and sorrows, hopes and*
*dreams for happiness lives there.*
*Our family is a bond of faith*
*that even time cannot sever,*
*A gift to last through out our lives,*
*The family of God is forever.*

*Anonymous*

## CHAPTER 16

## *Time Between*

So our clan became our family of nine. Even so we made it clear from the onset that if ever we felt we were ready to foster again we would like to be considered as foster parents. If the need was there and we could accommodate then we would. Fortunately we had the support of the Principal Worker for our five and the report she wrote for the adoption panel indicated our possible future intentions. Her report concluded as follows: -

*'Mr and Mrs Valdis have a great capacity to integrate children into their family and meet the individual needs of a number of children at once. They are certainly an extra-ordinary foster family and should be treated as such. I feel that their strengths lie in forming and building upon attachments and giving children a feeling of belonging to their family. This enormous strength can be a disadvantage in short term fostering but is of immeasurable value to children in long-term care. I feel that in a couple of years the Valdis' may wish to take on other children. I would recommend that if this happens their offer is seriously considered. It is not often that substitute parents of the Valdis' calibre are found.'*

Both Lawrence and I were pleased that our future intentions were documented, at least if we ever felt that our family was ready to begin again this just might give us the support we would need to be taken seriously. In the meantime, we had seven youngsters to keep us busy. They would provide us with more than our fair share of challenges; they would open our eyes and cause us to raise an eyebrow or two; they would also keep us up to date with youthful views at the same time as wearing us into the ground. Keeping open those lines of communication between us would have me on the lookout for new and interesting or different means to get our message through to them. Equally they would educate us through a minefield of difficulties faced in their lives. No one said it would be easy and they were right. We discovered all the schools in and out of the area, as we had to search further afield for appropriate, safe education for each child. We were also to understand just how big our family was as many of our previous children were to return for short bursts or for some much longer visits.

Extending the house was a must to give each child their own valuable personal space where they could feel safe and comfortable. This meant adding on another wing to the house to provide two additional bedrooms and a second upstairs bathroom, as well as a large second lounge downstairs and a study-cum-bedroom. We would also need to divide an existing bedroom into two smaller bedrooms, not to stop there, as we chose to extend the utility room (well we would need somewhere for all those boots, shoes and coats as well as the inevitable mountain of washing that came with having so many children), this allowed us to extend the bedroom above, so that part of it could become another bathroom, as we would lose the original bathroom to form a corridor to access the new bedrooms. We had no choice but to live in the house whilst all this work was going on for countless, endless months, as we had nowhere else to stay. The workmen had to work around us as much as we had to work around them. Fun and frustration sat side by side, as elements of our life to achieve our aim and retain some sanity. But gradually we emerged with a more practical home that offered everyone space to move, to breathe, and to have that all important personal space. We were not to realise until many years later when the house went up for sale, just how much it meant to all our children. It was a haven; a safe place to be that was filled with many, many memories. I think everyone of them at some point voiced their intention to buy it. When we were still at the building stage, our neighbour was asking Penny about the progress of the house, Penny explained that all was going well adding, "And when it is all finished all of us children will have our own bedroom but Mummy and Daddy will still have to share 'cos we will run out of rooms." The injustice of being a parent!

Over the next seven years our brood would grow, develop ideas of their own, not always to our liking, but always to be a part of us. Their trials and tribulations became ours; their joys and successes were also ours to celebrate. There were times when we ached and agonised for them, when their stage and age of life threw out another memory or perspective of their past. Like the majority of parents, we hung on for the ride of our lives with them, and though there have been the inevitable difficulties that tested us beyond endurance, we survived, not necessarily unscathed, but alive, alert, and still smiling! Life is a test, it does not come with instructions, and there have been times when we could or should have offered a different approach. But like all parents, we made the decisions at the time according to the facts to hand and the mood of the day, and anyway, hindsight is a wonderful attribute! Life was full; there was no time to get bored. We always had plenty of children for team games and companionship. They say that the family that eats together stays together; well our table could match the 'Walton's' any day for food, conversation and problem solving! Our budgeting skills excelled, and Christmas planning for so many as well as averaging a birthday per month within the family meant that I was always on the look out for a bargain, quality without the price! The designer world of teenagers took us by storm, and there were times when the word 'No' had to take on greater meaning.

Attendances at Parents' evenings in school filled us with dread and sometimes despair. Never knowing whether we would be facing an understanding teacher or one whose expectations of a child were far too great. But teachers are human too. Those with genuine experience knew the difficulties we as parents faced as well as those of our children and would support us completely, then there were some whose personal experiences left them struggling to cope with the exaggerated behaviours of our youngsters. The school environment could be the place where they could feel completely normal, at one with their peers, or it could be the place where they were made to feel different, be rejected or isolated. We rarely looked for huge strides of success, but small steady steps that lead to personal recognition of achievement meant as much to us, as to our children, and were always acknowledged.

We rapidly learnt to put names to behaviours; this helped to put their actions into perspective for all of us. So we had 'wobblers' when their foundations were shaken and there was still a chance of the child involved gaining control; 'mini-wobblers' which were slightly greater with some loss of control that would need reminders from us to help them find their self control; then there were the 'mega-wobblers' resulting in total loss of control and an unpredictability that relied on adult intervention, usually ours, to bring it back under control. The rise and fall of our emotions relied on quick scanning of a situation, to respond appropriately, and have the energy to know when to dive in to rescue, or when to stand on the edge and let the child solve it on their own. However a 'wobbler' in one of them could ripple through the others causing a 'mega-wobbler' in another further down the line. We would constantly be on the look out for signs of such trigger action and the possible effects.

Social growth was as valuable as physical growth and though they felt strong and capable when all together, we searched for ways to encourage them to follow their own interests, find their own friends and discover their own place in the world. This meant organising age appropriate escapes such as Children's summer camps, where for a week they could discover their own limitations and face their own self doubt, make their own expectations, meet new friends, and for a short time be totally responsible for their own actions and decisions. They would also have new experiences, gain new skills, take pride in who they were, and also learn to laugh at themselves or make fools of themselves. They were encouraged to go to after school activities of all kinds. Our local college organised Saturday courses for school age children such as cooking, woodwork, or photography that we enrolled them on. We had a definitive weekly timetable so we knew who was supposed to be at which venue, when and where. Timing and precision was all important. Swimming several times a week for most of them was an invaluable way of releasing pent up feelings and energy as well as offering a time for freedom of expression in a fun way.

They were to meet up with children we had previously looked after, the trio sets who had taken different routes away from our family were to come back as visitors, some more frequently than others. Those who moved South were to visit on occasions, and as their need to touch base with their roots emerged, one or another would stay for more prolonged visits. We discovered by pure chance that Jenna, Darren and Andrea attended the same school as our own two youngsters, their foster placement had broken down and they had returned to Mum, this resulted in weekly visits to us for Life Story Work to help two of them make sense of their own lives. Their involvement in our family became greater, often coming back to have an evening or two a week with us, though sometimes staying overnight at weekends. For the other family, a comfortable contact was maintained through letters and cards or the occasional visit when the family was passing through on their way to other parts of the country. Though one of the children went through a very difficult phase, which was traumatic for the whole family, we were asked by the social services of their area if we could offer a placement for a short time to that child in an endeavour to help them come to terms with their situation by revisiting their roots. We agreed, expecting a foreseeable plan to work with, so when I asked when would we expect the youngster to arrive it was quite a shock to discover they planned to put the youngster on a train that afternoon giving us less than four hours to organise ourselves! In later years another of the trio was to join us on an extended visit too.

Our home buzzed with the life and soul of youngsters, visiting friends usually meant impromptu parties or barbeques. I recall having two beautiful children from the Children's African Choir to stay for a couple of nights as they were performing at Andrew's school, they sang for us and encouraged ours to sing and dance for the evening. They were fascinated by our way of life and our big family. After their visit we sponsored Adika in Africa, receiving letters of his progress, his annual photo was stuck on the freezer door to include him in our clan and the children looked forward to writing to him and receiving his letters of progress. They also enjoyed the connection with an English family growing up in Italy who also became pen friends exchanging their different ways of life. Once or twice they were able to meet up when the family were staying in the area on their return to England for a holiday. We had a young man called Frasquito from Spain who stayed with us for a month as a teenager to learn more about Britain. He and Aaron became great friends. Frasquito fitted into our family so well, as his stay came to an end it was like losing a member of the family. Our friend asked us if we could offer a couple of weeks to some other overseas students who would be attending college during the summer months. We decided it would help our growing brood to reach out to the needs of others so agreed. We had two young lads from the Netherlands, Fransien and Marick who joined us for two weeks, Etienne and Francois from France, and Adele also from France. In and among our foreign students were our children's friends from school, Scouts, Guides, riding stables and as they became older from Air and Army cadets that they attended, so our house and home frequently heaved at the seams with visitors. Our garden became host for gatherings for Nathan's youth group. I have always been amused by the tenacity of youth and how they feel, and desperately want to sound 'grown up', as they move through their teens. Though my definition of a teenager is that they may be older experienced children at eighteen, never the less they are still naïve adults in their infancy with a great deal to learn! We enjoyed meeting most of their friends though voiced our opinions quite clearly about some, when the vibes they gave were less than comfortable. Quite a few of their friends seemed to live here and I often did a head count to check how many were hanging around. However I took the attitude that at least if they were here we knew what they were up to! Games of Rounders were well supported, as there were always plenty willing to play, and therefore were often played in the garden.

We tried to help them to pack as much as possible into their lives in the hope that they would be able to stand on their own two feet, feel strong enough, and capable enough, to realise how much they could achieve and go on achieving when they made the effort for themselves. If they made a mistake they were made to pay for it and learn from it without allowing it to hold them back. There were times when peer group pressure was a greater force than we were. They may not have always liked us or liked what we had to say, but I would always be truthful with them. But then we did not always approve of what they were doing or saying, love the child, dislike the action. As they found their inner strength they would at times turn this into physical strength and use it against us, which could be quite exhausting. When I felt that the spoken word was just falling on to deaf ears I would write letters or poems to them explaining how I felt about their behaviour, outlining the consequences and effects. These were very effective because it reduced the need to launch into an argument of any kind, they could read it more than once, and who wants to listen to nagging parents anyway? Many a clearing out session brought these letters to the surface so that was proof that they did not just bin them! Interestingly they learnt to write back to us too. I frequently found a short note or even a long epistle by my bedside from one or another of them proclaiming their love for us, and offering their heartfelt apologies for their latest heinous crime, telling us how they planned to correct their behaviour or pay for the damage caused, well that was until the next spate of poor behaviour! On the whole mutual trust, respect for each other, did emerge and would rise above most of the misdemeanours encountered as they attempted to take on our family values.

Aaron once disagreed with my way of handling a particular situation with Penny, he argued that when he was that age he would never have got away with what she was doing, and he made it clear that he felt I was far too lenient with her. I pointed out that as a parent I had to recognise the subtle differences in situations, and there were times when my expectation of one over another would be greater, as the experience of one was also greater so the outcome would be different. "Anyway,"

I said in my sternest voice, "perhaps as a parent I've gained experience too, and mellowed in my approach, maybe I realised where I went wrong when I handled your situation." "Oh, I see, what you're really saying is that you just practised on me then?" He announced. I thought momentarily about his words and decided to admit defeat as positively as possible. "Yes, I guess you are right, I suppose I did practise on you, after all you were my first, maybe by the time I get to Andrew I might just about get this parenting thing right." Feeling a little disgruntled and I expect badly done by, he walked away muttering to himself something to the effect of "I doubt it!"

Well whether our children agreed on our parenting ability or not was never really in question, they were stuck with us, and we were as tenacious as any parents could be. There were times when this would be to our advantage and at other times more to the children's. We did not suffer fools gladly but nor would we be made fools of!

Daily strife and life with seven moving closer towards the dominance of the turbulent teens was a whole new ball game, and some of their behaviours were to pale into insignificance alongside some of the performances we had to witness from the visiting teens who were also facing their own turbulence. Key adults readily manage a young child's anger, albeit uncomfortable to witness, and for the child to experience, but a teenager's warpath is trodden with full force and a physical strength that can rise within seconds, exploding unexpectedly in any direction, and the fall out can wipe out anyone in their wake or way! Life was never dull during this period though there were times when I would crave for the normality of the average family, or was everyone else going through similar situations? Maybe our household experiences were just magnified by the sheer numbers we were dealing with, our own seven plus the returning youngsters. So in 1997 how did we end up contemplating taking on yet another teenager? How did we slip into the situation of offering ourselves as a family for a young man of twelve? This was a question we often asked ourselves, but fate will have its way, and if his place with us was predestined then it was to be, so we accepted it, though his route to us was quite obscure!

I had called in at our village newsagent. Our situation as foster parents was well known as most of our older youngsters had delivered newspapers for them at some time. This particular morning I was asked if we still fostered. I questioned why, but clearly said, not at the moment, well at least not for new children, though we would never turn away children who had been with us in the past. The newsagent went on to expand her reason for asking. A regular customer had found herself having to accommodate her grandson as a family upset had resulted in him being unable to go home. However she genuinely had no space for him, he was sleeping on a temporary bed in her lounge, though this arrangement was completely unsatisfactory. She described the young lad as a nice boy, squeaky clean who caused no trouble. Was she naïve or trying to impress me? I was told the grandmother was very anxious and felt she had nowhere to turn to for advice. I agreed that she could pass on our telephone number to the family and I would offer some support regarding options that might be open to her through social services. I left the shop not thinking much more about it, not expecting to hear anymore about this rising teen.

Within a week I had indeed received a phone call from the grandmother of the young man in need of a home. We chatted on the telephone and she was genuinely upset about the situation but not wholly happy with the solution on offer by social services. Consequently we arranged for her to talk out the difficulties, as she perceived them and to look at alternative options if there were any! I really did not expect to have any helpful conclusions for her but I did feel that she needed a sounding block to air her own grievances. During her visit to us Grandma explained some of the family's differences and the reasons for young Peter's predicament. He would be celebrating his thirteenth birthday within a few weeks. Events in his life had led to a general deterioration in the relationship between himself and his father, this had culminated in Peter running away from home to another relative, this action was more than his father could take. To give everyone the necessary space, arrangements were made for him to stay with his paternal grandparents as a temporary measure. This was not to be an easy time for anyone, some of the lad's behaviours, born out of the separation from his family, were more than his grandparents were willing to cope with. Sadly this caused the relationship with their son, Peter's father, to deteriorate as he was prevaricating over taking him back. Eventually she tried to force the situation by various means, and in frustration abandoned him in the hands of the police, hoping they could make Peter's parents pick up on their responsibility. Instead the police were to ask his maternal Grandma to help out, leaving her with the same problem. So why were we left feeling so uncomfortable about their difficulty? Why was I so restless at night thinking about a young boy I had not met? Why was I prepared to contemplate compromising a change in our family dynamics when I knew from experience the upheavals that can occur by introducing another into our clan? In the words of our friend, "Don't you think you have enough teenage difficulties to handle without adding to them?" I believe my answer was in the lines of "well one more shouldn't make that much difference then, and at least he will have a home." But it was not going to happen that quickly!

> *"In each family a story is playing itself out, and each family's story embodies its hope and despair."*
>
> *Auguste Napier*
>
> *U.S. Family Therapist*

# CHAPTER 17
## Pushing The Limits

We had hoped Peter would join us in time to celebrate his thirteenth birthday, but after a lengthy discussion with the social worker discovered that we would have to go through the vetting stage all over again as he was living in a different authority. This would mean completing the work for the assessment form and being presented to their panel, to be accepted as foster carers all over again. The original plan for Peter, by social services, was for him to await a place in a children's home, it was this that convinced us we had made the right choice, at least for Peter's benefit. In the meantime we would eventually meet him to be sure we were able to care for his needs and start the process of establishing a rapport with him.

Peter had an aunt who took an interest in his situation and though unable to offer him a home was still prepared to support him in any way that she could. Arrangements for him to go to a short-term foster placement were made whilst we underwent our processing. The greatest sadness for both Peter and us was that this happened to take place on the eve of his birthday, so all of our hopes and plans to give him a memorable day as he entered the teenage years were lost. The thought of this young man entering his teens without being able to celebrate it with those he knew, really cut through the core of us, so I couldn't even begin to imagine or put into words how he would have felt. We were determined to make up for this when eventually he did join us. Until that day arrived, we needed to try to get to know him better. The frustration of waiting to meet him was infuriating and took a couple of months, though we had already made an effort on our part by acknowledging his birthday with a card and a small gift and also another letter to remind him of our existence and intentions. To us, it was important for him to realise that although he felt his natural family had turned their back on him, he was still wanted and very much needed by us.

Eventually the arrangements were set by the social worker, a short visit one evening prior to Christmas, so that we would become a reality to Peter and we could start to make plans for his stay with us. We had looked forward for so long for this moment but were not quite prepared for what would happen. He arrived with his aunt and the familial appearance between this young man and his aunt was very evident as they both had red hair and similar features. Peter had pure white eyebrows and plenty of freckles. A slim lad with frameless glasses, but his most striking feature of all was his need to be in the driving seat of this situation. His dominance was evident from the onset, and his determination to expect his own way was to be demonstrated on that first evening. Perhaps what he was not expecting was that we were experienced in the ways of teenagers and jangling their hormones at us did not get them very far! He was quietly but firmly spoken and withdrew a list of questions from his trouser pocket to ask us about our parenting. We were not sure whom if anyone was pulling his strings but one thing for certain was that if he planned to join our clan, those strings just might have to be tightened from our end! So we allowed this young fellow to 'interview' us, our answers had to be as exacting as his questions so that he gained insight into our intentions thereby laying our foundation for him too!

Peter asked about such things as how much pocket money he would be allowed; what time we would expect him to go to bed; was he allowed friends round? Then came a really important question, at least to him, "I like to play football especially on my way home from school which means my shoes and trousers can get very muddy, how would you feel about that and what would you do because I would not expect to go to school the next day with mud on my trousers." He looked at me very seriously waiting for my response and was a little non-plussed when he received it! "Well Peter, I would take the attitude that if you had the pleasure of getting the mud on your trousers in the first place, I would expect you to have the pleasure of getting the mud off your trousers by hand scrubbing it off before the trousers went into my washing machine." He stared at me or maybe it was a glare! "But that is what parents do!" He retorted. "Not really." I answered, "You see Peter, I take the view that you are old enough to take responsibility to make sure you wear the right clothes for whatever you are doing, which is why footballers wear shorts and shirts. However if you are not, then you must take responsibility and care for what you are wearing. Scuffs on your clothes I can handle, thick mud caused by inconsideration would be down to you." I was not quite certain whether he stared back with a look of deep shock or pure condemnation. But it was game, set and match!

So as the cherry blossom bloomed at the top of our drive we were accepted as foster parents specifically for

Peter. He joined us to be a part of our clan, ostensibly until he was sixteen, but in reality for a lifetime. Our biggest regret was that he had experienced several months in another placement that had coloured his view on life even more so than the effect from his own family experience. We spent a great deal of time unravelling the problems encountered in that home before we could begin to address some of the difficulties that had brought him into care in the first place. However the connection he held with that family in the initial weeks he was with us was based purely on the fact that to him they were now a known quantity and we were not! I also believed that he had gained a level of control in their household that he was unable to gain in ours. At his own admission, he did not like living there or living by their rules but he had learned to survive there and that was something he still had to gain with us. We were very quickly to discover how strong-minded Peter was, he had very high expectations of others and felt that he should have rights not to be afforded to other youngsters. In our eyes, he had a great deal to learn, and the first lesson was to step off his pedestal, and if he refused to, I'm afraid he would have to be knocked off it!

Peter had his own protective walls of defence built around him, he had found it hard in his natural family to cope with his own sibling, suddenly finding himself among so many must have felt exceptionally alien to him and hopelessly outnumbered. The others had siblings with them, whilst Peter presented as an only one.

Our house was not on a bus route and all of the other children had their own bicycles, which the older ones could use to go to the local shops in the village or meet up with friends, though living at the top of the hill always made them have second thoughts before going off, as they knew a downhill journey meant an uphill one on their return! Peter did not come with a bicycle, which made life a little awkward for him, so we decided fairly early on after his arrival that we could justify a new bicycle for him, after all, he had missed out on that all important thirteenth birthday. The one we chose was canary yellow with black trims, he loved it. Well at least he did until he hankered for a better model. But this was to be a theme of Peter, to always strive for that slightly bigger and better model of anything he or anyone else had.

Being so in touch with his own needs, as he discerned them, he was so very out of touch with the depth of feelings of others and the effects of his attitude. I felt that in his past, he had been so hurt by the actions of other people he now concentrated only on his own needs or desires, often to the detriment of family. We desperately needed to help him break down the walls he had built around himself, put his vulnerability on the frontline by facing his own hurt, to make him aware of those now close to him and their feelings too, especially when they made an effort for him regardless of how big or small that effort was.

Peter's aunt occasionally took him out to help maintain a bond between them and would buy him a gift or memento to come home with. On one such occasion, he came flying in to the house with the latest craze of a yoyo. To Peter this was the Rolls Royce version of a yoyo, and we were all to be told as much and have it endlessly demonstrated too. He expressed his love and devotion for his Aunt for giving him the best of the best. He was ecstatic and spent the rest of the evening irritating everyone with his fantastic, glorious yoyo. But this was also short lived. The very next day, he came home extolling the virtues of a cap given to him by a friend at school, when I asked about the yoyo he avoided eye contact completely, muttering quietly about something I could not hear, so I asked him again. This time he admitted he had swapped the yoyo for the hat. We discussed at length how he perceived his Aunt would feel about this. But Peter was unable to express any kind of remorse about his action and the following day swapped the hat for a pen, that he openly told us about, totally oblivious to our feelings towards his actions. He seemed so utterly detached from people, yet so in touch with his own self and his wants but not really his needs.

I strongly suspect he was used to working against adults rather than working with them and concluded that the rest of our children were like-minded. He must have been shocked to the core to discover they actually worked with us and their trust in us was paramount to their survival. Consequently they did not accept his lack of trust and his negativity towards Lawrence and me when we were not prepared to accept some of his demands. There was always one among them willing to 'inform' on his response and attitude of 'I'll get them done.' This was a phrase he often used to prove to the children that he had the 'upper hand' over us which often resulted in us calling for an impromptu review with his social worker much to his surprise and disgust, as he was to discover who really had the upper hand! He was a bright boy and a gifted artist who felt his all round abilities were better than everyone else's. Sadly he also thought he could achieve greater things without having to work and was also capable of making his teachers in school believe that too. Lame excuses would be used when he did not quite make the mark! The sadness was that he was unable to appreciate the gifts in others, as his insight was focused purely on himself. I found this rather strange and exceptionally sad because his intolerance of others only served to alienate him further. So I was even more surprised by the tolerance exerted towards him from our other youngsters.

From his behaviours we could guess that some of Peter's traits would have been difficult to tolerate, especially if one of his parents exhibited similar traits, and vied for that same dominant position in a family that Peter felt was rightly his. His jealousy of his sister was obvious through the way he spoke about her and also through some of the reports we received. Some of these traits were flaunted in front of our children but came over less as jealousy and more of intolerance. To them he exuded confidence which really hid his lack of confidence, and only served to highlight their own lack of self esteem stemming from their past history, which of course Peter had no understanding of.

Peter eventually found his own niche within our family, but he always struggled to cope with the group atmosphere of our lives, though I felt he gained a secure feeling with so many around him, as there was always someone there for him should he need someone to talk to, and believe me he could talk the hind leg off a donkey if the topic was of his choosing, and involved cars or football and he had you as a captive audience! Neither of these subjects was of any interest to me and he knew it, which is, I am certain, why he would collar me when I was on my own to launch into the latest news regarding either topic. He was a fully-fledged Leeds United Football Club supporter and football dominated our lives. Poor Lawrence spent many a cold afternoon at the football ground giving his support to Peter, not the team I hasten to add! He also joined a local football team, the colours were bright orange and black that matched his hair colouring so well. He felt he had the right to demand the latest new designer football boots, and I was to curse Beckham on a regular basis.

Social services were promoting their support of youngsters in care having the necessary support to achieve their aims in life. Peter saw this as an opportunity to exploit to get what he wanted. Consequently he told his social worker that he needed a guitar and a special pair of football boots. The request for the boots did not surprise us even though we had just bought him a good pair of football boots, however the guitar did, though we realised that it was only a need for 'pride of possession' as Aaron and Gareth both played and had them in their bedrooms. Each of these items was to cost about a hundred pounds. We were unaware of these requests until the social worker rang us to ascertain the actual models he wanted. I had no hesitation in telling him that if he planned to go ahead and provide Peter with the boots and the guitar at the cost of the tax payer then he would be looking for a new placement for him, as the one lesson in life Peter needed was to understand that he could not have everything in life unless he put some effort into working for it. I was livid. This would set Peter apart even more so and teach him absolutely nothing about life except how to con others. Peter was equally told in no uncertain terms that football skills were more important than boots, and designer boots would not make him a better football player, and until he wore out the recently bought boots there would be no others. He was also told that a guitar in a bedroom was an expensive decoration but if he wanted to learn to play, to have a few sessions with Gareth, to borrow one of his guitars, and if Peter was still serious about learning, we would then arrange lessons for him. Needless to say, all talk about guitar lessons faded completely but the green-eyed jealousy for designer football boots lingered a little longer. We did compromise that if he showed true commitment to his team and the game, he could have £50 towards the boots but he was to raise the other £50. Keeping one step ahead of Peter was all-important to keeping his feet firmly rooted on the ground! He had pushed boundaries to and beyond the limit in other homes; for the sake of fairness to all the children in our family our boundaries were firmly set. Peter just needed to learn where the comfort zone was.

Prior to Peter's arrival, we had been told he had occasional enuresis, which of course to a teenager was a huge embarrassment and great concern. He needed an enormous amount of support and reassurance to handle this almost on a nightly basis. This was never a problem to us as I had excellent washing facilities but persuading Peter to break his habit of hiding the evidence was not easy. We tried everything. Even though he would change the bed he would still hide the bedding, insisting he had stayed dry. Though inevitably we would find the offending sheets eventually. We tried patience, reasoning, discussion, brought in literature for him to read about the problem, but nothing brought him out of his world of denial. Finally I had no other way of getting through to Peter other than to leave the wet, odorous bedding found hidden under his bed in his room, bagged up waiting for his return, for him to realise we knew. He could not hide this as he realised we would want to know what he had done with it. He sheepishly brought it downstairs, I looked at him silently, he apologised! We had an admission! This was a breakthrough for Peter, so I showed him how easy it was to wash them. The enuresis continued but was more manageable as Peter now confronted the problem and helped to deal with it.

Peter continued to attend the school he was at whilst staying for those few weeks at his grandmother's home. This gave him continuation in his education, giving him stability in an all-important area of his life and was not a school we had previously dealt with. He had an excellent friend in a young man called Sam who also attended the school. They were good together, supportive, always 'there' for each other, vetting each other's girl friends, and quite positively partners in crime at times! But on the whole we trusted both of them and as we would ensure Sam towed the line when he was with us, his parents made sure Peter did when he visited their home. Their friendship took them through their school life and was retained thereafter even though their work experiences were in totally different directions.

Lawrence and I had many discussions on how to help Peter understand the work ethic of life, as he really did believe that parents were there purely to provide and fulfil his every demand. He took over a Sunday paper round for a short time, enjoyed the cash he earned, but found the effort needed was far greater than the reward. In time, Aaron was to encourage him to work for a couple of hours after school at his firm. Peter went headlong into this. The work boosted his self esteem as he felt this was 'real' work with 'real' pay. He was even prepared to work occasional Saturday mornings too. Now he was able to save for the things he wanted in life, placing a value and a worth on them. However he often felt demeaned by the company and could not recognise why they would not give him a pay increase as an invaluable staff member! We could see that one day this inflated ego would take him to higher places, but as a young man rising fourteen, it would land him at the bottom of the popularity poll. He was to be frequently reminded that there were many people who were not prepared to listen to or tolerate his cutting remarks or his disdainful looks thrown at lesser souls, and there were those who just might throw a punch his way and as someone who wore glasses he ought to think more carefully before speaking. My phrase was that God has given two eyes and two ears but only one mouth, that was intended for each of us to do twice as much listening and watching before we spoke! But Peter had the 'gift of the gab' and was determined to use it.

Throughout his stay with us and beyond, Peter was to struggle and agonise with the damaged relationship with his natural family, though we attempted to help him repair some of the damage with the grandparents, especially those that lived away, but they were so badly hurt by the events it was to take a very long time to achieve. I believe part of this was their difficulty in seeing us as Peter did, as his parents. In their eyes we were providing him with a home, no more than this. But from day one Peter had insisted on calling us 'Mum and Dad,' purely for aesthetic reasons to reduce embarrassing questions by others, or so he told me! Over time I would like to think those titles of ours had another more genuine meaning to him, as we became much closer. Peter may not have liked our down to earth policy of life, but adhering to it certainly earned his respect. They say truth hurts and Peter had to endure an awful lot of truths from us in order to step down from his pedestal as he learned to take real control of his life from another angle.

One of the hardest aspects of looking after Peter was constantly being compared to other parents. If they were redecorating their house he would insist that we should be doing this to ours. If friend's parents had a new car he could not grasp why we didn't, this could often lead to us feeling that we were never quite good enough for Peter. But we were who we were, and as adults we lead the way, at least for the time being. He could be infuriating, frustrating, the most difficult, but yet again I had to remind myself of the old adage, 'a child needs more loving when he least deserves it!' With gritted teeth we learned to smile, to not rise to his goading, and to reduce his elevated stance hopefully without reducing his self-esteem or future intentions. As he teetered on the edge of his pedestal, his cold, distanced exterior gradually thawed as his protective wall came down, brick by brick, to be replaced by a genuine warm-hearted soul who continued to ache for his loss but took pride in his gains, not least among those of our family. He may have a different surname, this preserves his identity and is to be proud of, but he is a part of our family 'that nought can sever'.

A real turning point for him was to be a testing trial for Lawrence. I had returned to nursing, working three shifts a week. Lawrence had arranged to help one of the older ones, who had moved out of our home, inviting Peter to help, as he did not want to leave him in the house alone. Peter felt this was beneath him and accused Lawrence of not trusting him. He reluctantly went along but had no intentions of helping and goaded Lawrence the whole time undermining him in all his efforts. By the time they returned to the house, Lawrence had listened to more than he wanted to and verbally tackled Peter stating clearly how he felt, pointing out Peter's selfishness. Peter was severely affronted by this and ran upstairs to pack his bags to leave. When Peter appeared downstairs, they had a headlong verbal collision of differences, as Lawrence recognised that Peter was falling back on old behaviours, running away especially from a father figure. Consequently Lawrence locked the door, removed the key and insisted Peter stayed to face the conflict. Though not Lawrence's style as a rule, it was necessary to break the cycle of events, to take away the control that Peter thought he had, and redress the balance of power to the rightful hands of the adults. Peter pushed beyond the limits demanding to be let out, each time he took his fury back upstairs he was reminded by some of the other children that Dad was right and he was wrong. Lawrence did something totally unexpected, he directed his fury towards me by contacting me at work to let me know what was happening, I knew I needed to be at home as quickly as I could but that would be a couple of hours. However I asked to speak to Peter, warned him he had gone too far this time, and if respect had gone out of the window, then he was to wait for me to get home so we could discuss his future with us if there was to be one! Lawrence and I had never allowed any of the children to drive a wedge between us so I knew that Peter had well and truly overstepped the limits. But in fact Lawrence's action to stop Peter from running had a huge impact on him. Lawrence had demonstrated how much he cared. That even though Peter had been a proverbial pain in the neck all evening, had been verbally abusive too, but Lawrence had still refused to let Peter go. He had unwittingly forced Peter into facing and confronting the situation, making him realise that running was not the answer, comments from the other youngsters had reiterated this for him too. By the time I arrived home both were feeling very sorry, licking their wounds, and both were ready to apologise for their reactions, not only to each other but also to me. Peter listened to what I had to say, admitted that he did want to stay with us and took that huge first step off his pedestal. We had a real breakthrough, an admission of feeling, of understanding hurt, not only one's own but also that of someone who cares and whom he cared for. The foundation stones were really laid and set in concrete.

Peter had pestered and plagued us for a pet since his arrival, but we were convinced this would only be a short lived love affair based on pride of possession. We had eight children did we really need pets as well that no doubt we would be left to look after? But we had kept various pets previously and on their demise had agreed not to replace them as the children lacked continual interest in them and the work became my responsibility. He really wanted a cat, which I felt might be to his advantage to take responsibility for and maybe to help him to get in touch with his inner feelings. This was in a way forced upon us when two young kittens were found in the laundry of the care home I worked in. The manager insisted they could not stay at the home and if new homes could not be found, then they would have to be taken to the vet to be terminated. So home for all waifs and strays the kittens came back with me. One became a family cat, the other Peter's personal treasure. He called him Ace, named after Ace Ventura, a film much loved and enjoyed by Peter. Peter did quite well to rise to his responsibilities for Ace including cleaning up any mess left by him. Ace encouraged Peter to understand selfishness from a different angle helping him to gain a perspective on some of his own selfish ways. Though Peter still broke the rules by hiding the cat in his bedroom at night telling us the cat was out and would not come in. Then in the middle of the night when Ace would wake up, Peter would open his door to let him out, ignoring the animal's real need to go outside, consequently Ace would come purring into our bedroom to awaken us!

Our children had always been given responsibility for daily and weekly chores within the house. Peter also had his share to fulfil. There were those among them who were more diligent than the others. Peter was not one of them! However he was expected to keep his own room tidy and clean it weekly, he was also expected to keep the toilet by his bedroom clean. Literally the smallest room in the house with a loo and a washbasin. I had taught him what to do, which products to use and as he was the only person to use this one I felt it was not expecting too much from him. However the ongoing struggle to achieve the level of cleanliness I expected was not worth the hassle we endured. But I was determined Peter would play his part and fulfil his obligations. Determined not to do his job for him was upsetting me and he knew it, and therefore Peter was all the more determined not to do it. An argument was brewing and this was one battle I had to win or else he had the answer to get out of every chore and responsibility in the future.

How was I to diffuse the situation, achieve cleanliness by Peter, giving him pride and praise for a job well done and keep the parental control in our hands? Well, writing to our offspring usually worked when all other forms of communication were not. I figured out a way of hoping to get Peter to notice the need in a manner that could not be easily ignored any longer. Whilst he was at school I wrote a note to stick to the underside of the toilet lid, it simply read: -

> *"Dear Peter, This toilet is rapidly becoming*
> *a health hazard. Please clean it before*
> *it affects yours! Thank you*
> *Love Mum"*

Peter came home from school at teatime, and as usual disappeared upstairs. We waited for the response. Would there be an almighty argument, would he run off in a state of fury? Thoughts ran through my head. Suddenly Peter ran downstairs, I waited with baited breath, and he pushed past everyone in his way en route to the utility room. He was muttering under his breath clearly objecting to my note. Then to my surprise instead of going outside to let off steam, he collected all the cleaning materials he needed, stormed back upstairs and turned his fury into positive cleaning power. In less than half an hour the room gleamed and at last was sweet smelling too! Not a harsh word had passed between us, both of us had achieved our aim. He may not have been pleased with me but where there is a will there is a way. Sometimes you just have to look for it!

I have never known anyone to have a relationship with his or her hair, especially not of the male domain!

But Peter did. He had a magnificent head of red hair that really was his hallmark. He endured the usual teasing and name calling about this, I suppose as much from within the family as he did out from outsiders. Most of the time he took this in his stride or treated those doing it with the contempt they probably deserved. But he was as much a fashion maker as a fashion follower and developed some interesting hairstyles. There was the swept back look, the parted curtains look, the stick it up in the air and let's see what every one thinks look, the long look, the short look. I could not keep up with it at all, but the most fascinating was the dreadlock look created by attaching hair extensions! When he told me the cost involved I could have cried, not least because red hair and false black dreadlocks looked quite ridiculous, but also I kept finding the offending locks in the strangest of places as they frequently fell out. He had more hair appointments than all the girls put together, but life was never dull and his hair was frequently the topic of the day!

Peter often frequented the town where he had previously lived to do his shopping; it was on one of these expeditions that he was to accidentally meet up with his natural mother and sister. Recognising his own family he reached out as they passed by to acknowledge them, but was met with total condemnation and abusive language. This was an unexpected public display of ridicule and humiliation that was to set him back phenomenally. He returned home that day pale, desperately upset with his ego and self esteem so bruised and battered. He wept as he told me what they had said and how he felt. Trying to help him recover from this was incredibly hard as he now faced the truth and reality of his family's position of totally rejecting him as one of them. He tried to brush the incident to one side but the hurt remained, at his own admission he had visited the area of their house in the hope of casually meeting up with them expecting everything to be all right, with the past forgotten. Peter was to continue to look for acceptance by other members of the family in search of making peace with his past. Each time he felt he was one step nearer to achieving it, something would happen or words were said that still smarted, only highlighting the state of the unhealed wound. The family feud had started long before Peter had appeared on the scene, their own wounds were deeper than Peter could yet understand and any attempts by him to reconcile the position were futile and ineffective. We felt that he carried a dream within himself that one day he would play a key role in repairing the family damage, perhaps he also carried guilt for their behaviour, blaming himself, as children in care often do. Until he reached his own acceptance of the family situation, all we could do was to support him in his quest. He yearned to feel the similarities between himself and his natural father, he felt scared of meeting up with his sister or finding himself in the position of being in her company as a teenager and not knowing whom she was. His vulnerability was more evident than he realised, and these were the times when we had to be strong for him, though there were many painful emotional moments shared between us.

Peter's need to feel in control of situations and hold a feeling of importance was to come to fruition for him and a co-student from his school when he was sponsored by the Rotary Club organisation to go on a leadership training course. This boosted his morale enormously and he threw himself into it whole-heartedly, wanting to shine like a beacon to prove his worth. However after the course he was invited to offer a shared presentation with the other student. This was to take place in a local hotel after a Rotary Club Dinner, Lawrence and I were invited to celebrate the occasion with him. I was never quite sure which of us was the most anxious at this nerve racking event, Peter for having to stand up to speak in public in the adult world or me for being the only female in this all male dominated world! Needless to say we both survived and enjoyed the pride we held for each other. Peter was more than capable of being a leader, hc just needed to believe in himself and remember to lead in the right direction.

That great gift in life, time, was to help us to tame Peter and help him to face his future that he would be responsible for, also to take the consequences of his own actions. We only had a few precious years to guide him before he would be launched into the big wide world, and during those years he was also to face the demons in his life and put them into perspective. I called it 'condensed parenting', tough love was needed at times, especially when Peter pulled in the opposite direction, which could be quite often. He was ambitious in mind but not always in practise, his ideas of grandeur would only be fulfilled when he put effort into the equation and accepted constructive criticism regardless of the direction it came from. He would also need to be more empathic towards others. He had the intelligence, and the ability, but he just needed the experience and the insight. Life, living and time would give him all of that, along with a nudge or two from a few folk!

He was nearing school leaving age and a review with social services was due, and Peter was about to be given options to choose from in life. He still presented to the world as the squeaky clean, upfront, confident young man, but this was a façade that he projected for appearances only. Whenever he had discussions with those in authority he carefully portrayed himself as a capable intelligent person able to make sensible decisions and carry them out. But once the captive audience had left, Peter would anxiously share his fears and agonise on the way forward. At this review he was to face the most difficult crossroad in his life yet.

He was informed that he was about to leave the care system and though there would be a level of support, it would be different to that he was accustomed to. The carrot dangled before him was to be assisted to find a home of his own, possibly a rented flat which he would be responsible for, though he would have an after care worker to guide him through the pitfalls of independence. He would be given a free hand to spend two thousand pounds to furnish his home and make it comfortable. The picture set before him was quite an attractive package. Peter smiled throughout, nodding appropriately at the review officer. She acknowledged some of the fractious moments and struggles that Peter had shared within our family, making it clear that such moments would be behind him and he could take full control of his life from the moment he stepped into his new world. Throughout the meeting Peter expressed confidence and understanding but his body language told Lawrence and I something else. I found myself explaining some of the difficulties he would encounter, pointing out the loneliness that Peter would find hard to handle. Each time I highlighted a negative that I knew Peter would struggle to handle, a counter argument was thrown back from his social worker about all young people struggling and learning from their mistakes. She was teaching her grandmother to suck eggs! We already had three of ours going through this phase but they were stronger than Peter and I truly felt that he was being set up to fail. They compared Peter to other youngsters in the care system, but Lawrence and I were seeing Peter with all his ideals, strengths and weaknesses laid out before him and we were afraid for him. We both lunged in to express our fears and concerns, stating clearly the struggles he had and how he would need more support and could not possibly cope with the scenario laid before him. We needed him to hear it from us as much as we needed the reviewing officer and his social worker to hear it. Peter was visualising a penthouse suite on offer and two thousand pounds was more than he had ever held, his materialistic world was forming before his own eyes. After a great deal of discussion they left us with a parting shot of arranging for an after care worker to visit Peter to help move him on. Peter nodded, thanked them and appeared to accept the situation. But as they drove away he stood in the kitchen backing against the kitchen cupboard saying, "Mum, why were they not listening to you? You were telling them the truth, you told them what a nerd I was, you told them why I wouldn't cope but they ignored you. Why?" I was still upset and annoyed about the bulldozer that had driven through my home and over one of my children. "Because Peter, they see you as someone stronger than the average, intelligent and clued up because that is what you want them to see. We know you and all your foibles. You have to choose Peter. Do you want to follow their lead or stay here? We will offer support whichever route you choose but you have to make the decision." Tears welled in his eyes, but he was a teenage lad that did not share his weaknesses easily. "Mum, I'm not ready to leave, I haven't been here long enough yet." I knew what he meant. "Then you have a phone call to make to your social worker in the morning, don't you?" He nodded, put his arms around me and thanked me. I believe my parting shot was "But you will tow the line young man!" He grinned from ear to ear. This was indeed a major turning point. Peter did stay with us, and certainly made an effort in all ways. If he had cause to apologise for a mistake made, he meant it and learnt from it. Growing up took on a new meaning and with his renewed outlook on life, feeling genuinely more settled and grounded as well as supported, he settled down to making his life the success he wanted it to be. When eventually he did move out a few years later, it was for the right reasons in a more natural way and he discovered two thousand pounds was indeed a great deal of money, but in terms of setting up a home it didn't actually stretch as far as he would have liked it to!

*"Good habits formed at youth
make all the difference."*

*Aristotle*

*Greek Philosopher
(384BC - 322BC)*

## CHAPTER 18

# Making Sense

During the previous year or so we had seen one or two of our earlier children return to us to rediscover some of their past before moving on once again. As individuals they were to stay for a few months, at separate times, offering their own trying and testing behaviours that would impact on the family. But our family was about supporting youngsters through troubled times and though many of those that knew us thought we were verging on the insane, they also truly supported us in their own way. Teenagers have their own way of bringing extras to add to the collection of characters or in finding those in need of a spare bed! Our son Gareth befriended a particularly lovely girl who came to stay with us for quite a lengthy time, interestingly she came with the understanding she could stay while she found a flat of her own, but in the end Gareth found a house to rent with a friend, whilst the girl friend stayed with us for many more months whilst we supported her to find a house of her own to buy. Social Services were able and willing to explore ways of using our bedrooms too! So once again we maintained our clan status.

Having stated that we had no further intentions to foster, given our work responsibilities and Lawrence moving towards retirement age, we were asked if we would consider some form of respite service. We felt this was a possibility, as we knew only too well how strained relationships could be at times. There are always occasions when young folk need that all-important break, to allow both parties to regain perspective in their lives, in order to keep the relationship going. One such youngster, a little girl, came to stay for a week whilst her parents went away. She was a lively soul but had limited understanding into the negative effect of her behaviour on the family she was living with. She was much younger than Penny and Laura and they loved mothering her, she revelled in this attention and viewed the week's experience as a holiday, as we took her on outings virtually every day she was with us. Another young teenager had slightly different needs for he had an ongoing arrangement to join us on alternate weekends and proved to be quite a handful. I could certainly understand why his parents needed a break!

I recall taking a telephone call asking if we could possibly consider a rather difficult toddler, in turmoil, of about eighteen months old. How refreshing I thought, after dealing with the tiresome teens the terrible two's stage would be a doddle in comparison. After all just how difficult could one small toddler be? However I explained that I would love to be in the position to take on this tot but unfortunately our work commitments could no longer work around one so young. The social workers comment was "Well this one is quite a problem as he has rampaged three sets of foster parents and they have all given up on him." I gulped. Had I just escaped an experience no parent would want or had I just missed out on the challenge of the new century? I would never know, but I have often thought of that little chap because

I would have loved to have him as part of our clan. Then a few weeks later came another call from the social worker:

*"Mrs Valdis, we have a ten year old who is in need of a placement for a limited period of time. I know this is no longer part of your remit as you now do respite, however he is waiting for a placement in a children's home and one is expected to be available in about three weeks time. Consequently we are just looking to fill the gap. So it will be time limited. He can be quite a handful and really needs experienced parents so we wondered if you would feel you could help?"*

I thought about it, he would be younger than those still living with us, and I felt we had a lot to offer in that short period of time. "Tell me a little more about him, what is he like?" I asked.

She explained that his name was Jake that he was the middle child of three boys. The three boys were brothers through adoption. The couple that had adopted them had, like us, been foster parents too. Jake had not been an easy child to care for, and though he had been with his adoptive parents since babyhood he had proved to be quite a challenge. "He is small, slim and slippery and has a poor relationship with school." She added. Well so had Nathan, and we had survived his school days even though we terminated them early! What could this lad offer in three weeks that Nathan hadn't? In any case I told myself, whatever he threw at us would be over in three weeks and we had a holiday in Tenerife already booked shortly afterwards. "You must be realistic." She said. "I know he is unlikely to give you an easy time." What child ever did! Now who was being unrealistic? My rose coloured glasses had long since been put away!

With this in mind I had no hesitation in saying "Yes, of course we would take him." Now I needed to find the courage to tell Lawrence what I had agreed to. It was to be the longest three weeks of our lives, and perhaps the most daunting and the most exhilarating too. If we thought our lives had simulated a roller coaster ride then this was to be the real thing, and the speed of the ride was uncontrollable by those on board.

Jake was a city lad, street wise and worldly wise. His attendance in school had been virtually non-existent during the previous two years. He took what he wanted, when he wanted, in any way that he could. He was one of life's non-conformists. He had walked all over his adoptive parents and not given an easy time to his brothers either. His language could be colourful with expletives we had yet to learn! Schools had found him impossible. His reluctance to attend was only made worse by his attendance, as he was there purely to cause maximum disruption. His adoptive parents had struggled to cope with many unexpected behaviours, and these were getting harder to handle the older he became. Hurling furniture down the stairs was something he would do to make his point, that he would not comply with a request to get ready for school! Stealing the deputy headmaster's car keys in an attempt to drive his car away was a recent occurrence. Jake had broken in and out of his parents' home preferring to walk the city streets rather than be comfortable at home, or hide in the roof, only coming down when the family were out or asleep, in order to take food from the kitchen. Stealing from his own family, and lying, were the traits that his family struggled with, along with destructive sibling rivalry of the extreme. His attention seeking or attention craving notions knew no bounds, another recent performance included Jake climbing on the rooftop of his home and staging a sit-in. Most boys go through a phase of risk taking behaviour, but Jake constantly looked for greater risks to take, searching for ways to shock or create disharmony. Running away when life seemed tough was his answer to many problems, and he only ever came back on his own terms!

Is there any wonder that the parents felt they were at the end of their tether and despite all the support they had gained over the years felt they could take no more. Jake had been taken in to care on a few occasions to give everyone a break. But his parents had clearly screamed out enough was enough, and perhaps Jake needed to hear that. They had two other sons to consider, one older with Asperger's Syndrome and a younger one that clearly was not benefiting from Jake's example. There was a danger in the whole family collapsing as a direct result of Jake's negative behaviours. With his removal they had a chance to salvage and change their own family dynamics.

But at this stage we knew none of this, and our family dynamics were to be flung into oblivion. Jake was to discover another side to life, redefine his expectations, discover more of his capabilities and skills, and recognise that in life you can make choices, but you also have to take the consequences of those choices. He was to push everyone to their limits, play on their weaknesses and witness his own. He demanded centre stage but discovered it was not always as comfortable as he thought especially when the police were involved. He established just how big this world was and how small his city was to prove to be. Jake had a love hate relationship with the world, he feared for his place in it. An intelligent lad who had facts to his fingertips but never knew where he had learned them. He was an incredible natural artist who could express himself through his art and often did. Jake had an insight into everyone else's problems but lacked insight into his own, except on a good day. He had a natural desire to go with the flow of life but Jake rarely stopped to discover which direction the flow was coming from or going to. This left those trying to help him, struggling to contend with which direction they needed to face to best support him. He could bring out the very best or the very worst of himself on the turn of a coin. He was capable of making you stand on mountains to be proud of him or he could sink you to the bottom of the deepest waters to drown your aspirations and hopes for him.

But Jake was Jake, love the boy not the deed, this lovable rogue had entered our lives, our clan, and life would never be the same again.

So on a cold wet autumn day in 2001, Jake was brought to our home. Lawrence was to be at the receiving end as I was working until eight in the evening. As soon as the necessary paperwork had been completed Lawrence brought Jake to my place of work to meet me. He had left Jake in the reception area of the care home whilst he talked to me first. His eyes welled and he choked on his words, "He's a lovely lad Dani, he's not a boy that should be in a children's home. I can't put my finger on it but there is something about this lad you can't help but like." He had been in our care all of half an hour and Lawrence was hooked by this beguiling young man. I went to meet him. The moment I saw him I knew exactly what Lawrence meant. We were considered experienced parents but we were about to discover how naive we really were! But for the moment we were delighted to have him with us. He was indeed small and slim, but the slippery side of him was yet to be seen. Jake was smaller than the average boy of his age, his pallor was white and his cheek muscles were tense, which matched his strained demeanour. He kept his hands in his pockets, stared at the floor with an occasional glance up to me: his shoulders drooped but stiffened. He had short medium brown hair and he was dressed in jogging bottoms, a baggy necked tee shirt and a hooded jacket. He sheepishly greeted me and I welcomed him to our home apologising for still being at work. He was exceptionally quiet and a little withdrawn or maybe overwhelmed by all that had happened. He gave a half smile of acknowledgement as I suggested that he went back with Lawrence and I would see him as soon as possible. There was huskiness to his voice, a rasping that we would learn would change according to his mood and dependent on how much shouting he had done. For such a streetwise character, Jake portrayed a capturing innocence and I was convinced this was a misunderstood young man. He was soon to earn the nickname of Smiler because when his half smile gave way to a full smile Jake could captivate anyone, it was certainly a feature that emanated life and all things positive. Unfortunately there was another facet to Jake's character, this one created a very dark cloud that engulfed anyone in his way, but sadly I felt the main person he targeted was himself, though the projection did not always appear that way.

Jake had a few days at home getting accustomed to his surroundings and of course our family, which he struggled with, as he had not yet made his niche. During this 'honeymoon' period his behaviour was exemplary, keen to show us his manners, social abilities and his level of intelligence. He was incredibly impressive and it was so easy to enjoy the company of this very clever lad. He had opinions and willingly shared them. He could offer a counter argument in any debate and could clearly see all sides of any discussion, often questioning his own thoughts; this gave us insight into Jake's depth of thinking. But we also witnessed how easily his temper could rise and the struggle he had to keep it under control. We decided to find a school prepared to give him a chance, we were taking a risk of upsetting the equilibrium, and so would the school. But to help Jake get back into education we would have to give it our best, having others who willingly went to school was a great help, because it gave him the example and the motivation to do likewise. Jake talked openly about his situation and his own stupidities. Having distanced himself away from his own home and family he confidently shared with us some of his wrong-doings and even went as far as to discuss with us how his parents must have felt too. He was able to show remorse, he was angry with himself for what he had done, but some of this anger was noticeably aimed at his parents because he felt they should have been stronger. He certainly had no idea how exhausted they were with dealing with his perpetual anti-social behaviours.

We chose a school in the neighbouring district, not too far away from us. We explained as fully as possible the problems Jake had regarding school. He was given the chance he needed and was accepted. Uniform bought, start date set. We prepared his mind for this event as much as we were able. We also told him we would like him to consider staying with us for as long as he would like. This came as a shock to Jake, as he was dreading the day he was to go to the allocated place in the children's home. We spoke with his social worker; she felt we needed to know more about Jake to see if we felt differently. Pre-conceived ideas may have stopped us taking Jake in the first place, but we had now met him, could see the potential and in little more than a week felt we could move forward with him. What was important was to stop Jake slip-sliding backwards, because convincing him that progress was good frightened him and inevitably set him back temporarily. Jake expressed his fear of going into school and meeting everyone, both teaching staff and pupils. But his fears melted when he met Mr B, as all the pupils knew this teacher. He was just the right person for Jake. A dominant male, Mr B was easy to relate to, firm but fair to every pupil with a determination to make learning fun. Jake entered the classroom on his first day and was welcomed and introduced to everyone. His teacher afforded Jake the respect he needed and hoped Jake would reciprocate, and in time he would. The first day went well and Jake even did his homework at the kitchen table with everyone else. One successful day behind him! We had decided to only take care of one day at a time to reduce the pressure on Jake, and try to lay his educational foundations gradually by building on each successful day he managed.

Over the following week Jake had a few minor fracas as he found his place within the peer group, but there was to be an ongoing situation between himself and another boy, who also had struggles in his life not altogether dissimilar to Jake's. These two were to frequently have head to head arguments, which left Mr B having to separate them and no doubt help them to come to terms with each other's presence. My own theory was that they mirrored each other's traits and neither liked what they saw.

One day behind him, then another, before we knew it he had successfully achieved one whole week, which of course we celebrated, and praised Jake, to encourage him. This may have been one small step for mankind but for Jake it was a huge stride in his life. He was truly proud and thrilled that it had been easier than he thought possible. Then half way through the second week, Lawrence took him to school in the usual manner. Parked the car and walked with Jake to the school gate where they said their farewells. Lawrence watched and waved to Jake as he entered the school, Jake smiled and waved back. But as Lawrence arrived back home he heard the telephone ringing, it was the school to explain that Jake had been seen by staff entering the school but had not arrived at the classroom. Staff had searched the school but there was no sign of the boy. Where on earth had he gone and which way did he leave the school?

The rest of the day was spent searching for him after notifying social services and the police of his disappearing act. They may have been used to this pattern of Jake, but he was still a vulnerable boy of ten, loose on the town or heading for the city. By early evening we were informed of the area he had been sighted. I opted to drive around the area in the hope of seeing him to persuade him to come back. After an hour or so I spotted a group of younger teenagers with a small lad swaggering alongside of them wearing a cap, it had to be Jake, it was definitely his stance. I watched them from a distance go into a house. A few minutes later I rang the doorbell of the house, a woman answered it, when I asked if I could speak to Jake, she was hesitant, but then the youngsters, including

Jake, peered inquisitively around the door. The look on Jake's face was a mixture of total disbelief and relief. I explained that I had come to take him home, as he had a long way to go, Jake stared. The woman explained that her daughter had said he had nowhere to stay that night and had asked if he could stay with them. I also explained that this was true, which was why Jake was to stay at our house and I had offered to collect him after his night out. Now it was the mother's turn to look relieved. Jake was annoyed at my approach and even more shocked that I did not appear angry, though when we were both in the car he realised that I was not best pleased with this antic. He huffed and puffed in the car all the way back, torn between trying to show me the 'tough-guy' stance, and astounded that we had found him. But by the time we were home and the police were sitting in front of him explaining his selfishness and foolishness he was far too tired and hungry to argue. The policemen eventually left, and Jake and I had a chat about disappointments, feelings of being let down and the meaning of trust, along with trying to discover what had caused him to leave school and at which point he had made the decision to run. We felt it was important to have some answers whilst he still felt tired and vulnerable, simply because a night's sleep would strengthen his reasoning for everything that he did. He was given supper, reminded of our commitment to him, and that tomorrow was another day to prove that he could carry on where he had left off. He was certain that the school would be against him and not let him back.

The following morning Lawrence was to speak to the headmistress, who insisted that Jake was to attend school ready to start all over again. The head spoke at length with Jake to establish strategies. Jake made a sort of promise to make more effort but added that he might not be able to keep to the promise! He was right, over the next week or two we were to have a problem knowing whether Jake was in school or not. Lawrence would take the willing, smiling boy to school, wave him goodbye at the front door, but before he had even got back to his car, Jake had left by the back door, and school would be ringing him yet again. Many times we would trawl the streets in search of him and haul him back late at night. His so-called friends were not a good influence and we somehow needed to cut the ties between them. But as any parent knows the more you try to do that, the thicker the band of friendship grows. Jake was intrigued as to how we always found out where he was, and his reluctance to come back to us lessened on each occasion. He began to talk openly about the friendship not being all that good and if he wanted to make something of his life he would need to make changes. We leapt to support this, highlighting his strengths and skills and what he could achieve. In support the headmistress felt she needed to have an agreement with Jake signed by all parties involved. Jake rose to this, especially as the cold nights were drawing in and walking the streets with his friends was not so much fun any longer and in any case we always brought him back! With the help of Mr B and Jake's supportive peers he began to enjoy school and took pride in any achievements he gained. The pressure and concern was still with us but we felt there was a chance that we might be able to take him to Tenerife with us. The holiday experience might just help to seal a bond with him and take away some of the hurt he felt after receiving a card from his mother stating that there was no possibility of him ever returning home. We believe this to be Mum's intention to help Jake to focus on settling into our family and helping him to move forward in his education as he moved towards the teenage years. Perhaps our only concern was if he chose to run away whilst on holiday.

With the success he was having in school we had good reason to include him on our holiday. He would have young company with Andrew and Laura around and the holiday would be beneficial to all of us. Both Lawrence and I knew we would be on tenterhooks with Jake joining us in case he took the notion to run, but we also felt that as Jake had never been abroad nor flown before, there was a good chance that for a week he could tow the line. We stressed the need for a passport to travel but also knew we would have to keep his safely in our keeping. Flying was a little daunting for him and his first impression at the airport was one of fear. But he only needed a little coaxing and plenty of reassurance, particularly from Andrew, in order to feel able to board. He loved the island, the sun, fun, the time spent together and meeting new friends as well as the freedom to meet with these friends in the evening. It was a whole new experience and one he revelled in and was sorry to leave behind. But it helped to keep him focused and moving forward on our return.

So we moved towards Christmas with Jake having regular attendance in school. Though not totally without problem he was proving his worth, his abilities and his intelligence. He still challenged the system but he also realised that we worked on his behalf with the school. Conforming to expectation was not always a comfortable place for him. He battled with his own feelings about his achievements. One day he could stand so pleased and proud, on another day he would be so angry and annoyed because he had complied, that he would take those feelings out on anyone. But we were also aware that these foundations to his life were very new and therefore not very strong, they were already being shaken along with his confidence, as we were expected to consider the next school for him. Even if he was able to maintain his attendance through to the end of the summer term there was no way he would be ready for any of the large comprehensive schools on offer. We had to have some serious thought and make decisions in the early part of the following term. But where would we go? The ideal would have been another year at his present school but his age was against him and would have been an insult to his intelligence. We chose to defer our decision until Christmas was over.

Another difficulty of Jake's was his light-fingered ways. He never meant to be malicious but would fall back on old ways. Jake would target the bedrooms of the other children, which was grossly unfair. I suspect it was his way of aiming at their vulnerability, he aimed small, and usually minor things were taken but it was as though he could not stop himself breezing into their rooms, spotting an item and just taking it. Despite all the children we had cared for, we had never felt the need for locks on any door, until now. It was essential to protect our other children and their belongings. Jake was not impressed, especially as we allowed the others to have a key for their door but not him until he could show greater respect. When he did, he had a key, if he let himself down or showed disrespect it was confiscated. He could use this against us too by locking himself out of the room several times a day just so we were inconvenienced by having to unlock it. If Jake thought for one moment we would not have the stamina to handle that he was mistaken after all there were two of us to share the load and only one of him!

His relationships with our other children were quite reasonable, though Jake quickly played on their lack of knowledge; they had the upper hand on social graces and toleration of his negative behaviour. His mood swings were hard to cope with, and Peter, who was seven years Jake's senior, struggled at times to accept his presence, as Jake would make constant remarks about Peter's various hairstyles. They should have been united in their support of Leeds United Football Club but this only developed into a competition of who had the greatest knowledge of the latest footballers. Jake goaded and Peter rose to it showing his intolerance of this kid type brother. Perhaps Peter saw something of himself in Jake as much as Jake used Peter as a big brother alternative in the absence of his own. I am convinced that there was also an element of jealousy from Jake over Peter being on the brink of leaving care, which emphasised how much further he still had to go.

Jake was ready for the Christmas holidays, and those itchy, edgy feet of his were struggling not to be on the run. We really would have to find a way to use that surplus energy! But in truth Jake had no reason to run which also confused him. He would try arguing over silly trivialities, and when others could reason their way around it or simply refrain from rising to his taunting, Jake would be so annoyed but only with himself and successfully take his feelings out on others in the household. He was still very demanding of both time and attention. He often changed character many times in a day from being a real darling of a boy to being an angry belligerent hooligan.

Huge efforts were put into helping our other children learn to handle their own feelings and reactions to Jake's demeanour. We worked as positively as we could with him and it appeared to be reaping rewards. We had tremendous support from our liaison worker and also from Jake's social worker. We concentrated on the good he did and used the not so good as examples of how not to behave. He still found success hard to accept as this almost went against the grain of life for him. But one of his remorseful expressions could make anyone truly believe he did not approve of himself or of his own ways, which is why he made such a huge effort to change. Equally one of Jake's smiles could dissolve any negative feelings that might be harboured against him. 'Small, slim and slippery,' a good description for 'Our Jake,' which is how we now thought of him. But Jake was his own person and would always hold an affinity but never to be 'owned' by anyone. He was a free spirit.

*"Each forward step we take we leave some phantom of ourselves behind."*

*John Lancaster Spalding*

*Roman Catholic Bishop of Peoria (1840 - 1916)*

# CHAPTER 19

## Spread My Wings

Jake was having occasional organised visits from his parents, which were initially very stressful for both parties. There was an obvious attachment and a love between them but, to an outsider, it appeared that trust and respect was no longer a part of their relationship. Jake could not rise to his parents expectations but nor could they meet his. Communication bordered on each giving instructions to the other and the tension could be easily sensed at this time. Jake was unable to manage stress at any level, becoming tense his body bristled, his face paled and his cheeks were very taught. The sadness always showed in his eyes. He constantly thrust his hands deep into his pockets, avoiding eye contact. He had shared enough with me for me to surmise that he was ashamed of his behaviour towards his parents, but found it hard to break the pattern of misdemeanours he offered them. His older brother came on the first visit but was so anti-social and revengeful towards Jake the decision was taken not to include him in subsequent visits. His younger brother also came, which pleased Jake, but our concern was that Jake displayed arrogance towards him and was overly rough in much the same way as his older sibling was towards Jake. This was all very worrying, as we had not met this side of him. He was subjected to a hefty beating from his brother, which we witnessed, breaking up the boys making it clear this was totally unacceptable. But Jake's brother had been determined to have revenge over an incident in their home involving a pet. But it gave us some insight into the strength of feeling or lack of it that existed among the boys. This would be another aspect of his character to watch out for, and work with, as we were acutely aware of how quickly his temper or anger could escalate and he was now sharing his life with some very sensitive teenagers.

The arrival of another New Year was celebrated with friends and family around. Jake had coped well with his first Christmas with us. This would always be a crippling emotional time for youngsters away from their families and we had anticipated some problems and the possibility of him 'doing a runner,' but Jake had surprised us and kept amazingly calm, enjoying all aspects of the festivities and family frivolities. He certainly knew how to enjoy himself on high days and holidays, such times brought out the best in him, the pure childlike innocence and his generosity shined through. We had our first grandson at this time, an active toddler of two years old, who lived with his parents not too far away and Jake liked nothing more than to race and chase him as he toddled around emanating happy squeals and giggling endlessly. He was beginning to enjoy the role of a much younger ten year old and would let down his guard becoming very protective of the baby.

He began to relax, to smile and laugh more. The tenseness in his cheeks faded a little. Jake's natural humour surfaced and his view on life's situations held a comedic charm. His deep gravelly laughter was very infectious and, as long as we steered him away from using any of our teenagers from being the focus of his fun, he was to prove that he was great company to be with. He and Andrew got on exceptionally well; unfortunately Jake's influence was not always beneficial. Though Jake was younger than Andrew his worldly knowledge and exciting ways did cause some problems over the coming years.

Whenever I was out and about with Jake he would ask about the various schools we would drive past. It was as if he was eliminating them from his potential list of possibilities for the senior school option. On one such occasion nearing the new school term we passed the local private grammar school, Jake asked about this one. I explained that both Aaron and Gareth had attended that school and went on to extol its virtues. "Why can't I go then?" he said. I discussed the difference between the types of schools available, the cost involved with this one and the need to take an examination for selection purposes. "Well that's ok, if I don't pass the test I won't be able to go will I? So I might as well at least have a try?" Jake was to continually mither me about giving him a chance to do the test. In fact he would not let up about it. Lawrence and I were afraid that we would be setting him up for failure and this could have a knock-back effect on him but he was so determined. Consequently we spoke with his social worker, she felt he could at least try, but as his school attendance had been so poor for so long the chance of him passing was so very remote. "And what if he does pass?" I asked, not wishing to underestimate this young man who was always full of surprises. "We cross that bridge when we come to it." She truthfully answered. We could see the benefits for Jake, the level of education would be right and challenging for him, he would cope with the smaller class numbers and we knew their ways of handling discipline would be acceptable to Jake. The extra-curricular activities were ideal and he would have a chance of joining one of the cadet forces as he became older, which had appealed to him. They had contained Gareth successfully so there was a chance that Jake could do really well too. We also knew they would clamp down heavily on any of Jake's stupidities without quelling his desires.

On the eighth of January Lawrence rang the school to ask when the entrance examination was due to take place and establish if there were still places available. He was to be told that the exam was to occur on the twelfth, the following Saturday! Four days to prepare him! Jake's attendance in school had not yet been put to the test that term. Added to which, that particular week was the first full week of the new term, so Jake would be looking forward to having his weekend off. So how would he accept having to spend the Saturday in another school to cope with examination conditions? What if he erupted causing problems for the other pupils? What if he ran away during the day? How would this bode for getting him back to school the following week? As fast as our minds managed one scenario, another was set before us. But the bottom line was giving him the chance, the opportunity to carry out his intentions, and possibly succeed, to simply prove to himself that he could move forward. This was his initiative, so he had the control, now he had to see that he had the drive and determination to see it through. We just had to support him and have trust in him.

He was glad to be back at school for the new term, meeting up with his friends and telling Mr B about his intentions to take the entrance examination. Mr B shared his own doubts with us but supported Jake wholeheartedly throughout that week, encouraging him in all ways to be confident in himself, to enjoy it, offering tips to succeed yet at the same time endeavouring to take away some of the pressure from Jake should he not make the grade. At home he was also being built up to do his best, regardless of the outcome. Both Aaron and Gareth shared their experiences telling him what to expect and also enthused about the school in general. Jake asked relevant questions and seemed to accept the answers he was given.

Saturday the twelfth finally arrived, armed with his pencil case and maths tools he was required to take, along with his green pass card, Jake was duly taken to the school. "Will you be upset if I don't pass?" He said as I parked the car, "I will be upset for you, because I think I know how much this means to you, but I realise you can only do the best you can, and there are an awful lot of children coming who have spent months practising for today, all hoping for the same and not everyone can get a place in this school." I answered. Jake smiled. "I will try, I promise." He had a final hug of both love and encouragement and I reminded him one of us would collect him at the end of the day. Like a 'lamb to the slaughter' he strutted in to the school and the only thought I had at that time was would he still be there when I came back and can he contain his frustration if it arises!

I don't believe any of our family relaxed that day, nor could we settle to anything constructive. Not only did the house feel hollow and empty without Jake's presence, we were all on edge wondering what the end of the day would bring and the effect on him. Lawrence and I also had concerns for the future effects resulting from today.

But 3pm finally arrived and I was duly parked outside the school eagerly waiting to greet Jake. I strolled into the playground to stand with all the other strained looking parents awaiting the arrival of their prodigies. They hoped for a place in the school, I just hoped Jake was still there! Eventually the first batch of potential high flyers were released to find their parents, some were thrilled, others looked worried but all were relieved it was over. Jake was not among them. The second batch appeared, still no Jake. I checked my watch for the time. Perhaps he had not managed to stay the day, stragglers appeared from the school door, but still no sign of Jake. The playground was emptying, the majority had dispersed, there was only a handful of parents left and most of them had a child sharing their views on the examination with each other. I felt I was the only one without. Perhaps he has disgraced himself. Perhaps he is hiding in the school and plans to trash it later. Where was my trust in Jake? Then out of the corner of my eye I saw a confident familiar young man walking towards me. Shoulders back, walking tall, and smiling the biggest grin in my direction. "Sorry for being late out, had to go to the toilet, it's been a good day, think I've messed up one question though, which was annoying, 'cos I knew the answer when I thought about it. I like the teachers, they are really good." And so he chatted on, garrulous beyond belief, and not an ounce of stress showed in his body, he was amazingly relaxed. At that moment I really could not have cared less if he had messed up every question, the fact was, here he was, here standing in front of me. No different from any other child in that playground, he had sustained the day. That was achievement enough for me, another huge stride forward for this young lad. What did the future really hold for him? Enthusiasm exuded from him, if only he could be like this all of the time. He had opened his eyes to see the world differently, if we could help him to stop retreating and hiding in his shell, like Peter he had leadership qualities that needed to be harnessed and utilised but he would need to get through the turbulent teen stage, let go of his hang-ups, and more than anything else believe in himself. It was the latter that was to be the hardest to do.

We had to wait three weeks to see if Jake would be offered a place in the school, in the meantime he went from strength to strength in his present school under the guidance of Mr B and the Head. He more than fulfilled his educational needs, his thirst for knowledge was great and his ability to retain information was excellent. Jake attended school willingly, with confidence, and there was a noticeable improvement in his emotional and physical development. It was quite impressive how well he adapted to an alternative lifestyle. He even took a new child in class under his wing when he realised someone was teasing him. He continued to carry the 'don't mess with me' stance whenever he felt the need but this could easily be dissolved with a stern eye and a firm reminder. We encouraged him to go swimming regularly to use his excess energy and enrolled him for junior weight-training sessions in an effort to stem those edgy feet of his but whilst winter was about he was less inclined to want to walk the streets.

Three weeks passed, the letter arrived; Jake slowly, teasingly opened the letter. The tension in his face showed.

Then he let out an almighty 'whoop' of joy that resounded throughout our village! He had proven his worth, he had passed and been offered a place. This to him was the most fantastic news and more than he had expected. We all celebrated his news, genuinely thrilled and delighted for him. But there was another side to this, who would pay for the fees? We only had a week in which to respond to the school confirming that he would or would not be taking up the place. Jake could not wait to get into school to tell his friends, but most of all to let Mr B know he had succeeded.

Meanwhile we contacted his social worker who was delighted with his success but very concerned about the expected fees. However we decided to go ahead with accepting the place, putting our faith in the system that commonsense would prevail and there would be money available for the fees. After all, the original plan was for Jake to be contained in a children's home and, before Christmas, there had been talk of the need for a secure unit placement at vast cost and reduced chance of success! If not we would appeal for a sponsorship, we hadn't a clue where from or how to achieve this but we had until September to do so. In the meantime I drafted a lengthy letter to appeal to the Director of Social Services explaining the full circumstances of Jake's situation. He had the opportunity to be a success, he was still emotionally fragile but his self-esteem was rising. All talk of sending him to a secure unit was dissipating, as his running away seemed more controllable. We stressed that we truly felt that fulfilling his potential was dependent on this school placement. We had another long wait for the answer to our appeal during which time we followed up other alternatives through various charities. But eventually we were told that the finances could be found to allow Jake to attend the school of his choice. Jake was fully aware of how fortunate he was and vowed to work extremely hard to achieve his aim to succeed.

He certainly continued to make the effort throughout the rest of his last year in the junior school. He still struggled to keep his anger under control and we had raised the possibility of an anger management course to help him but there wasn't a place available. So we worked with him, along with our support worker, to help him discover the triggers and offer strategies of control. He could cope when those he trusted were around but at other times he was so speedily engulfed by his rising anger, and at his own admission would lash out or search for a fight with someone. Just one look from another child or adult was enough to set him off, as his paranoia misinterpreted the expression, and Jake would insist they harboured thoughts against him. We were often left wondering whether this was part of his hang-ups over his past or associated with an illness. But given that each day he showed an improvement we chose to believe the former.

We were called into school to see a piece of work that he had done. His headmistress and Mr B were so proud of him. In fact the Headmistress had a copy of his work pinned to the outside of her door as a real show of her pride in Jake. The children had been talking about aspirations and achievements, how to aim high in life and do well. They had been given the first line "When I spread my wings and fly…." They were then asked to complete it to show their own personal views and feelings. Jake wrote: -

## <u>When I Spread my Wings and Fly</u>

*When I spread my wings and fly*
*I would like to be a social worker*
*So that I can help children like myself*
*That struggle and sometimes cannot cope in life.*
*I think that I would make a very good social worker*
*Because I have experienced the pains that you go through.*
*I have also experienced the heartache that you go through.*
*So when I spread my wings and fly*
*I will help kids like me and I will be a social worker*
*When I spread my wings and fly.*

Jake would always spread his wings and fly, his intentions were honourable but carrying them out was not always easy. His school report at the end of the year made references to the fact that he wrote from the heart, was a fast learner and accurate, there were no negative comments. Mr B wrote.

*"It's been interesting and a challenge working with Jake. He's clearly gone through some tough times yet obviously believes in looking forward."*

So with his wings spread wide he flew on to the Grammar School to discover new ground, new rules, new friends and new opportunities. We tried to offer him a little more independence as a sign of him growing up. But Jake was afraid of leaving his childhood; he wasn't ready, even though he put on an act of bravado. At his previous school he was a big fish in a little pond but now he was floundering as a little fish in a big sea. In moments of insecurity he donned his tough image, displayed his anger and appeared not to care about anyone. Then as the temper waned he would be eternally sorry, hurt and upset for what he had done. He tried to prove that he was better than others as a way of covering his real feelings of insecurity and despair. The school was right for Jake, he made an excellent friend who accepted him 'warts and all.' The friend's family were brilliant with him and for once Jake felt life was good. In that first year there were occasional difficulties but on the whole he was moving forward. He was chosen for the cricket team and the football team. Most of the time he worked hard and played hard. Since coming to us he had experienced two schools, both so different, but he needed that second year in the one place to gain a sense of belonging within the school environment. His second year started well, though at times he became overconfident in his position and started to push the boundaries both in school and at home. We were managing to rein him in most of the time whilst the school did more than play their part. He was suspended for a couple of days over one incident and this really upset Jake, so we felt there was a real feeling of determination to succeed ready to surface.

Towards the end of his second year Jake's struggle with life became ever more noticeable, the anger would rear itself and the triggers seemed various. At home his need to take off was still evident and there were the odd occasions, more often in the school holidays, when we would need support from the police to have him brought home. Two steps forward, three steps back, followed by a giant leap ahead rapidly became the pattern of success for Jake. But the hormones of puberty were kicking in too, and his need to question his roots to discover his true identity was stirring and churning him up. To him everyone else around had a good life, he constantly questioned his own and why his natural Mum had given him up. He had a Life Story book that he frequently read, searching for answers about his parents. He knew his Mum was a single mum and struggled to manage to care for him though she had kept his half sister. There was less information about his father but Jake was aware that his natural father had a drug and drink problem. He had learned that he had been a fractious baby and interpreted this as his difficulties began at birth. He felt perturbed about the way he treated people not least his adoptive parents and also us. He recognised that he chose to hurt people he could befriend by rejecting them before they had a chance to reject him. During the summer holiday Jake began to pull strongly in the opposite direction. We tried hard to understand what was happening, not certain whether he was trying to reject us for some reason, or whether he was testing our powers of endurance. He was certainly encouraging Andrew to walk the wrong path, but then he knew only too well the vulnerability of individuals.

He started to revert back to old habits of stealing and smoking. His deviousness bordered on the criminal. We desperately wanted to believe in him and have him sense that, which I am sure he did. Consequently he started to take his anti-social behaviours further afield. He targeted teenagers in the neighbouring vicinity causing quite a stir with his language and threats. On one occasion when he took umbrage at what we had to say about this, Jake escaped through his bedroom window, and it was two days before he came back feeling very sorry for himself with promises of making amends. But before long his slippery habits were becoming more regular, he would be all prepared for Lawrence to take him to school and as Lawrence was ready to lock the house door to take him in the car Jake would say he needed the toilet. What he was actually doing was setting the window of the shower room slightly ajar so that later in the day, after Lawrence had left for work, he could climb back in, sometimes with a friend in tow, whereupon he would take something to sell. The items he chose were expensive electrical equipment that were not used too regularly, so we would not notice they were missing until we needed to use them. He always left the boxes neatly in place so aesthetically their going was unnoticed.

His moods became darker and lasted longer and we realised we were witnessing similar patterns of behaviour to those experienced by his parents. School continued to support him, frequently calling us in or writing to us about his recent misdemeanours. He loved his school and on occasions when he was suspended for a few days missed it dreadfully. We knew his behaviour would not be acceptable in the school for the sake of the other pupils. He was a popular young man with the other pupils but not always with their parents!

The misdemeanours escalated. He created an enormous stir within the neighbouring community who formed an almost mob-like response to gain revenge, this culminated in quite a fight between Jake and another boy, and though Jake was the smaller of the two it was the other boy who came off the worst. The police were involved yet again, this time Jake had to go to court; he was given a roasting and a caution. Lawrence had gone with him to support him. We kept our roles quite separate, Jake would need someone to talk to when he returned and that was likely to be me. But he never quite got his head around this episode and the part he had played, and could not forgive himself for what he had done. He now convinced himself he was a 'bad lot' all together. Around this time Peter was moving on and Jake was kicking against him horrendously, he had to reject others but deep down he was actually rejecting himself. Discussions or talking helped him over each difficulty he faced but the undercurrent and strength of emotion still lingered and only increased with the next episode of trouble. He struggled to cope with his contact visits with his parents, and felt there was no purpose to the visits as he was so stressed before he went and that stress stayed with him for several days. He wanted the visits terminated. Then he would have deep moments of guilt for shutting them out of his life.

His pilfering became more widespread as others complained that after Jake had visited them something would be missing. Talk of trust was harder to achieve especially after I had caught him with his hand in my handbag helping himself to my purse. Jake began trashing his bedroom; the rot was setting in. No amount of help could release that pent up frustration and anger. But we hung on in hope.

Then came the ultimate, Jake had caused many rumbles in school and they had been talking of asking him to leave, Jake knew this but felt it was no more than an idle threat and would never happen. He had an altercation with one or two other youngsters, usually older and much taller ones that had culminated in yet more fights. Then he locked a member of staff out of the classroom with some of the pupils inside and this was viewed as a hostage-like situation. Jake had insisted that it was an accident, but we knew Jake and his strategies were well practised and accidents rarely happened. He escaped from the school and ran off in his inimitable fashion. Only this time he could not be found.

I was convinced that given a day or two to calm down he would re-appear but as more days went by and there were still no sightings, I began to fear for him. But Jake was a survivor. After about eight or nine days a boy knocked on our door to tell us that Jake had been seen in their area, that he was living rough in a shed though he would not say where. We searched at all times of the day and night, sent a message back with the lad to tell Jake to come home. Eventually the father of the boy that had called brought Jake back. We also deduced that the lad had probably been sent by Jake to test the waters in our home to establish if he was still welcome! He knew he had overstepped the mark and had let us down as well as the school but most of all he had demeaned himself. The school chose to ask Jake to leave and this was something he now really hated himself for. He could not pull himself around from this and the darkness of his mood filled the household and penetrated every person within it. He no longer talked, he only shouted and swore, throwing out his anger and frustration in all directions, he wanted us to reject him and he despaired as we held on to support him through this awful stage. He kicked, fought and caused considerable damage but more to himself and his own belongings. Jake was no longer a small boy he was a strong teenager and his flailing was painful if you were in his way and if you were not, then he would make sure he was in yours.

We tried to talk with him about trying another school, but he would not even entertain the idea. Lawrence persuaded him to at least look at alternatives and Jake reluctantly agreed providing there was no pressure. But on the evening before the school interview was set, Jake sparked off in all directions, he hated us, his parents, wished he had never been born. Friends were false and schools were the pits! We allowed him to let off steam but suggested he went to his room to do it. He did so, turning it upside down, breaking items he valued. Now even more annoyed, he needed to take it out on us, his hate for himself was so strong he desperately wanted us to reject him and we refused. Our tenacity would not let us though living with this anger, damage and darkness was so awful, we still had hope that Jake would work through it and come out the other side a stronger individual. Never the less he did go for the school interviews and held himself well, only to return home to indulge in his dark moods and retreat into his inner world. He longed to be hugged, yet rejected any attempts as he told me he did not deserve them. We promised him endlessly that he would get through this and we would continue to support him. Perhaps that was not what he wanted to hear as he was convinced that we should be giving up on him. He had several sessions with Diane, from the after adoption support team whom he had a great deal of trust in. He claimed he wanted more freedom, stating that he was never meant to be in a family and was looking for his independence. We were heading for crisis point and were running out of ideas and energy to prevent it. Each day was filled with dread, wondering what he would do, how far he would go. We still had so much love for him, continued to support him but I dreaded going to work as Jake was now goading Lawrence so badly, constantly undermining him and aiming at his vulnerability. Then one evening I smelt burning on the corridor outside of his bedroom. I accused Jake of smoking, we had smoke detectors but he would take the batteries out. He insisted that he had not smoked, as he did not have any cigarettes. I began to check his bedroom, as the smell of burning was so strong. He was livid with me, but this was our home and I felt I had the right to find out what he had done. I pulled back the duvet on his bed to discover a burning hole on the sheet, and underneath that a smouldering burn in the mattress. This time he had gone too far, he had tried to extinguish it. He claimed he did not intend to set the house on fire, I would have believed this if he had been ten years of age but at fourteen he knew well the consequence of his action.

A review was called and Jake made it clear to everyone that he felt it was time to move on, that he was sorry for all that had happened and all that he had done, we felt he desperately needed to be away from this situation to enable him to move forward once again, much as he had to leave his parents in the beginning. Our only concern was that this would be his pattern in life, we stressed to Jake and the appropriate workers that we still wanted to be a part of his life, to support him as much as possible. We realised that Jake's way of living at this moment was not compatible with our way of living. He had another court appearance to attend and it was agreed that Lawrence would give him full support. Once he had settled down in the alternative environment we could have an arrangement to visit Jake. We also agreed that he could have arranged visits to us.

Jake was found an alternative placement, he was there for a few weeks but caused more problems for himself, though the heat had been taken out of his situation, and we missed him desperately. Love the child not the deed, and we did. Jake came back to us for a short time but it was around this time he was given the news of the death of his natural father. His belief and chance of meeting this person was never going to happen and this cut deeply into Jake. He had wanted to know if he looked like his father, had the same interests, if he had the same faults. But now all his hope had faded, and his only reaction was to emulate the person he had lost. Jake had already thrown caution to the wind walking on the wild side of life. I don't think he was comfortable with it as the hardened strained expression crept back into his life. He began to drink though never at home, his petty thieving was supporting his need to play with drugs. I strongly felt it was his way of being in touch with his natural father, to feel as he felt his father did. But everything became too much for him and for us, as Jake's free spirit demanded more freedom and we could no longer comply. He left us again returning to the children's home. Lawrence supported him in the court appearances; I visited him at least once a week, occasionally taking him out or bringing him home for the day or to have an overnight stay. But the company he kept, continually brought him court appearances, along with the other miscreants he brought problems to the home, then sadly got roped into a very heavy handed crime, his part was minimal and he was encouraged by older ones, no doubt his need to impress and be a part of it was enough to entice Jake to follow their lead. He had also met up with his adoptive parents once again and was trying to build up his relationship with them. Jake knew that whatever he did we would always be there for him, only from now on it would have to be on our terms, as his behaviour needed to be strongly curbed and controlled. We knew from past experience he could not handle two sets of parents at once; it was time for us to bow out. We had an arranged meeting with him, reminded him how much he still meant to us and how much we still cared and loved him, he explained how genuinely sorry he was for the things he had done and the way everything had turned out. We felt he just needed a little more space, a chance to get schooling out of the way and to find some success of his own as well as coming to terms or at least accepting his past. We parted on good terms wishing him the very best for his future and hoping to see him again soon when he felt ready to see us again.

His struggles did not end there, anymore than his contact with us, though the latter was less direct as Jake would telephone us often late at night or visit the house in the daytime when he felt certain we were not in. I felt it was his way of touching base. His brother allegedly made some of the calls, but Jake would be in the background telling him what to say. Sometimes the calls were mildly abusive when he would be letting off steam or perhaps had a drink or two. The visitations to the house were evident by the way things were strewn around the garden. Perhaps he was annoyed that we were not there for him to speak to or maybe he needed to 'vent his spleen.' We would find garden lights thrown onto the lawn similar to when he was here and needed to make a point. On one such occasion I drove up the drive reaching the top just in time to catch a glimpse of someone turning the corner of the other end of the house as they ran off. As I parked the car I realised someone had been watering the garden with the hosepipe that was still gushing water. Again that is the sort of thing Jake on a good day would think to do. There was a particular day when he rang and was very sensible asking if he could collect more of his belongings. We had an arrangement with him and the articles he wanted were brought downstairs ready for him to call, he actually talked at length on that occasion about thinking of joining the army. We finished by wishing him well and wondering if his attitude to authority had changed. He never called, at least not whilst we were in. The items were not collected, but several months later we were to find a box of his belongings hidden at the back of the garage, interestingly this was not long after we had appeared to have had a break in, as the window at the back of the garage was broken but we could not establish that anything had actually been taken. We assumed Jake had left the box for safekeeping.

Those phone calls and visitations became less frequent and we hoped that it was because Jake was truly making the effort to sort his life out and to use his intelligence and skills more beneficially. We sincerely hoped that the better times in life for him had taken over those painful dark moods and that having had a taste of walking on the wild side he now had a brighter view on life. During 2008 we were being prepared for deregistering from fostering, the next generation was fast putting in an appearance and it was time for us to enjoy their innocence. We had a long chat with Diane to be sure of our position for her to carry this out. Naturally we talked of Jake and she too knew of his intentions of joining the army. She smiled and said, "You know, one day that young man will come knocking on your door to thank you for all that you did and to show you what a success he has become." Together we shared our feelings, hopes and aspirations for Jake and his future and I longed for that day to come when I could open the door and meet the man in Jake.

About six weeks later we returned from a holiday in the Lake District, one of Jake's favourite places. I opened the mail to find a card from someone whose names initially meant nothing to us; it asked if we were feeling better over the recent situation. I checked the envelope it was definitely for us. We were a little perplexed but put it to one side whilst we continued to unpack. Lawrence then listened to the telephone messages, there was one from Diane insisting we should ring her as soon as possible, we assumed it was to do with our retiring from fostering as she had promised to be in touch with us. It was a Saturday evening. We planned to contact her on the Monday. Then the following day I puzzled over the card and Diane's message, I listened to it again, there was a definite note of urgency in her voice and she had left us her home number too. I chose to ring her in the evening rather than disturb her day off.

The emotion in her voice told me before the words came out. Jake had taken his own life. This young man had made the very ultimate decision; it had been a purposeful action. I then realised the card had been sent by his friend from the Grammar School.

The crematorium was packed with youngsters of Jake's age all paying their respects. But the greatest privilege of all was meeting and talking to his birth Mum. I hope he saw her. He would have realised it was not his birth Father that he looked like. But he was the absolute image of his Mother. I would like to believe that would have pleased him.

> *"Life can only be understood backwards,*
> *but it must be lived forwards."*

*Soren Kierkegaard*

*Danish Philosopher (1813 – 1855)*

# CHAPTER 20

# Consequences of Choices

Jake may have been an irascible youth, but he was also one of life's charmers. His death left so many questions unanswered for so many people. Why did he choose to end his life just as he was on the very edge of leaving his childhood and entering manhood? Jake's desperate struggle through all of his life, constantly holding on to his past, had tormented him. Though during his last year he had settled down taken control of himself, resulting in a problem free year, no police involvement or court appearances. He had a flat of his own, a girlfriend he really cared for and was employed. His destiny was in his own hands, his choices were his own. He had curbed his drinking considerably and drugs did not contribute to his death. Those who were close to him around that time comment on the positive changes in his life and that he was a good companion. Jake had made great strides and efforts to reconcile his relationship with his adoptive parents and brothers. He had applied to join the army eagerly awaiting their decision. So why? What happened that day for him to leave without saying goodbye? Only Jake would know the real reasons if he was in a position to rationalise his actions. The rest of us of can only surmise.

We know he was bitterly disappointed when the Army gave him a refusal, allegedly based on his lack of confidence. Jake found this rejection hard to take as he always thought he exuded confidence, not realising he was actually covering up his lack of confidence. A day or two prior to being found Jake had had an argument with his girlfriend and she had returned to her parents. Having done so well for so long had he seen these two incidents as 'everything in life going wrong', and being on his own not known how to handle the hurt he felt? Did the dark cloud of depression descend over him as it had many times in the past and if so was it a part of something undiagnosed in Jake that in the right hands could have been supported? Did he try to reach out to anyone before he carried out his final act? I have frequently wondered whether he had tried to contact us, but if he did there was no one in as we were away on holiday. On our return there had been a couple of calls that had gone on to record messages but no one had spoken, no messages left.

During life Jake had constantly run away from situations of stress and difficulty. He had fought back at such times on the very people trying to help him and put the blame on those people. But deep down he had always known that he was responsible for his own actions, and in those rational moments then blamed himself and punished himself. His self-esteem would be so low he could not and frequently would not accept the support he needed; this was a part of his own self-punishment. So in those last few hours did those past patterns of behaviour and thinking take over Jake once again? He was now in his own place of his own choosing with people he wanted to be with and situations he made for himself. Did that edgy 'need to run' feeling return, and if it did how do you run from yourself?

Our questions can never be truly answered, to allow us the peace of mind we would all prefer to have. But then Jake lived his life leaving everyone with unanswered questions in his wake. Love the child not the deed, and as I said before, we did.

At his funeral his adoptive Mum and I hugged, for we had both played a part in this young man's life. She told me that Jake really wanted to be successful and so wanted to go into the army. "He used to talk of coming to your house in his uniform and knocking on your door to show you." We both struggled to hold back the tears as we spoke.

------------------------

Our fostering years had stretched beyond our own expectations. When asked the question of 'How many children do you have?' I have never quite known how to answer. I often felt like asking them to define the question! Our lives have been all the richer for the children we have cared for and the experiences they've given us. I daresay we could have done without some of those experiences but what is life without a challenge? Maybe we could have done things differently, but like all parents we based our decisions on the 'here and now' of the time. Perhaps we are a little possessive, but so many of the children have maintained their contact with us, that we still consider them as ours, especially as Aaron and Gareth refer to them as their brother or sister! We could not always give them what they wanted or expected, but we did give them what we felt they needed. There is a huge difference in the two! We offered them a different lifestyle to the one they had. We've been accused of being a culture shock to some. But if we gave them an alternative lifestyle that included values and standards and they chose to live by those then our efforts were not wasted. At least they are now hopefully in a position to make better choices but also to take the consequences of those choices. We have always endeavoured to support them, perhaps not always the way they would like to be, after all support comes in many different ways. Sometimes it was with a smile and a helpful hand, other times it was making them achieve through their own efforts so they could have the self-satisfaction of knowing they could. There were always the times when a stern 'no' would be given, meant and adhered to especially when boundaries were tested for their flexibility! We had moments of taking youngsters off to far flung areas as they each reached for their independence, and guided to aim as high as they felt they dare, but there were also times when we brought them back to touch base, to find the strength to enable them to leave again. And of course there were also times when we dragged them back too, when we felt they had slipped a little off the rails we had set them on and were floundering in life!

We have had a phenomenal amount of support from so many people over the years; there have been those who have touched the edges of our family yet left their mark. My dear friends from my nursing days, who became more like a third set of grandparents, who entered the very heart of our clan and more than left their stamp on our lives. Our own parents who never questioned all the additional grandchildren in their lives. Our own sisters and brothers, albeit from a distance, offered their support too in accepting this oversized family. My nieces, especially one of the older ones who periodically would stay at our home and look after some of the children so Lawrence and I could escape for a day or two to 'recharge our batteries.' So many friends who thought we were out of our minds, including those who struggled so much when we continued to foster, when the family was almost torn apart. But the old adage of what doesn't break you makes you stronger must be true. Church members, social workers, teachers, health visitors, our work colleagues, the list is endless but each person who touched our lives also touched the lives of our children, teaching them in some way or showing them a positive aspect of life. The two exceptionally patient support workers allocated to us from the two authorities we fostered for, who steadfastly stuck with us to the bitter end. I am left saying where does the list end? What I do know was though there were those who may have wondered what we were doing or why we continued to foster, yet all of them gave their time and efforts to the benefit of our children and helped Lawrence and me to find the strength within ourselves to keep on going.

Fostering provided its challenges, made us discover alternative solutions to similar situations according to each child's needs. We had moments of pure desperation that would bring us to our knees, take us to the very edge of our sanity, our patience and our determination. We would be forced to face metaphorical mountains and climb them to the top before descending at speed headlong into equally metaphorical bottomless pits, and be expected to scrape ourselves off the floor, to get up and start again. Sometimes it was hard to know if we were at the beginning of a day or at the end of one! We learned to smile when we really wanted to cry, to be stern when we would have preferred to laugh. We learned that what is said is not necessarily what is meant! Our children taught us to hold on, hang on and not let go so we could reap the rewards with them, to enjoy their growth and their love as well as their successes in life. The mixed emotions we have experienced have at times left us totally drained of energy but also injected renewed determination and drive in us. Our coping mechanism was switched on permanent standby, as we never knew what the children would throw out at us or what would trigger their distress. But fostering has also given us the opportunity to enjoy visiting so many places, some many times as we showed them off with different groups of children. To explore different ways of communicating with our youngsters and maintain it, especially when working on their Life Story Books, which has been an interesting exercise in building rapport to regain harmony. We learned the language of teenagers but also taught them ours! We were to enjoy unexpected skills in children who thought themselves to be less than able. We witnessed some amazing moments, as their eyes were opened to another side to life, when they found their confidence to discover their surroundings wherever we were. I honestly believe that over the years between our children and us we wore out the full range of human emotions possible.

We may have craved for a peaceful life at times but nothing would ever make us want to change our lives, only some of the events! Every child was loved, but each one for different reasons as each brought something different to our family. The dynamics between them changed as dramatically as the characters themselves did.

If a child is a gift, to play a part in a child's life, or look after someone else's gift, is a great privilege. To meet the adult that emerges from their childhood must be the greatest privilege of all. Some just take a little longer to get there, as their journey seems more perilous!

Imagine, we could have been the average family, but how mundane, perhaps that is why we chose our alternative life style! Fostering has given us so much more in life and I suspect our children have taught us far more than we taught them. Life has its ups and downs and I suspect that we just had a few more than most ever have!

*"Like all the best families, we have*
*our share of eccentricities, of impetuous*
*and wayward youngsters and of family*
*disagreements."*

*H.M. Queen Elizabeth II*

# About The Author

The author, Dani Valdis, writes under a pseudonym. Primarily a mum, and now a proud grandma, she is also a nurse. Dani lives with her husband Lawrence and along with their two young sons chose to foster sibling groups in need of care, love and support. Though having written many odes, rhymes and poems as gifts for family, friends and colleagues this is her first book.

*Find out more by visiting*

*www.cherryblossomchildren.com*

Lightning Source UK Ltd.
Milton Keynes UK
UKOW051935240412

191375UK00001B/1/P

9 781781 487549